DATE DUE

OCT 2 0 1997			

GEMCO

BATTLE LINES

BATTLE LINES

The American Media and the Intifada

JIM LEDERMAN

HENRY HOLT
AND COMPANY
NEW YORK

Library of Congress Cataloging-in-Publication Data
Lederman, Jim.
    Battle lines : the American media and the intifada / by Jim
    Lederman.—1st ed.
        p. cm.
    Includes index.
1. Jewish-Arab relations in the press—United States. 2. Intifada,
1987–   3. Foreign correspondents—Israel—Influence. 4. Foreign news—United States—Objectivity. 5. Television broadcasting of news—Social aspects—United States.
    I. Title.
    PN4888.J48L4   1991
    070.4'49956953044—dc20   91-11488
    ISBN 0-8050-1602-3   CIP

First Edition—1992

Book design by Claire Vaccaro
Printed in the United States of America
Recognizing the importance of preserving
the written word, Henry Holt and Company, Inc.,
by policy, prints all of its first editions
on acid-free paper.∞
10 9 8 7 6 5 4 3 2 1

In memory of my father, Jack,
a passionate news consumer

Contents

Acknowledgments

No matter how much effort an author expends in researching and writing, no book is a purely individual effort. Many of those who aided in the production of this book, from typesetters to copy editors, I have never met. But I would like to thank them all. Particular thanks are due to those who in one way or another actively supported this project and shepherded this volume from its infancy as an idea, through the innumerable rewrites, to the concrete object you hold in your hands. Marvin Kalb, Gary Orren, and Ellen Hume, who directed and administered the Shorenstein Barone Center at Harvard University while I was in residence as a fellow, provided the environment and research facilities that allowed me to begin the work. Nathan Appleman provided the seed money to begin the research. Several fellow fellows at the Center, especially Timothy Cook, David Yepsin, and Beth Knobel, took the time and effort to read and comment on parts of the manuscript. I also received invaluable comments from Yitzchak Oron. Harry Sindel provided important technical assistance. Thanks are also due to all the journalists and spokespersons who agreed to be interviewed.

My agent, Mildred Marmur, and my editor, Marian Wood, deserve special praise for their commitment and help.

However, all their efforts would have been for nought had it not been for the support I received from my family. I am deeply grateful to my mother, Florence, and my sister and brother-in-law Dinah and Mervin Kerzner, for their backing; to my children, Shai, Rachel, Micha, and David, whose patience I sorely tried; and most of all, to my wife, Miriam, who read and critiqued almost every draft.

To anyone whom I may have forgotten to mention, I offer my most sincere apologies.

                                        Jim Lederman
                                        Jerusalem, Israel.
                                        March 1991

Introduction

There is nothing more difficult to take in hand, more perilous to conduct, or more uncertain in its success than to take the lead in the introduction of a new order of things.

—Machiavelli

On December 8, 1987, an Israeli semitrailer smashed into a battered Peugeot near the Erez military checkpost that divides the Gaza Strip from Israel. Four Palestinians riding in the car were killed. In itself, the incident was hardly newsworthy. It was but one of more than six hundred fatal accidents that occur on Israeli roads each year. But this accident would prove different. The following day, a rumor spread through the Jabalya refugee camp near the site of the accident that the crash had been no accident. It had been a deliberate act of revenge for the murder of Shlomo Sakle, a forty-five-year-old Israeli businessman, in the city of Gaza the previous Sunday. As this rumor spread, a crowd gathered in the center of Jabalya and began to demonstrate. An Israeli patrol sent in to restore order was soon surrounded by a crowd of young Palestinians hurling bottles and bits of rubble.

The soldiers shot their way out, killing a seventeen-year-old youth and wounding an estimated sixteen others.

The next day, the demonstrations were repeated. By the third day, when demonstrations had spread to the West Bank, the U.S. press, especially television, had begun arriving to record the events. At the end of the third day, when the journalists went back to their offices to file their stories, six Palestinians had been killed by Israeli army gunfire, including an eleven-year-old boy and a fifty-seven-year-old woman. That was enough to convert a local incident into an international news event. More violence was soon to come. A chain reaction that eventually was to become known as the "intifada"—an Arabic word meaning "to shake" or "to shake off"—had begun.

The intifada, the popular uprising of the Palestinians in the Israeli-occupied territories, was political theater, carried out in the streets and broadcast by television to an audience of millions. It was a superb example of the interaction of the press, domestic politics, and international relations in the new information age. Although the word *intifada* continues to be used to describe the ongoing violence in the Israeli-occupied territories, the actual period of the shake-up of old concepts and old ideas was relatively short, lasting only a few months. By April 1988, the revolt against the old, established leadership in the West Bank and Gaza and the Israeli occupation had been largely institutionalized. All of the political and social trends within the Palestinian community, like the competition for power between secular nationalists and Moslem fundamentalists, had become well established. All of the organizations that were to take part in the ongoing struggle had carved out roles and positions for themselves.

It took the Israelis somewhat longer to realize the extent, the depth, and the staying power of the rebellion, but by June, Israeli attitudes and military practices had largely solidified as well. So, too, in June, after months of probing and experimenting with various formulas in the hope of finding a political breakthrough, the position of the United States was set, and the basic principles guiding Washington's actions did not change in the two years to come.

Although the foreign press was among the first to recognize and to publicize the extent, breadth, and depth of the rebellion, its coverage went through a number of phases before becoming fully routinized in a lasting form in the fall of 1988.

The Palestine Liberation Organization (PLO), the slowest of all of the political bodies to react, took until February 1989 before its position was more or less clarified. But by November 1988, the trends within the organization already were apparent.

Thus, by the end of the first year of the revolt, and certainly since early 1989, what we have seen on the streets, in the political back rooms, in the newspapers, and on our television screens are repetitions of, or variations on, basic themes, attitudes, and practices that had developed in each of the protagonists during the first year of the uprising.

The U.S. foreign press played a leading role both in raising the subject of the uprising as a matter for international public discourse and debate and in projecting the ebb and flow of the rebellion to the world. But the press coverage was not the result of some sudden, inexplicable, volcanic upwelling. Like the intifada itself, the reporting was the product of processes that had been under way for many years. In regional terms, the personal and professional baggage the resident correspondents brought to their tasks was the product of innumerable small and large confrontations they had had with the other players over previous years, anticipations of what their editors would expect from them under the circumstances, prior experiences they had had elsewhere, and their own perception of what modern foreign journalism entails. In global terms, the press's coverage of the intifada was a major way station in the development of modern foreign reporting, situated between the fall of the shah of Iran and the massacre in Tiananmen Square and the demise of communism in Eastern Europe; some of the journalists who covered the intifada also had covered the events in Tehran, and others were to report later on the events in Beijing and in Eastern Europe.

In many ways, the conditions under which journalists operated during the intifada were considerably different from those found in Iran, China, and Eastern Europe. Unlike most of the countries in Eastern Europe and Iran, almost all of the major American news organizations had full-time bureaus in Israel. Unlike places like Romania and Bulgaria, Israel had excellent communications facilities. Unlike Iran or the Eastern European countries, the distances between the scenes of events were relatively short and therefore the most important events could be easily covered. Unlike all three other venues, Israel had an established, active, and relatively free press on which the foreign journalists could lean. Israel is a democracy with a wide range of public voices and a plethora of publicly active institutions. (While not free to vote and lacking a free press, the Palestinians are free to speak out as individuals and many are thoughtful and articulate.) Israel has well-established technical and journalistic support services, like stringers, translators, television technicians, and camera crews. Journalists are also free to import almost any equipment they need that is not available locally. Thus, in a purely technical sense, the press was working under best-case-scenario conditions when the uprising broke out.

The same cannot be said for the other four protagonists in the drama: the Israelis, the Palestinians in the occupied territories, the United States, and the PLO. The Israeli government was seriously divided over policy and the direction the country should take. Its planning mechanisms were sorely wanting. And its systems of co-optation and control over the Palestinians and the foreign press had broken down. The Israeli army and police force were ill equipped and untrained to deal with a large-scale popular uprising. But most of all, the nation as a whole, from its top leadership down, was psychologically unprepared to cope with the shock that comes when the myths, conventional wisdom, and wishful thinking that had guided Israeli actions for years finally were shown to be ethereal props.

The Palestinians in the occupied territories blundered into a media success of remarkable proportions. But just as the Israelis were unable to react imaginatively to changed circumstances, the Palestinians were unable to capitalize on their own achievements. Early on, they understood the roots of their success and they had a bedrock of public institutions on which to build and consolidate their gains. But they lacked both the experience and the moxie to move beyond rebellion. Having overthrown the old order, the youngsters in the streets had little more to offer than their tenaciousness. Divided, drunk on the euphoria of the moment, and chained to their own myths and wishful thinking, the new leaders were unable to make the existential leap from anarchic, violent conflict to political opportunism. Instead they soon staggered from one self-destructive act to another.

The United States, which had adopted a policy of benign neglect toward the Israeli-Arab dispute for the previous two years, found that its appreciation of how to deal with the Middle East conflict also was bankrupt. The old techniques of government-to-government and elites-to-elites intervention were unsuitable for a popular uprising like the intifada. Bound by the constraints of traditional diplomatic practice, lacking a clear, realistic policy in the region as a whole and in the occupied territories in particular, the State Department was vulnerable to pressures from vested interest groups and the press as well as incapable of developing new models for mediation that the dynamic situation demanded.

The PLO also was caught by surprise by the uprising. But it, too, was so entrapped by its ideology, by its past, and by its modus operandi, that it could not react imaginatively to the opportunities being presented. More ponderous in its decision-making processes, and more risk averse and hidebound in its attitudes than any of the other parties, the organization failed to adapt. Although it had the potential to play a major role in guiding the rebellion to a political denouement, its inability to create new concepts and new lines forced it to remain largely in the wings.

Such widespread unpreparedness inevitably leads to "surprises" and crises. And the intifada was a crisis of the first order for all of the participants.

As a dramatic story with a broad cast of characters, set against the backdrop of the Holy Land, the intifada probably was destined to become a major news story. But additionally, in recent years, public, press, and diplomatic interest has shifted away from the traditional focus on great power contests to the ethnic and regional conflicts and sudden popular uprisings against traditional authority that threaten to be more internationally destabilizing in the long term. In this age of increasing international interdependence, small, seemingly localized conflicts can have a disproportionate impact on the lives of people thousands of miles away.

Beyond this, new, cheap, user-friendly imaging technologies and high-speed communications have changed the very nature of journalism, international diplomacy, and public perceptions of the world. The intifada was one of the first major regional, interethnic conflicts—to which the press had wide access—to arise following the advent of the new information age. It is thus a signpost to the kinds of international events that may await us in the future. How each participant reacted to the events is a case study in itself. Of greater import, however, is how they reacted to each other, at a time of confusion, when old beliefs were collapsing all around them.

Coming as it did at the beginning of a period of enormous change in the fine matrix of international politics, it was inevitable that the intifada would raise disturbing and provocative issues about patterns of political behavior, international diplomacy, and foreign reporting in the late twentieth century. Indeed, among other subjects, it threw into sharp relief some basic questions about established concepts of political crisis management, the capacity of the public and special-interest groups to shape governmental policy, the ability of outside powers to intervene effectively in intraregional disputes, the role of foreign reporters, the nature of foreign reporting, journalistic ethics, the relationship between reporters and those in authority in countries of which the reporters are not citizens, and the impact new communications technology is having on political and social processes.

I had been a foreign correspondent in the Middle East for twenty years when the intifada broke out, having worked over the years for such organizations as the Canadian Broadcasting Corporation, the *New York Post*, and National Public Radio. I had covered seven wars and innumerable public demonstrations. But when I went to Gaza during the first week of the rebellion, I realized that this time things were different. This was not a demonstration of strength, organized by some leadership from above. This was a popular uprising. Children, some no older than seven, were in control of the streets. My car window was smashed by a rock thrown by a child who might not have been even that old. As I interviewed members of the elite and the older generation, I quickly realized that in only a few days, the social structure of Gaza had changed beyond recognition. Leadership had passed from men and women in their sixties and seventies to those in their teens or barely into their twenties. It was a situation for which almost no one was psychologically prepared, including the press.

When I was awarded an Appleman Fellowship by the Joan Shorenstein Barone Center for the Press, Politics and Public Policy at Harvard University in September 1989, I decided to do my research on those early days of the rebellion. I was aware that the coverage had been very controversial and had generated a great deal of criticism both in the United States and in Israel. However, until I arrived in Cambridge, I had not seen or read any of my colleagues' work. I had spent the previous six months interviewing many of my colleagues and had assumed that my only major obligation to the Joan Shorenstein Barone Center—the writing of a short discussion paper—would present few difficulties. I could not have been more wrong. The material proved to be extraordinarily rich. As the body of research material grew, virtually every premise with which I had begun this project had to be discarded. Instead of a short discussion paper, this book-length study is the result.

The central question I began with was what happens in a democracy when a government faces a major political crisis with important and potentially damaging international implications, and when there is an established foreign press corps operating under best-case-scenario circumstances. In particular, I wanted to explore how American foreign policy and the domestic political decision-making process in foreign countries has been influenced by the new information age—when the time for rational consideration of problems is compressed and secrets are few.

To ensure that I would be dealing with a true best-case scenario, I established the following criteria for my study. Each media outlet studied had to have had a bureau in Israel for at least ten years, with an orderly change of correspondents and bureau chiefs during that time. This eliminated most of the parachutists—except those working within the framework of an established bureau. It also eliminated some news organizations that had undergone internal traumas. The bureau had to file on an almost daily basis, without the advantage of an end-of-week opportunity for synthesis. The individual journalists had to be personally responsible for their work by having a byline or an on-air introduction. This eliminated the weekly newsmagazines. The media outlets had to have had a record of influencing Washington's political decisions on the Middle East. I therefore chose not to deal with the regional American newspapers that have full-time correspondents in Israel. Finally, since this was to be a story of the American foreign press, I wanted all of the outlets to be American owned and operated. Moreover, they had to have had a recent record of financial and administrative institutional stability. This eliminated operations like Reuters and UPI.

For practical purposes, I needed organizations whose work was recorded in a public archive that was easily accessible. Thus, both the radio networks and Cable News Network (CNN) had to be eliminated from the project, too. All of the television material, for example, was taken from the excellent Vanderbilt Archive. I wanted my focus to be on daily foreign journalism and so I ignored magazines, week-in-review sections, special documentaries, op-ed pieces, editorials, cartoons, and columns.

Altogether, I watched, logged, and analyzed tapes of about eight hundred nightly newscasts by the three main commercial television networks in the United States. Some of the more complex broadcasts had to be viewed more than forty times each. In addition, I reviewed more than two thousand dispatches from the Associated Press (AP) and fifteen hundred reports from the *New York Times*, the *Washington Post*, and the *Los Angeles Times* as well as, for comparative purposes, about one thousand articles that appeared in the Israeli press. This material was supplemented by my own notes and the radio reports I sent at that time.

I have used few quotes from journalists in this book because once I began my archival research in depth, I discovered that there was an enormous gap between what most of my interviewees said they had done or had intended to do and what I actually found in the public record. I therefore chose to let the material I found speak for itself. The interpretations are my own and I take full responsibility for them.

What I found after months of bleary eyes was surprising, enlightening, and at times frightening. The material I chose to include in the book represents only the highlights of the press's coverage of the first year of the uprising, but I think that it accurately represents all of the important journalistic and political trends that developed during that time—and the effect those trends had on all of the main participants.

Journalists often are accused of being ahistorical. From my interviews, it is clear that that allegation certainly is true of the correspondents' and spokespersons' perceptions of how coverage of the Middle East developed. Because most reporters and spokespeople are rotated frequently, only a very few could remember back to the period before 1982 and the start of the Lebanese War. For almost all, it was as though this one single event changed the course of coverage in the Middle East. Nothing could be further from the truth. I therefore chose to devote a large section of this book to tracing the cumulative, incremental changes that took place in the nature of the coverage and journalists' perceptions of the story over a period of two decades. Without this historical background, the events and actions of the participants often are inexplicable.

I also set out to discover how adherence to established story lines—and in the case of the broadcast media, technology and production values—influenced the substance of the reports being sent. In other words, events tend to be interpreted in the light of preconceived themes—even when those themes no longer apply in whole or in part. In television and radio, the accepted and preconceived production style and the technologies available to reporters also play an enormous role in how a story is presented. Therefore I also have devoted considerable space to analyzing the story lines, the technologies, and the production styles used by the various reporters.

All of this background information would be little more than a curiosity, however, were it not for the fact that news reports can and do influence public perceptions and the acts of public policy makers. The intifada is an almost classic case of how the press influences public policy and is, in return, influenced by policy makers.

As I have mentioned, the intifada was a political crisis of considerable proportions. During crises, many well-established defenses designed to protect the participants in normal times break down. It is then that hidden attitudes, modes of thought, inherent weaknesses, and even the defense structures themselves become most apparent. The book concludes by looking at some of the issues that arise when these usually ignored or misinterpreted phenomena become apparent to the careful observer.

In toto, this is a critical insider's look at how and why we who participated in presenting the intifada to the world behaved in a particular place and at a particular time. The journalists who took part in these events can count a considerable number of successes in bringing to light and explaining the events that occurred. There were, however, a notable number of failures. And they have been dealt with in depth. A few of the basic questions raised by this study may, in the end, be unanswerable. But there are many lessons that can be learned from the press coverage of the intifada that go beyond the relatively narrow confines of the Middle East and the period of December 1987 to December 1988. If we as journalists are to fulfill our designated roles in society and to learn from our mistakes, we must be open to thoughtful criticism—and the criticism should start with ourselves.

The Israeli presence in the areas known as the West Bank and Gaza began in 1967, in the wake of the Six-Day War. Since 1948, the West Bank had been held by Jordan and the Gaza Strip by Egypt, and the capture of these lands occasioned euphoria among Israelis. Not only had they survived after weeks of tension and hostility, but also they now could return to the lands of their religious and national roots from which they had been excluded for the previous nineteen years.

Initially, most Israelis viewed the occupation as a temporary one, with the territories as but another bargaining chip to be cashed in when the "inevitable" peace negotiations with the Arabs began. And indeed, these were heady times: peace seemed to be just around the corner. But late that summer, at an Arab summit conference held in the Sudanese capital of Khartoum, it was decided that there

O · N · E

Trapped in a Story Line

would be no recognition of Israel, no negotiations with the Zionist state, and no peace with it. That resolution unleashed a number of processes that, individually and collectively, were to have a profound effect on the area for the next two decades.

The first, and most important, was to give official pan-Arab sanction to perpetuating the conflict between Jews and Arabs that had been going on in the region since 1929. Major confrontations between the two sides had erupted every decade, and smaller political and armed skirmishes had been a way of life for almost forty years. Now the armed struggle was to continue indefinitely. In the immediate post-Khartoum period, the violence took two main forms: massed military confrontation, as expressed in the 1969–70 War of Attrition along the Suez Canal and the 1973 Yom Kippur War; and terrorist raids, mainly by Palestinians, inside Israel and the occupied territories, along Israel's borders, and in other parts of the world.

The Khartoum resolution had a major effect on Israelis, for whom the fleeting summer days of unfounded euphoria quickly vanished. For journalists, the war story, which once had seemed to culminate with the Six-Day War, in reality had only just begun.

That conflict is news, is no news. And the extended Arab-Israeli conflict was to become one of the major international news stories for more than two decades. Conflict, as a news story, has all of the elements a journalist seeks: well-defined characters, occasional novelty as tactics change, and a strong and dramatic story line (especially if violence is involved) that reporters can build on every day. It is this last element— the story line—that gives reporting its sense of continuity. The story line is a frame into which a journalist can place seemingly random events and give them coherence. It simplifies the narrative thread, reducing it to manageable dimensions by using a single overarching theme so that each dramatic incident can be highlighted as it occurs and each "chapter" of the ongoing story can be slotted in easily and given a context. It gives all who use it, be we hacks, ideologues, area specialists, diplomats, or scholars, a common reference point, a set of agreed bearings from which to set out into the unknown and through which to communicate with our audiences.

When a story line works—and is a reasonably accurate shorthand representation of reality—it becomes the crucial underlay for everything that follows. From the Six-Day War onward, and especially after the Khartoum resolution, the central story line for Arab and Israeli leaders, diplomats, and journalists alike was to be "Israeli-Arab violent conflict over possession of land."[1]

However, as subsequent events in the Middle East were to show repeatedly, and the intifada was to highlight, story lines, particularly when adopted in haste, also can become a snare, distorting both the journalist's and the public's perception of events. Our problem as analysts is that once a story line does become widely accepted, we rarely question it. To do so poses the danger of possibly stepping into mental quicksand. The longer an incorrect story line remains in use, the more people begin to accept it as truth—and the more difficult it is to change the thrust of the theme or to find an acceptable alternative narrative thread. For some people, it becomes a vested interest on which their futures may depend. Editorials are written and government policies are formulated based on the accepted story line. If enough people believe in it, it becomes self-sustaining. Television, which has become the prime source of foreign news for most people, is particularly susceptible to the charms of a well-defined story line because, since there is never enough air time on the nightly news to discuss complicated subjects in depth, television reporters need a simple and clear narrative with vivid characters in order to describe an event. Good, thoughtful television correspondents are aware of the problem, but after fighting it for a while, they usually just give up. The psychological wear and tear of fighting the groupthink at the head office can be too much personal strain—and can endanger their careers. As one very experienced Middle East hand once told me, "I fought with [the senior editors] in New York for six years, but it didn't help. Now I just give them what they want."

Foreign correspondents, of course, are as susceptible to groupthink as their editors. From the moment journalists new to a particular area

---

[1]By "violent conflict," I am not referring merely to what frequently is called "point violence"— riots, terrorist attacks, and the like—although television often is obsessed by such confrontations. Violent conflict as a story line means that reports are fashioned in a way that will cause many otherwise nonviolent stories to be "hooked" onto the ongoing narrative. Thus, a report about Christmas in Bethlehem will emphasize the security aspects rather than the religious experience; or an analysis of higher education in Israel often will make reference to the budgetary fights between the Defence Ministry and the Education Ministry or the need of many university students to take time from their studies to do reserve army duty.

begin their research through their company's archive, they cannot help absorbing all that has been written before. The more a particular story line is repeated from different media outlets, the greater the credence it acquires. Because senior editors are so far away from the site of events—and the nuances—they have to rely heavily on the story line. In some cases, it is all the supervisors have to go on and it is all they know about the subject. By a natural process of osmosis, then, reporters, whether just going through the morgue or already out in the field, will fashion their material to fit what seem to be the established criteria so that they can insure they will get maximum "play" in the fight for recognition. And once in the field, the reporter quickly learns just how difficult it is to carry on a fight over the phone with an editor who is seven thousand miles away. Groupthink is reinforced in the field at the local "journalists' bar," at press conferences, at parties and discussions with the local elite, and in conversations with other journalists, where they either justify what they have written or seek reassurance that what they have written is right.

In the case of the Arab-Israeli dispute, the conflict was not the real issue. Conflict was and is a symptom, not the disease. The real story was the need by the residents of the region to face and then agree on their national self-images. Without such an image, there could be no tolerance. Many states, like Iraq and Lebanon, had no geographic or ethnic rationale. Their borders are the products of past colonial masters. With no national self-identity, social cohesion in the Arab states could be found only within the confines of the clan, a pan-Islamic or pan-Arab ideology, or through the imposition of strong antidemocratic (usually minority controlled) central regimes. Each of these solutions is, by its very nature, exclusivist and cannot tolerate competition. Conflict was an inevitable consequence of the battle for survival and supremacy in a sea of political absolutes created to cope with the absence of national self-images. It is no coincidence that Egypt, the only Arab state to make peace with Israel, is the Arab state with the strongest, most atavistic self-identity. The creation of Israel exacerbated the already existing situation because, in addition to sustaining itself as an independent, competitive, Jewish-ruled enterprise in an Arab midst (something fundamentalist Islam would not tolerate), its leaders chose to emphasize their Western rather than Semitic roots. Conflicts between all of the parties, whether as part of the Lebanese Civil War or the Israeli-Palestinian dispute, were the result of politicians throughout the region not facing up to the challenges domestic and international tolerance demand. Doing battle was an escape. And all of those who subscribed to the story line the politicians put forward were merely assisting them to escape their responsibilities by reinforcing the stereotypes and the oversimplification of events that storytelling produces. The end product of this process is what often is termed "conventional wisdom." If foreign correspondents working in the Middle East have a single common fault, it is that we allowed ourselves to be sucked in to support and validate these mass Middle Eastern exercises in political escapism.

Well-aged story lines feel good. They go down the throat as smoothly as fine sour mash. They can lull the most skilled journalistic and political practitioners into a kind of trance in which events are automatically slotted into the frame of the story line without considering that the story line may not be appropriate for the events being described. In the case of the intifada, why were we seduced by the old story line of "Arab-Israeli violent conflict over land"? Many reasons can be given. For one, so much reporting about the Israeli-Palestinian dispute in the past had legitimately been about blood-drenched disputes over land. Every knowledgeable foreign correspondent in the Middle East has had to consider the PLO dogma of "armed struggle" as a potential factor in any circumstance that involves violent conflict in the region. Then, too, common alternative story lines— such as "factional disputes within the PLO are leading to extreme violent behavior"—were patently untrue of the intifada because the events were purely local and the PLO had been caught by surprise when the uprising began.

Yet another reason for falling back on the story line is that most reporting in the Middle East is events-driven, and individual events-driven stories demand some sort of narrative glue if they are to be given any sense of continuity and context. Elie Abel, an experienced television reporter, explains the impact of events reporting this way:

> An event, however defined, is easier to report than a trend or an idea. It takes less time, meets the definition of hard news more squarely, and is, of course, inherently visual. . . . TV is a storytelling medium. It abhors ragged edges, ambiguities, and

> unresolved issues. . . . The effect all too frequently is to impose
> upon an event a preconceived form that alters reality, height-
> ening one aspect at the expense of another for the sake of a more
> compelling story, blocking out complications that get in the way
> of a narrative.[2]

It is not only television that abhors ragged edges and ambiguity. A newspaper reporter tied to a six-hundred-word slot on the foreign news page
and the radio reporter limited to thirty-five seconds have little opportunity
to explain complicated issues that may lie behind an event.

Fixed story lines also are popular because it is extraordinarily hard
for any journalist to get an overview when events happen in rapid succession and have to be tracked in detail. As one critic has pointed out,
"Journalists are fixated on the present. . . . [They] see individual or group
action, not structural or other impersonal long run forces, at the root of
most occurrences; and simplify and reduce stories to conventional symbols
for easy assimilation by audiences."[3] Added to this is the exhaustion that
comes from covering an extended and fast-breaking story in a complex
society, day after day—a natural occupational hazard. The situation is
further complicated by foreign journalists sent to the Middle East with
little or no understanding of the languages or the multitude of cultures
of the region.

I think that another, less obvious factor is at work as well. The vast
majority of Western journalists working in Israel come from nation-states
with strong national self-identities derived from a relatively homogeneous
population or with a long-accepted and respected constitution that defines
their national self-image. While we may be able to understand intellectually the idea of citizens of a state lacking a self-identity, we cannot relate
to it emotionally. We cannot conceive of the fears and even terrors pro-
voked by tribal and ethnic competition within a single nation-state or
territory, and thus we shy away from trying to relate to it in depth because

---

[2]Elie Abel, "Television in International Conflict," in *The News Media in National and International Conflict*, ed. Andrew Arno and Wimal Dissanyake (Boulder, Colo., and London:
Westview Press, 1984).
[3]David L. Paletz and Robert M. Entman, *Media. Power. Politics.* (New York: Free Press, 1981),
21.

it is not within our own life experience. The story line thus serves as a psychological shield and a cover for reporters' personal inadequacies.

The story line addiction can be broken only by asking "dumb" questions and then actually following up on the questions to see if they have real answers. It is not just a matter of questioning the facts being presented (although that is an important part of the job). It is a matter of dissecting the assumptions that are being used to tie the facts together. If the resulting pathology report contradicts conventional wisdom, the journalist has to have the guts to say aloud "The emperor has no clothes"—not easy when one is up against a powerful editor and the expenses involved in sending the kids through college.

In the case of the intifada, many hard-working, knowledgeable journalists got their individual stories right—accurate in every detail, able to be slotted into the story line with ease—and yet misrepresented the Palestinian uprising in a major way because the frame itself was no longer valid. A more accurate representation of reality would have been: "There is a social revolution going on inside the Palestinian community in the occupied territories and the actions of Israelis, together with those of Jordan and the PLO, are among the major factors contributing to the unrest."

It may seem surprising that journalists did not consider this story line of "domestic social disorder" at an early stage in the uprising. It is, particularly in the United States, one of the most common journalistic narrative threads. And it was not as though the revolution lay hidden. It was a major subject of discussion among most Palestinians. Within a couple of weeks of the start of the rioting, I was discussing the subject in depth with a wide cross-section of the Palestinian community in the occupied territories. The evidence was everywhere. Sons would not talk to their fathers—an almost unheard of phenomenon in such a patriarchal society. Worse still, they would openly contradict their fathers in public—an incredible slight. Children would talk of their grandfathers as "corrupt old men who sold us out in the 1930s and 1940s."

The problem for journalists was that in order to uncover these real, festering sores, they needed time to probe and examine, to ask the "dumb" questions. But time was at a premium because of the tyranny of the daily or, in the case of radio reporters, hourly deadlines. Television had a special problem. As ABC's bureau chief Bill Seamans noted, "Telling a background story like that takes too long, and there are no pictures." Virtually the only way a television reporter can break the hold a story line has on his or her editors is by bringing pictures to disprove the conventional wisdom. But what if there are no specific pictures to prove the point? The real story, all too often, goes untold.

The apparent unity of the uprising's leaders, who came from a number of different Palestinian factions, also served to befuddle things. This social revolution was not a clash between factions or classes or religions, places where journalists had been taught in the past to look for causes of violence in the Middle East. It was between generations within the same class, or the same religion.

However, if journalists become trapped by story lines, they also tend to become entranced by story characters, the more colorful and stereotypical the better. Journalists, as professional storytellers, need sharply defined and vivid characters, preferably ones that can be identified easily by the audience as good guys and bad guys. Reporters don't have to make value judgments of their own as to the merits of each character. They merely have to etch each protagonist sharply in words or pictures. In the Middle East, that was not hard. Even if the reporters themselves did not use labels (and many of them did), the audience, each member carrying his or her own cultural baggage and perceptions, was always quick to use terms like "aggressor," or "victim," or "fanatic."

Other processes, which began after the Six-Day War, could not but create the characters needed to support what was to become the story line. The most notable was the emergence of the Israeli army as an ideal subject for reportage. Prior to the 1967 war, it had portrayed itself as a small, light-footed scrapper ready to take on cumbersome, blowhard thugs in defense of its turf. By the time of the intifada, it was presenting an image of a big, strong, cocky, undefeated prizefighter—a modern fighting force, the best in the region and maybe, man for man, the best in the world. This self-portrait made it a large target for the press, a perfect stereotype to reinforce the story line, a highly visible lightning rod in times of crisis, and an ideal foil for all of the other protagonists in the ongoing drama.

Deliberately, the image the army rejected out of hand was that of a beat cop. Nonetheless, the role of neighborhood flatfoot was precisely what Israeli officials would assign the army when they could find no political solutions to policy problems. After the Khartoum resolution, this involved the imposition of a wide series of measures designed to exert authority over more than a million Palestinians. This is a task the commanders have never particularly relished. Promotion to general staff rank, the best and the brightest young officers know, comes not to those who prove themselves competent and imaginative in dealing with alien civilians, it goes to those who have proven themselves as warriors leading fighting units.[4] These fighting officers know that there is no greater trap for a battlefield officer than to bring a force designed to fight in open terrain into a civilian area. Therefore, where possible, these officers tried to keep their units away from civilian areas.

The Israel Defence Forces (IDF) has always viewed its primary mission as defending the nation from the threat of other armies—all the more reason why internal police actions were to be avoided almost at all cost. The exception was where there was a well-defined threat of terrorism from within the occupied territories that fitted in with the army's self-image as an armed force defending the country from other armed forces, as occurred between 1968 and 1970.[5] This inherent distaste for police work and administration was furthered later by the army's experience in Lebanon, where it was forced to deal with a hostile civilian population for which it was unprepared. The "lesson" for the army from its disastrous experience in dealing with Shiite civilians was that it should not train for crowd control or policing actions lest it be diverted from its primary missions and be asked to do police work. The job of preventing terrorism was to be left to the *Shabak*, the domestic security service, and criminal investigations were to remain within the purview of the local police units in the West Bank and the Gaza Strip.

[4]This phenomenon is not restricted just to officers working in the occupied territories but is almost a central tenet of the army. Few chiefs of the crucial and highly specialized area of military intelligence, for example, have come from *within* the intelligence system. Most were "parachuted" in after serving long periods in fighting units.
[5]During this period, the Palestinian saboteurs from within the occupied territories made extensive use of what often are termed "hot" weapons—guns and explosives smuggled in from abroad. This, in turn, led to an extensive, no-holds-barred response by the Israeli army, especially in Gaza. Because it was a case of guns against guns, media coverage generally was neutral, and even tilted slightly in favor of support for a policy of law and order, although, for example, Israeli tactics included the demolition of dozens of homes to widen streets and alleyways. Twenty years later, during the initial phase of the intifada, the Palestinians learned from their prior mistakes and kept to using "cold" weapons like rocks and bottles.

One process that was to develop out of the fighters' dislike of civilian administration was the growth of the Israeli bureaucracy in the occupied areas and the vested interests created by that bureaucracy. Under international law, governance of the occupied territories was placed in the hands of the Israeli military, and a separate bureaucratic apparatus was established to rule over and to provide services to the local Arab population. As the Israeli presence within the occupied territories solidified, the number of Israeli civil servants (mostly young military officers) grew apace. As the bureaucracy aged, and in some cases ossified, jobs originally thought of as temporary became sinecures that required defending. People who had worked in these jobs for several years knew that their chances of advancement within the regular "fighting" army system were limited and they were concerned with holding on to what they had. Although these administrators were the primary, and often the only, contacts Palestinians had with the Israeli authorities, developing imaginative solutions to the Palestinians' social and economic problems was of less concern to these bureaucrats-in-uniform ("jobniks" in Israeli slang) than maintaining the status quo through administrative means. It was patently obvious to all who worked in the military administration that the promotions available went to those best able to maintain stability at the least cost and with the least effort. These administrators were to become the natural allies of Jordan's King Hussein. For both him and his allies, administrative control over the Palestinians and risk avoidance were to become a well-honed profession. And for many years—until the intifada—the king and the Israelis worked together in what came to be called "the condominium of the occupied territories."

Another process was the emergence of a clearly defined sense of "peoplehood" among the Palestinians living under the Israeli occupation. The burgeoning feeling of specific Palestinian nationalism provided a perfect foil for Israel's Zionist vision. Unfortunately for the Palestinians, this growing national identity was not accompanied by a leadership structure capable of dealing with the real social and political problems that arose in the wake of the occupation.

The traditional form of leadership centered around a system developed by the Ottoman Turks as a means of controlling their large, widely dispersed, and ethnically diverse subjects. After the Turks were expelled from the Levant during World War I, this system was adopted by the successor rulers—the British, the Jordanians, and finally the Israelis. The system was based on the *mukhtar*, a village or clan headman who was appointed by the authorities in consultation with the local families. He was paid a small sum by whoever was in power at the time, but made much of his money as the intermediary between the family and the authorities and as the authorized signatory on many legal documents. The *mukhtar*, for example, was required to sign the survey maps that accompanied land titles. In return, the *mukhtar* often was held responsible for the actions of members of his clan and was expected to control their excesses.

Although the Israelis wanted to maintain the *mukhtar* system as a convenient method of political control, they inadvertently undermined it. For example, the Israelis wanted to control the inflow of workers coming to find employment in Israel, so they set up labor exchanges. Once those exchanges were established, the need for family connections or intervention by the *mukhtars* in finding work became far less important. Furthermore, the *mukhtars* found time and again that they had become singularly ineffective in intervening with the Israeli administrators on a whole series of painful issues—for example, the issuance of permits for Palestinians living outside the occupied territories to be reunited with their families. Many *mukhtars*, used to the old, traditional ways, did not have the tools to understand what was happening or to influence the Israeli authorities. And if they could not deliver the goods, they could have no legitimacy. By the time the intifada broke out, most of the *mukhtars* had been discredited by the youngsters in their own families.

Another form of leadership rested in the oligarchy that controlled much of the trade and commerce in the West Bank and Gaza. Collectively, they were called "the notables." They often were called in for consultations to discuss government policy, and during the period of Jordanian rule, they often were awarded seats in the government or the upper house of Parliament. The growing radicalization of Palestinian youngsters and the oft-repeated question "Why did you lose the [1948] war?" did much to diminish the informal authority the heads of the leading families once had wielded. It did not help that most of these families, for economic and social reasons, were closely allied with King Hussein, whom a majority of the young Palestinians despised.

During the occupation, a small coterie of local leaders did develop. Some were moderates, many were not. Some were awarded formal authority as mayors, trade union leaders, or heads of institutions. Others were content with the informal authority they could wield. Most of these individuals were authentic voices, able to mobilize constituencies and to raise issues in public. In one way or another, though, almost all were silenced, either by Israel, or by the Jordanians, or by the PLO. The Israeli tack was to imprison or expel. The Jordanians restricted movement over the bridges across the Jordan River that connected the West Bank to Jordan. And the PLO either threatened violence or killed whomever its leaders opposed.

Complicating the problem was the fact that the interests of the Palestinians under Israeli occupation always took at least second place in the list of concerns of those outside the occupied territories who might have been in a position to represent them on the world stage. At a very early period in the history of the occupation, the Palestine Liberation Organization appropriated to itself the mantle of "the sole legitimate representative of the Palestinian people." That role was given official sanction at the 1974 Fez Arab League summit conference. However, from the outset, the leaders of the PLO viewed the two-thirds of all Palestinians living outside the occupied territories as their primary constituency. That diaspora constituency was not interested in a separate settlement with Israel that would include only the West Bank and the Gaza Strip within a Palestinian-controlled entity. The Palestinians living in the refugee camps in Lebanon, Syria, and Jordan or working in the Arabian Peninsula were not interested in the overcrowded warrens of Gaza or the large desert areas of the Jordan Valley Rift. They wanted to go back to their original homes in Haifa and Jaffa and Lydda—which meant dismantling the Jewish State. Without a willingness to compromise by the expatriates who controlled and still control the PLO, the issues of relevance to the Palestinians under occupation could not even be addressed by those who purported to speak on their behalf.

King Hussein attempted to address some of those issues—notably education, health, and welfare matters and financial transfers—out of a personal and national self-interest. His primary concern was to insure that large-scale Palestinian unrest did not slop over from the occupied territories into Jordan and threaten his regime. He had historical precedents to remind him of his vulnerability. His grandfather, King Abdullah, was assassinated by a Palestinian outside Jerusalem's al-Aksa mosque, and there had been dozens of attempts on Hussein's life as well.

Although no census has been taken in Jordan, it is commonly believed that the Palestinians now form a majority of the population in the kingdom. In 1969 and throughout most of 1970, the Palestinians had threatened Hussein's throne by creating what amounted to an independent, separate state within the kingdom, complete with an armed militia and a considerable degree of self-rule, especially within the refugee camps. That threat to the king's throne was quashed only in 1970, as part of the big, bloody, and bitter military confrontation that Palestinians have come to call "the Black September." To the king, the question that was always uppermost was how the Palestinians could be controlled so that there would not be a repetition of 1969–70. He believed that he was too weak to compromise with Israel without the approval of the PLO and the other Arab states. Thus, in the end, he, too, could not deal with the deep-rooted social problems that would soon grow in the occupied territories.

The other Arab countries were also too preoccupied with their matters of state to take up the cudgels on behalf of the Palestinians under occupation—except when it suited their national purposes. Egypt usually was preoccupied with internal matters or with securing the withdrawal of the Israeli army from the Sinai desert. Even after the withdrawal of the Israelis was complete, Cairo had little leverage to use with Israel. Iraq was at first preoccupied with its long-standing dispute with its neighbor Syria, and later was busily at war with Iran. Lebanon had no influence at all and, at a later stage, became engaged in an exercise in self-dismemberment. And Syria was at odds with everyone.

That they could do little to help the Palestinians did not prevent the outside Arab nations from trying to influence or control the Palestinians under occupation by money or threats. What little political assistance they did provide was usually in the form of military or verbal threats directed against Israel and the United States—ideally suited to maintain the story line and the escapism of the principal actors.

Yet another process was the slow creep of Israeli settlement in the occupied areas. The more time that went by without a solution, the more time annexationists had to plan and execute strategies. Although relatively few in number, these ideologues more than made up for their demographic deficiencies with a fervor that forced the government to bow to their wishes. With the advent of the Likud-led government in 1977, settlement expanded rapidly. Large government loans and a promise of a "quality life" drew Israeli city dwellers to the West Bank. This new type of settler was drawn to the occupied areas not for ideological reasons but by the promise of a single-family house with a little garden and the absence of automobile exhaust fumes that were choking Tel Aviv. Once ensconced in their new homes, however, they formed the basis of a whole new constituency within the Israeli electorate with a stake in the status quo, in real competition for, and in conflict with, the Palestinians over the control of land.

All of these processes, in turn, created another: a continuous international focus on the region by major world states. Every major Western country—particularly after the 1973 oil embargo—had a "Middle East policy," which it would enunciate at regular intervals. The constant publicity these nations gave to the Middle East—for various domestic political reasons—kept the dispute before the public eye. The primary concern for most of these nations was not a resolution of the Arab-Israeli dispute but the maintenance of assured supplies of petroleum products. Since it was the Yom Kippur War that had provided the catalyst for massive oil price rises, the focus of many of these policy statements was on the prevention of future conflicts. The most frequently offered diplomatic solution to the dispute was usually termed "land for peace": an Israeli withdrawal from the occupied territories in return for recognition of Israel's right to exist. This formula, however, had the effect of reinforcing the already-accepted story line among both diplomats and journalists. "Land for peace" is just the flip side of "Arab-Israeli conflict over land." Media events, such as television debates between advocates of the Israeli or Arab position, the visits of officials from the various Middle Eastern states to foreign capitals, and intense coverage of terrorist hijackings, aided in maintaining the focus of public attention on that which was either militarily or verbally violent.

The end result of all of these processes was inevitable: a strong presence by the foreign press corps in the area, a desire by the Israeli authorities to maintain control over the Arabs at as low a cost as possible, an un-willingness to compromise on critical issues by the PLO leadership, risk avoidance by all of the Jordanian and Israeli actors, and growing frustration among Palestinians within the territories.

Had the Palestinians in the territories been able to raise their own voices publicly without the threat of death or expulsion hanging over them, and had they been given an opportunity to deal with their problems, the story line as projected by both the local Palestinians and the press might well have changed. But that was not to be. The result was an explosion in the streets by the young and the disenfranchised.

By the time the intifada broke out, approximately 70 percent of the Palestinians in the occupied territories were under the age of twenty-four. They had known life only under the conditions created by the Israeli occupation. These young Palestinians perceived not only an inability to direct their own futures but also an ongoing breakdown of the most basic socioeconomic survival mechanisms used by their elders for at least two generations—and in some cases, for hundreds of years. Those mutually supportive mechanisms, which combined advanced education and free movement with traditional social rights, the protection offered by extended families and clans, and norms of property holding and local leadership, had once provided Palestinians with a workable social safety net. During the years of the Israeli occupation, however, that fine web had come apart.

To understand the processes and concerns within the Palestinian community, a researcher had to go out into the field before the social volcano blew—a thing done by few Israeli officials, journalists, diplomats, or academics. Such research requires hours of small talk over coffee and repeated meetings before trust can be developed. Instead, in a mutually supportive way and with the self-interested support of the Palestinian elite, those who might have reexamined the situation on behalf of the public continued to work on the basis of the original story line—that of Arab-Israeli conflict. Few of those to whom I spoke over the last few years—all claiming to be close observers of the scene in the occupied territories—were even aware that a critical mass of unrest had been built up. They were suffering from tunnel vision created by the cossetting effect of the agreed upon story line.

When the intifada broke out, there was an opportunity to alter the old story line or to substitute a different one. Chaotic times, when the course of events is uncertain, are often the ideal moment for a reexamination of cherished beliefs. They are also, however, the very moment when people seek an easy lifeline that can be held on to in the face of such uncertain situations. The craving for a lifeline would overpower the need for a reexamination of old presumptions. And so the story line continued to play its insidious role, as all of those involved focused almost entirely on how to fit the events that were occurring into the basic narrative. The stonings of Israeli soldiers and the shooting of Palestinians were reported almost entirely within the context of an Arab-Israeli dispute. In fact, the situation was considerably different. More than just an expression of rage against the Israeli occupation, the intifada was an outward manifestation of the social revolution that had been under way on the West Bank and in Gaza for more than a decade. The Israelis became the public focus when the rebellion went aboveground, but the rebellion essentially was directed at reforming Palestinian society from within so that the major social and political interests of the residents of the territories finally could be addressed, and so that the Palestinians could throw off the shackles of control from without. The Israelis were simply the only ones against whom the young Palestinians could express their sense of outrage. And so naturally, it was against the symbols of Israeli authority— the soldiers—that the stones were directed.

The Israelis, for all their political and social myopia, were by no means the only figures responsible for the outbreak of the unrest. The dissolution of the Palestinian social fabric stemmed to a large extent from a belief common to Israel, the Arab states, and the PLO that it was in each one's interest to control Palestinian actions in the occupied territories. Using a combination of incentives, threats, and administrative controls, each group was intent on preventing the Palestinian heads of households from openly rejecting the authority from without that was being imposed on them. What none of these outside parties realized was that the cumulative effect of each of their efforts was to lift the level of fear among the young Palestinians to the point of despair, until the youngsters believed that they had nothing to lose. The outsiders also failed to take into account that the move to rebellion could jump an entire generation. When the rioting broke out in December 1987, the Israelis and the Arabs were caught totally by surprise. So, too, were the foreign reporters.

Indeed, none of the major social issues with which the Palestinians were concerned most was aired publicly or had become the subject for open debate in the six months prior to the outbreak of the rioting. Even the Arab summit meeting in Amman in November 1987 did not address these issues. The old story line had done its unseen job again. What was not conflict was not considered news. *Time* magazine's Jamil Hamad relates that he submitted a story in May 1987 on the West Bank and had to wait until October before it was published. Other longtime reporters say that from the beginning of the 1982 Israeli war in Lebanon, the Palestinians in the occupied territories had become a "nonstory," one for which they could find no interest among their editors except during peak periods of demonstrations and "point violence." The story line that was supposed to aid the analyst and the audience to make events more understandable was, in fact, holding back both the reporter and the audience from acquiring new perceptions.

It is a truism of news coverage of Israel that anytime there is a superstable political or social situation, and therefore a drought of hard news, a major explosion can be expected within six months. The period immediately prior to the outbreak of rioting in the occupied territories was precisely one of deep drought. Yet in a survey I conducted of thirty foreign correspondents, only one besides myself had used that drought to explore in depth what was happening in the occupied territories—and he had specific reasons for doing so: he was returning to Jerusalem after several years in the home office and wanted to get reacquainted with old friends. The vast majority of the reporters I spoke to said they either did no work there because they couldn't interest their editors in anything, or they produced the kind of soft feature stories often called "fluff" or "puff pieces" in the trade.

This lack of preparatory work meant that the vast majority of reporters were ill equipped to analyze the intifada in depth when the rioting broke out. Deep-seated issues, like Palestinian emigration due to lack of jobs, the drop in per capita income in Gaza and the slowdown in the growth of per capita income in the West Bank, the breakdown in the system of traditional leadership among Palestinians, and the inability of the traditional leadership to persuade the Israelis to permit 150,000 expatriate Palestinians to be reunited with their families, went unreported. What was reported was the violence, because it could be slotted so easily into a widely accepted story line. The journalists, particularly in the early stages of the uprising, retreated into events reporting, reinforcing the story line. It should act as a warning to all of us in the field. If present trends continue and ethnically based conflicts between two cultures that are unfamiliar to us grow in number, we will be facing similar circumstances in the future—but more often.

I cannot think of a more complex, uneasy, and misunderstood ménage à trois than that which exists between the Israelis, the Palestinians living in the occupied territories, and the foreign press. We are all bound together, not out of love but out of necessity. We have difficulty living with one another but know that we cannot live without one another. The result is an enduring contentiousness in which each party feels itself under attack and besieged by a power that it cannot fully control—but that it can and must use in order to serve its own interests. Within this tricornered adversarial embrace, each party tries to increase its own freedom of movement, while at the same time trying to set limits on what the other two can do to it. It is an unending fight for an oxymoronic ideal—that of a dynamic stability.

What makes the battle for survival all the more dif-

T · W · O

Caught in a Cage of Their Own Design

ficult is the fact that, especially during crises, each party cannot but come face to face with some of the central myths that usually help to sustain it in times of distress and uncertainty—and invariably the myths are found wanting. The reality that pursues each party relentlessly is inescapable. And often unlikable.

To understand how this marriage of convenience works—and often doesn't work—one has to look at the histories and backgrounds of each of the partners and how they were brought together in the first place.

From the very beginning of the Zionist enterprise, the basic motto of the major Israeli political parties was "co-opt or control." Centralization and the capacity to apply sanctions within the various political groupings, and eventually within the state, provided the means of control. Proportional representation by vested interest groups within each party and in the larger political fora became the vehicle for co-optation. Any group could find a niche for itself—and have that niche legitimized by others— so long as it undertook to play by the existing rules. The preferred choice was co-optation because, inevitably, it was easier to buy someone off than to fight with him or her. Moreover, those who could be persuaded to join in the enterprise then had a stake in sustaining the prevailing system. That did not mean that Israeli political leaders were averse to using control measures. The political parties and other public organizations did and still do use a variety of sanctions and penalties against political heretics and ideological deviants. Control, however, simply was more inconvenient and required centralized policing techniques, whereas co-optation usually was self-policing, as each partner sought jealously to protect its share—and to ensure that no one else got too much.

It is difficult for someone who has not lived with the system for some time to understand just how pervasive it is. The political parties are not merely vehicles for political expression, they are surrogate extended families. Although much of their power over social institutions has waned in recent years, their tentacles still reach down deep into everyday life. From the moment a child is born, he or she is brought into the system. The political parties control health-fund clinics where the child will receive doctors' care, they run the youth movement or sports club where the youngster will play and be socialized into his or her peer group, and they control wide patronage systems and even large businesses and banks that provide jobs and credit. Membership in the system is predicated on the acceptance by the individual of the Zionist ideal of a Jewish state run by Jews for Jews and of the supremacy of the political leadership, whether elected or not, to make decisions that affect the personal lives of all those within the community. Those individuals who choose to remain outside the system, who never learn how it works, or who break its tangle of minute, tacit rules, are isolated or punished.

A central tenet of the centralized system is that knowledge provides power, and information is a commodity to be centrally controlled and regulated. When combined with the preoccupation with national security and the security services' natural penchant for secrecy and their belief that almost any data that even remotely relates to national defense is the stuff spies thrive on, this tenet provides a very considerable obstacle to the free flow of information. Another tenet is summed up in the word Israeli officials use for public relations: *hasbara*, meaning, literally, "explanation." The assumption is that if Israel only explains its position well enough, any rational person cannot but agree with the government's position.

A very good example of co-optation is the means used to bring and to keep the local press under the bureaucratic umbrella. The stage was set long before Israel became a state. The editors and senior journalists on both the Jewish and Palestinian sides in mandatory Palestine saw themselves not as checks on their politicians but as activists deeply involved in their individual national struggles for independence. When Israel was founded, the Jewish press continued to view its role as that of a participant in the task of building up the country—as aides to the government "in helping to implement policy."[1] It formed a closed club that came to be known as the Editors' Committee. In return for regular, high-level background briefings on the affairs of state, the leaders of the Israeli press agreed to voluntary self-censorship. This technique of providing access in order to silence is neither new nor restricted to Israel. It was used successfully, for example, by General George Patton, who briefed American military correspondents prior to the invasion of Italy in World War II. In

[1]Moshe Negbi, "Paper Tiger: The Struggle for Press Freedom in Israel," *Jerusalem Quarterly* 39 (1986): 17–32.

a somewhat different form, it was used by the British during the Falklands War and by the United States during the invasions of Grenada and Panama. In these cases, reporters attached to the invading forces simply were sequestered in camps or on board ships—permitted to talk freely to the soldiers but forbidden either to file reports on military plans or to see most of the action on the ground.

In Israel, the system has at times reached monumentally absurd proportions. Perhaps the most egregious, although certainly not the only example I witnessed, occurred on the eve of the 1973 Yom Kippur War. In the first week of October, foreign media reports outside Israel began describing massive troop buildups along Israel's borders with Syria and Egypt. On October 3, Chief of Staff Lieutenant General David Elazar convened a meeting with the Editors' Committee at which he confirmed the buildup—but asked the editors not to use the story, which already had been reported around the world. Not only did the editors agree, but they also withheld crucial information from their own military correspondents about what had transpired during the briefing.

The system of editorial co-optation began to break down with the election of Menachem Begin as prime minister in 1977. He refused to meet with the editors. Instead, he either appealed to the public directly in speeches at public gatherings and appearances on radio and television, or he held background briefings with a few selected reporters and editors with whom he had developed close ideological ties during his time in the political wilderness. When Ariel Sharon became defense minister in 1981, the breakdown in the system of co-optation advanced even further, since he not only refused to meet with the editors, he forbade his chief of staff to do so as well. This adversarial relationship may have been one of the major contributing factors in the highly critical coverage the Israeli press delivered during the 1982 war in Lebanon.

The system of co-optation does not merely begin at the top and filter down. It is all-inclusive. "Beat" journalists in Israel are divided into *ta'im*, or cells. Each reporter who joins a *ta* requires special accreditation and is given special access to newsmaking institutions, such as the Knesset, the police, or the army. In return, no matter how personally outspoken or politically contentious he or she may want to be, each reporter is subject to certain strictures and subtle pressures. Despite these pressures, the country has produced a goodly number of serious critics and independent investigative reporters who deal with domestic issues. However, reporters assigned to beats that somehow relate to national security issues are far less free. "It is a world of 'gentlemen's agreements,' " one longtime local reporter relates. "They always call on our national loyalties, or the effects a particular story may have on foreign relations, in order to try to get us to kill reports they don't like."

The military correspondents are a special case in point, an almost idealized example of how Israeli officialdom would like the entire system to work. For these press practitioners, not only "gentlemen's agreements"[2] apply. Military field reporters are treated as though they are an integral part of the army, and in wartime, they are mobilized, put into uniform, and subject to all military strictures and military law. Even during peacetime, however, reports filed by these correspondents, according to Deputy Chief Military Spokesman Raanan Gissin, must be vetted not only by the military censors but by the military spokesman as well. "Israeli military correspondents have a special status," he says. "But they have to pay for it."

Two other aspects of the press system in Israel deserve special note. The first is that the broadcast media are a government monopoly—with the boards of directors of the Israel Broadcasting Authority (IBA) appointed according to a parliamentary political key. Each major party nominates a given number of board members in direct proportion to its strength in the Knesset. The powerful director general of the authority is appointed only after consultations within the government—and usually is expected to adhere to a particular political hue. Thus, the broadcast media are viewed not so much as a service to the public—although that is what is publicly professed by the politicians—but as a tool of the government.

The second aspect is the special role played by the Arabic language service of the IBA. This service is treated specifically as a propaganda arm of the government. All of the material it broadcasts is thoroughly vetted for the total message it carries. Thus, as would be expected, Israel's successes, rather than its failures, are highlighted. Deterrence is stressed, not sympathy. With the appointment of a Likud-oriented management in the early 1980s, the service's freedom to report was further restricted. For

---

[2]The term is a great misnomer because, at the time of writing, two of the leading military correspondents were women.

example, for almost three decades, the IBA's English- and French-language news services had been broadcast on the Arabic language's powerful transmitter. However, under the new right-wing management, the English and French news reports were seen to be insufficiently under control. The reporters, born and trained abroad, had a different, more questioning ethos. As a result, a decision was made to remove the two news services from the Arabic-language station. IBA officials admitted at the time that the two news services did have large audiences in the Arab countries. Nonetheless, the two services were downgraded to a low-power transmitter on a different station.

For decades, the overall system of co-opt or control worked, if imperfectly. A state was created, hundreds of thousands of immigrants were given new homes, farms were carved out of swamp and desert lands, and industries were built—primarily through centralized planning. The Six-Day War, however, brought with it fundamental changes in the society that were to have a deep and lasting effect on the system of co-optation and control. Among those changes was the introduction into the Israeli body politic of two groups that could neither be co-opted on a long-term basis nor be totally controlled: the Palestinians in the occupied territories and the foreign press corps.

In keeping with previous practice, the Israelis did set out to co-opt these two new foreign bodies.[3] The problem for the Israelis was that neither the foreign press nor the Palestinians were interested in entering into the system, and the Israelis never were willing or capable of offering enough inducements in return to draw these two groups willy-nilly into the system. Unlike the local press, the foreigners did not accept the premise that they should be part of the nation-building enterprise. Their loyalties were to the story itself, to their professional reputations, and, in some cases, to their home governments. And, unlike the Arabs living within the pre-1967 boundaries of the state, the Palestinians in the occupied territories accepted neither the legitimacy of the state nor the right of the political

---

[3]It is not my intention to pass judgment on whether co-optation is a "good" or "bad" thing. It is, however, an important fact of life of which every journalist must be aware. Award-winning American journalists like Edward R. Murrow and Drew Middleton certainly were co-opted by the British as part of Winston Churchill's efforts to draw the United States into World War II, and they were lauded for their efforts.

leaders to govern them. Their loyalty was to themselves and their desire for a country that they could call their own.

The Israelis, for their part, were unable to come up with comprehensive strategies for dealing with these aliens. They couldn't get rid of either of these foreign bodies without serious international consequences. Nonetheless, they believed that they had to manage the "threat" each group posed. The result was a string of short-term, tactically based programs that had the pretense to policy but that led to actions that were haphazard in both planning and execution.

Within Israeli officialdom, there was no consensus on what to do with the foreign journalists who streamed into the country in the wake of the Six-Day War. The foreign press had played a very prominent and important role in Israel's formative years, and thus, foreign correspondents were viewed as an important public relations tool that could not be ignored. It was the foreign press that had displayed to the world the crimes committed against the Jews in the Nazi concentration camps, and in doing so had created an international atmosphere supportive of the establishment of the state. The press had helped mythologize the young pioneers in the kibbutzim, the new immigrants flowing into the country from around the world, and the new Jewish army. The press was an essential communications link in Israel's search for international recognition and legitimacy. And yet, it was not a part of the society. In Israel, however, there was, and is, no formal or legal definition of the role the press should play— or be allowed to play—such as that defined in the United States under the First Amendment. Fortunately for Israeli officials, until 1967, this did not have to be a matter of concern. The foreign press corps in Israel was small and manned largely by local stringers who were part of the system.

In the initial period following the Six-Day War, the foreign press corps was looked on as a wonderful public relations device—so long as the journalists could be kept in their place and remain docile and servile. There is little doubt that the foreign press corps in Israel was co-opted during the 1967 war and in the three years that followed. For U.S. correspondents in particular, Israel initially seemed to mirror and embody all of the most dearly held American values. It was a democracy in a political sea of dictatorships, monarchies, or oligarchies. It prided itself on its sense of community, self-reliance, modern scientific and educational institutions, rural and small-town values, and egalitarianism, and on being a bulwark against Soviet expansionism in the Middle East. Although a young nation, Israel was able to present itself as the heir to the ancient Judeo-Christian tradition. The image it projected was of a politically moderate, morally upright, fiscally responsible state with a strong, independent judiciary. Americans like winners, and Israel was a winner in the battle for national liberty. And most of all, it was the site of the Holy Land, with all that that brought to mind. The initial infatuation, however, was not to last. The foreign press could not and would not play the role the Israelis wanted to assign it: that of a simple mouthpiece.

For politicians anywhere to be able to co-opt Western journalists over time, certain conditions need to be met. Not all of the conditions need be present at all times, but the more there are, the more favorable is the environment for co-optation.

There must be a consensus between the reporters and the politicians on a shared value system. There must be a shared perception that those enduring values are threatened by an enemy that is implacably opposed to them. There should be a joint recognition that the nation involved has no moral or other alternative but to fight if it is to protect that value system. There should be a sense that victory for the "enemy" offers only two alternatives: total submission or death. The journalists also must believe that the "rewards" for being co-opted are at least equal to or greater than those that may accrue from opposing the system. And the leadership of the country involved needs to be respected by both the journalists and the country's citizens and be considered legitimate under the shared value system. There should be a belief by the journalists that the leadership has a clear mandate for action from its constituency, with an agreed-on set of "rules of the game" and an agreed-on set of limits on the leadership's freedom of action. There has to be a presumption that any violence the leadership needs to use in order to protect the nation or to execute policy will be proportionate, reasonable under the circumstances, and deliberately designed to avoid injuring the innocent. Finally, the leadership needs to prove constantly that it has information that is unavailable from any other source, or information that cannot readily be challenged by another legitimate source.

Almost all of these conditions prevailed in Israel up to September 1970. It was therefore hard for a foreign correspondent not to be co-opted. It would have taken superhuman qualities, for example, not to identify with the position of the individual Israeli soldier trying to survive in his bunker at the Suez Canal. A reporter's trip to the canal zone usually would begin at about 2:30 A.M. The journalist would drive down from Tel Aviv with an army escort officer and reach the Baluza crossroads—just outside the range of Egyptian guns—just before daybreak. One could hear the rumble of tank and artillery fire in the background and watch the soldiers nervously waiting around for the signal to move. After a while, the Egyptians would halt their fire to let their big guns cool down. Then the order would come to move down to the waterline. These respites usually did not last more than twenty minutes—and every second was precious. The army vehicles would careen wildly down the narrow, sand-swept paved road to the front. When the command cars and jeeps reached their destination—usually about two hundred yards from the forward bunkers—everyone would jump out and make a mad dash for the cover provided by the ties and rails of the Sinai railroad, which had been torn up to provide roofs and joists for the bunkers. And then the fighting would begin again. First would come the bursts of machine-gun fire, then the mortars, and finally the heavy guns. The din was deafening, the fear of a direct hit intense and palpable. It was the terror of World War I trench warfare in instant replay. One could not but be drawn to identify with the fears, false bravado, and shock the eighteen- and nineteen-year-old conscripts were undergoing. Anyone present was bound in a brotherhood whose only requirement for entry was the desire to survive.

The incident that stands out most in my mind from that period, because it illustrates so well the bond created by a realization of our common human frailty, was a conversation with a medic. The biggest problem he had to deal with among the soldiers, he told me, was constipation. Soon I was to see why. There were no underground toilets. Anyone who had to relieve himself had to do so in crude latrines and outhouses. At each break in the shelling, the first priority had to go to checking the defenses to see if there had been any damage—or if the shelling had been just a cover for a commando raid. If supplies were coming in, unloading them had to take high priority, too. Only then, after group needs had been taken care of, could the soldiers take a moment for personal necessities. If the Egyptians kept to their schedule, the machine-gun fire would provide enough warning to allow anyone caught out in the open to reach cover in time. But the Egyptians were not always so obliging and often would begin their barrages with mortar fire. Unlike guns, with their instant ra-ta-ta-tat and high-pitched whine in flight, mortar bombs are silent—until they explode. There is no warning. And many Israeli soldiers, literally having been caught with their pants down once, dared not try a second time—even when almost deathly ill. After only a day in the trenches, one could not but feel for the real agony these soldiers were undergoing.

Away from the front lines, there was the excitement of covering a major and exotic political story and of being carried along by—indeed, being a part of—a tidal wave of events. For foreign correspondents, the years that followed the passage of the Khartoum resolution were heady. There was a battle for the survival of the pan-Arabist ideology in Egypt, a fight for personal and dynastic survival in Jordan, a reawakening of fervent Palestinian nationalism in refugee camps throughout the Arab world, and confusion about the future direction of public and social policy in Israel. This was not back room or salon politics. It was not the politics of measured debate. Each public declaration, each event, each campaign, was part of an extended raw battle for political supremacy and survival that was lubricated by bloodied bodies. To Israel's east, Palestinian saboteurs began making raids across the Jordan River. The western desert slopes of the Jordan rift became known as "the land of the chases" as Israeli military units scurried hither and yon trying to trap the saboteurs who had crossed the frontier during the night. The Gaza Strip became a scene of daily shoot-outs, Wild West style, between Palestinians and Israeli soldiers. To the north, Lebanon's once-placid border became a pathway for infiltrators. In the south, Egypt declared a war of attrition along the Suez Canal that every day would see as many as fifty thousand artillery and mortar shells flying over the canal each way. The Israelis retaliated with deep-penetration bombing raids in the Jordan Valley and the Egyptian heartland. Each day seemed to bring with it a new escalation in the level of violence, and what the journalists in Israel saw and reported on could not have been anything but one-sided.

No less a reason for co-optation was the fact that the journalists who came to Israel after 1967 did not yet know the country well enough to be able to interpret domestic events accurately and fully. As they became familiar with the society, they began to see some of the warts. Later, particularly after the Yom Kippur War, Israeli society was in a state of flux, and as the nature of the society changed, so did journalists' perceptions of it. Demographic changes, including the rise to political preeminence by the Sephardic Jews (those of Asian and African origin), brought with them a political worldview vastly different from that of Israel's European-bred founding fathers—and of the United States. The increasing power of the various religious groups plying their worldly political wares came into conflict with fundamental attitudes and perceptions among American correspondents regarding the separation of church and state. The appearance of mystic nationalists and true believers in the vanguard of Israeli subjugation of the Palestinians made Westerners uncomfortable and critical.

Clashes became inevitable between the press and Israeli officials who continued to try to sell the ideal rather than the real. There was a fundamental lack of understanding by Israeli officials of how the foreign press viewed its mission and what it was supposed to do. When coupled with a fear of what those journalists might do, the attitude of many Israeli officials toward the foreign press corps became one of ambivalence at best, and open hostility at worst.

The foreign press corps was treated, in general, as though it were a pipe, capped at both ends by valves. One valve was to be opened by spokesmen to allow a trickle of self-serving information to enter. Once the information had passed through the pipe, a second valve, operated by the military censors, was designed to prevent the outflow of information that might have leaked into the pipe and might cause what often was called "damage to national security." It was a system that had been developed by the British Mandatory Authorities during World War II and had been slightly refined after Israel first became a state in 1948. However, this control mechanism could work only so long as the conditions prevalent in World War II remained constant. For the system of controls to operate effectively, the Israeli bureaucracy needed to maintain an information monopoly and control both over access to information and over the means to deliver information abroad—and it had to have the capability to impose real and effective sanctions against journalists who broke the rules.

The Israeli bureaucrats were aided immensely in this particular endeavor by the wall-to-wall government in power in Jerusalem during and immediately after the 1967 war, by communications links that had not improved much since World War II, and especially by their Arab counterparts. So long as foreign journalists had to contend with borders sealed by the Arabs to anyone who was known to have served in Israel, a system of political control by one large governing coalition in Jerusalem, and a primitive Israeli communications system, this mechanism could work.

In the days and years that followed the Six-Day War, these conditions changed. The barbed wire separating Israel from the West Bank was torn down, and eventually, the Arab states' boycott of Israeli-based journalists was honored more in the breach than in the practice—which allowed journalists to seek out alternative points of view. Increasing fragmentation within the Israeli political system, changes in regional political processes, and social upheavals within Israeli society meant that sources of information no longer could be centrally controlled. And eventually, sophisticated communications technology made the foreign press corps largely independent in its ability to transmit information abroad. The Israeli system of co-optation and control, like some prehistoric dinosaur, could not adapt quickly enough to changed environmental conditions.

Within Israel during the two decades that followed the Six-Day War, there were frequent calls for changes in the system. An Information Ministry was established in 1974 but died after an intense campaign against it by the Foreign Ministry. Also in 1974, a military committee studied the handling of the press during wartime. In 1976, a report from the National Command and Staff College of the Israel Defence Forces recommended that senior commanders consider the press to be an integral part of their "operational environment." In other words, the potential actions and reactions of the press should be given significant consideration in tactical and strategic planning. In 1989, yet another military commission, this time headed by the widely respected former director of Military Intelligence, Shlomo Gazit, submitted a report on how the army should deal with the press. In between 1974 and 1989, there were innumerable discussions in public and in the press over the role of journalists, both local and foreign, in Israeli society.

What is striking about almost every governmental report and most of the public discussion, however, is that the "solutions" proposed were almost completely technical and bureaucratic in nature rather than conceptual and substantive. They dealt with subjects like where to place offices and how the internal bureaucratic chain of command should be organized. Difficult as it is to believe of a country that attracts widespread media attention, few spokesmen in Israel have had any training in either journalism or public relations, and only one, Dan Pattir, who was a media adviser to prime ministers Yitzchak Rabin and Menachem Begin, had ever been a correspondent for a foreign media outlet. Spokesmanship, as a trade, was never considered as a career track within the Israeli system. It was either a dead-end job for someone about to retire, an interim job slot for someone wanting to work elsewhere, or a short stepping-stone for a careerist with other, high-flying objectives. There have been some spokesmen, like American-born Ze'ev Chafetz, who became director of the Government Press Office when Prime Minister Begin came to power, who were notable for their openness, thoughtfulness, and understanding of the foreign reporter's trade. But there were also many others who were as thickheaded, defensive, and risk-averse as one could conceive of.

Those who sat on the various committees investigating the spokesmanship system were usually products of the Israeli system and thus simply ignorant of what makes a foreign journalist tick. They therefore made no real attempt to explore the ethos of the foreign press, a prerequisite for understanding how and why it functions as it does. Just as someone who has not been a soldier will find it more difficult to comprehend the depth of fear, the sweaty relief at remaining alive after a close encounter with death, the intensity of fatigue after battle, and the smell of dust, mud, and gunpowder, so, too, it is difficult for someone who has not been a foreign reporter to identify with the visceral and emotional element of journalism—the frustrations of a promising story that does not pan out, the intellectual challenge of trying to understand the workings of an alien society, the deadening fatigue that comes from working simultaneously in two different time zones seven hours apart, and the elation that comes with insight into what seemed to be an intractable problem of comprehension.

In reading the Israeli committee reports, one gets the impression that the Israelis also did not recognize the impact that changes in Israel and the region were having on the foreign press corps, and therefore, the committee members did not plan for the consequences. Each discussion on the role of the foreign press seemed to take as its starting point the need to perpetuate the status quo. There was no sense of the dynamic in reporting as a whole, and of foreign reporting from Israel in particular. Committee members, as a result, only tinkered with the mechanical aspects of control without questioning the assumptions and presumptions on which the system rested. By failing to recognize and to deal with the evolving situation realistically, the Israeli system of co-optation and control became progressively weaker over the years and collapsed entirely when the intifada broke out.

The basic Israeli method for handling the foreign press rests on the assumption that more than half the battle for control can be won if access to newsmaking events can be regulated—thus forcing the journalists into a posture of dependency.[4] The task of regulation was given to the spokes-people. All requests for information or interviews had to go through the official spokesperson of each ministry or department, and, at least until the mid-1970s, foreign journalists who tried to contact civil servants directly, and were caught, usually were called into the spokesperson's office for a dressing down. Sanctions could be imposed by the simple procedure of denying a journalist access to a newsmaker or to an official with information. The mechanism of control could survive, however, only so long as the monopoly on information distribution remained intact and so long as the information emanating from each department was timely, had been coordinated, was coherent, was of better quality than that available from any other source, was evenly and fairly distributed to all of the reporters, and, most of all, was credible. By the end of the 1973 Yom Kippur War, none of these conditions prevailed.

The breakdown process was slow and incremental. After the 1967 war ended, the country continued to be deluged with journalists, Jewish dignitaries, and Jewish philanthropists, all seeking the same thing: access to the newly occupied territories and to the country's leaders. The demands

---

[4]This was the same philosophy and tack that guided the U.S. military in Saudi Arabia during the Iraqi War.

they made on government officials would have been too much for any large public relations outfit to cope with, and they were even more difficult for one as unskilled in handling the new crop of journalists from abroad as was the Israeli government. In the confusion of wartime, the journalists were more or less equal in their capacity to gather information. In the immediate postwar period, however, the drive by the Israelis to assert centralized control was renewed. To reassert the old order in the face of this torrent of people and demands, priorities had to be set; otherwise the system would be overwhelmed. The choice was to put most of the emphasis into cultivating those it was thought would best serve the government's immediate needs. First priority of access to decision makers and to the sites of events was given to the international media stars and Jewish dignitaries. Second priority went to visiting contributors to Israel Bonds and the United Israel Appeal or journalists on short trips who had made prior requests through the Israeli embassy in their home country. Third priority was assigned to what was then the relatively small number of true foreign correspondents stationed in Israel.

Those stationed in Israel after 1967 were further, tacitly subdivided into two groups—those with major media connections and those whose media outlets were considered to be of lesser importance. Among those considered to be of lesser importance were the Canadian, Scandinavian, and Dutch press, plus any journalist reporting to Asia and Africa. In other words, because of their workload, lack of money, lack of time, and lack of skills, these officials had to give up the very idea of trying to co-opt large chunks of the foreign press corps. A kind of triage system developed. Foreign reporters were slotted into one of three categories: work on to co-opt; help when necessary; ignore where possible.

There were officials within the system who were aware of the inequities and the long-term negative effects on Israel's image that these policies produced, but they seemed to have had little impact on the perceptions of their superiors. And so, for example, it was difficult for one of the journalists considered to be of lesser importance to get a seat on a trip going to the Sinai if there was a shortage of space. Requests to interview the prime minister or the foreign minister routinely were turned down. So, too, were requests to interview senior military officers.

That situation had two important long-term repercussions that helped erode the system of co-optation and control. It made some of the "minor correspondents" (many of whom were experienced journalists working for large-circulation media outlets) more skeptical of official statements—simply because the journalists did not have the access to officials (other than the spokespeople) who independently could confirm, deny, or provide further explanations about a particular policy. In later years, by way of compensation, many of these lower-ranked reporters, especially those from Europe, were to seek out "the other side of the story" among those Palestinians willing to talk. The feeling that they were being treated as second-class journalists made many of these reporters more aggressive and inquiring in those public fora—such as press conferences—that they could attend. This, in turn, confirmed the officials' deep suspicions that these journalists were inherently uncontrollable, hostile to Israel and sympathetic to the Arabs, and therefore doubly undeserving of any consideration or special attention. It was a wondrous case of a self-fulfilling prophecy.

The consequence of this allocation of second-class status was that it made these journalists more aggressive in the field. To maintain their positions within their own organizations and to preserve their self-esteem as craftspeople, they were forced to go beyond the simple contact building that is an essential part of any journalist's tradecraft. They had to make a special effort to build up wholly independent, unofficial information pipelines and networks. To a large extent, these networks were made up of officials in middle-ranking managerial positions. To get to those officials, a journalist had to sidestep the spokespeople. Officials were waylaid in public places, like in the corridors of the Knesset. Friendships often were struck with members of the Israeli elite who either were in government and dissented from official policy or were outside government and could provide informal introductions to those within the system. These officials, because they often became close personal acquaintances with the journalists, were usually more forthcoming outside their offices than they would have been in the more formal precincts of their ministry. No less important were the everyday contacts journalists made with simple, gregarious Israelis. Almost every adult Israeli male serves in the military reserves and is a potential goldmine of information. Many in industry work on contracts for one or another government department. Also, those who work in hospitals where victims of terrorist attacks are taken are useful sources in times of crisis. But friendships also were struck with local journalists who sometimes were willing to provide information on a collegial basis—but more usually for financial consideration. Payment for information eventually became a pervasive part of the system. Military correspondents or those living along sensitive border areas, for example, who were forbidden by the army spokesman to print certain pieces of information in their own reports, routinely would pass material on to foreign journalists for a fee. Some even took retainers for their services. Those journalists with large corporate resources could pay. Those with small or nonexistent expense accounts could not. With the acquiescence of the Israeli officials involved, inequalities in the system of information distribution and the class system were thus reinforced. Censors, under their mandate, could not prevent the sale of information, only its distribution beyond Israel's borders. Money, therefore, became a criterion for access to information.

By creating a class system of journalists, the Israelis helped to undermine two legs upon which their system stood: equal access to news and the maintenance of a monopoly on the supply of news stories. So long as the Israeli actions affected only a portion of the press corps (and therefore did not cause the entire foreign press corps to rise as one body in revolt), and so long as news coverage was primarily events-driven by forces outside Israel's immediate control, the relationship between the authorities and the foreign press corps remained relatively stable. The real results of the Israeli officials' actions would only be seen many years later.

No less a cause for the breakdown in the system was the lack of coherence in the way newsworthy material was released to the press. Coherence means not only that there is a consensus among all departments about what the common theme of a public relations campaign should be, but that any material bearing on the theme is made equally available to all journalists covering the particular story. The Israeli ambivalence about the foreign press often led officials to withhold information from journalists for no apparent reason, thus alienating correspondents unnecessarily.

A good example, but hardly unique, occurred in the early 1980s. The Israelis, as usual, were on a Qadaffi-bashing jag. Anything that was remotely connected with the Libyan leader was considered grist for the Israeli public relations mill. Israeli radio then had a weekly program on military news. One of the items broadcast was an interview with an Israeli intelligence officer that dealt with advertisements Libya had placed in Arabic-language media in Europe seeking mercenaries. It sounded like a good story, one worth following up. I called the army spokesman's office and asked for the names of the magazines so that I could check out the story further. I got no reply. Further requests also were ignored. This was quite incredible because the story had been broadcast. It was based on public, not covert, sources. And it was potentially embarrassing to one of Israel's opponents. Nonetheless, the army refused to release the material to me. Eventually I was able to confirm the story and to get copies of the advertisements from other sources. But I have never been able to figure out why the army was so reluctant to answer questions or to allow me to interview the intelligence officer involved.

Timeliness during the post-1967 period was not a major problem for Israeli news managers. Many of the military actions of the period, like bombing or commando raids, were initiated by Israel. Raids by saboteurs across the border usually took place at night or at daybreak and often were over by the time the foreign press corps awoke. If the chases lasted longer, they usually would take place in isolated desert areas that had been sealed off by the army. The limited access journalists had to the front lines meant that unless there was an announcement from the Arab side, the Israelis often could delay releasing news of an event for as long as they liked. What pressure there was to be timely came more from a need to respond to Israel's national rumor mill (an often accurate, if incomplete, source of information) and a need to placate the local press. Press announcements, therefore, usually were geared to the deadlines of the local journalists rather than to those of the foreign reporters.

While speed in relaying information to the foreign press was obviously not a priority (announcements often would be given to local journalists hours before they were released to foreign correspondents), having to cope with an ever-increasing quantity of material was. The increase in the number of events brought with it an increase in the number of official announcements from the Arab side, many claiming victories and attacks that never happened. In order to maintain national morale and to prevent the Arabs from achieving a monopoly in the verbal warfare that accompanied the military conflict, the Israelis had to respond quickly with their own version of the facts.

To cope with the situation, the government was forced to introduce a major change in its system of information dissemination. By 1969, the army alone was crafting a dozen or more press releases every day—and they had to be passed on to the ever-growing foreign press corps. The Government Press Office was overwhelmed with work. Journalists were complaining of delays in receiving announcements. There were simply too many people to call individually, and there were fierce arguments over who should be called first. The solution was to introduce a device, promptly labeled the "Golem," that enabled all of the journalists who subscribed to it to be telephoned simultaneously.

This new technological tool, however, would have had far less impact had the Israelis not hoarded and protected their most important public relations resource—credibility. While the Arabs often would make wild and unfounded claims, Israeli announcements were comparatively truthful and often verifiable by the journalist on the ground. This meant that journalists would wait, sometimes for hours, to get the Israeli side of the story before filing a report about an Arab claim. Such enormous trust in the veracity of the Israeli statements nullified much of the public relations effect that Arab statements otherwise might have had. It was a trust that was soon to be squandered, and never really was recovered.

What the Israelis failed to grasp was that credibility is a strategic asset that must be cultivated over time, and it is easily lost once opportunism takes priority over strategic planning in any organization. Credibility is patently one of the most important elements in the source-journalist-audience nexus, but it is extraordinarily difficult to describe and to define. It is one of the most fragile of human constructs because it is based on nothing more than a presumption by one party that another party is trustworthy. And what is trust? Is it boundless or circumscribed? If it is the latter, what are its parameters? What are the criteria for establishing and judging those parameters?

We can sense when a person has lost credibility, but can we say for certain when he has gained it? We can list some of the attributes of credibility—reliability, accuracy, good judgment, comprehensiveness, candidness—but they all seem insufficient to describe what is at once

intensely personal and subjective and, at the same time, the very basis
for open public discourse. It seems to me that credibility is not just an
outgrowth of a source's (or journalist's) reputation for transmitting accurate
data; it is the product of the respect a source (or journalist) brings to the
information available, to the process of transmitting that information, and
to the person to whom the information is transmitted. Thus, a source can
retain personal credibility even when his or her department's policies are
less than wholly credible, by the simple procedure of honest, if discreet,
dissent. For credibility is built largely on that most tenuous of founda-
tions—faith. And in the case of a source-journalist relationship, it is the
result of a process of constant testing by one person of the other. Implicit
in the whole concept is the belief that the person dispensing information
is truly a repository of accurate information and that, while still pursuing
his or her own agenda, the individual has dispassionately considered the
long-term consequences of his or her statements and actions in all of their
conceivable permutations and combinations.

Building credibility is an ongoing process that should preoccupy every
journalist and every official source. In the case of government spokespersons, it means not just relating the truth, but seeking out the truth. It
means understanding that individual pieces of data that are accurate are
not necessarily "the truth." It means initiating the search for information—not merely reacting to requests or events. Credibility is built on the
coherence of the story the spokesperson is trying to project over time—
an ability to leave an impression that there is a logic tying together different
parts of a government's policies and a predictability to a government's
actions. Credible spokespeople constantly must carry with them a sense
of urgency and accountability; they must recognize that if they do not
come up with accurate information, journalists will seek out alternative
sources—and there is always someone who is willing to fill an information
vacuum. Building credibility requires skill, time, and dedication.

While Israeli officials and spokespeople understood the importance
of credibility, they failed to consider or to grasp its true nature. Officials
working within Israel's centralized bureaucratic system have always assumed that a person appointed to a position of authority is ipso facto
"authoritative." To Western journalists, nothing could be further from
the truth. To be authoritative, a person must be considered by his or her
audience to be the definitive speaker on a particular subject. A person in

a position of authority may be in a position to acquire the information to become authoritative, but it is the audience to whom a person speaks that decides, in the end, whether that person is, in fact, the definitive source of information. It is the audience that invests the speaker with the authority to speak and the privilege of being taken at his or her word. In a monopolistic system, a person's credibility is measured against the facts a journalist can gather on the ground. In a competitive system, a person's credibility is measured not only by a comparison of his or her statements with objective facts but also by comparing those statements against the comprehensiveness and truthfulness of the statements of others. So long as official statements emanating from Arab states were, for the most part, not believable, the Israelis had little or no competition. But beginning with President Anwar al-Sadat's peace initiative and following later with the Israeli spokesmen's performance during the Lebanese War and the intifada, comparison, and therefore competition for credibility, became the name of the game—and Israeli officials, for the most part, were found to be wanting and, at times, outright bush leaguers.

It is surprising that Israeli officials were so obtuse, since Hebrew journalistic terminology makes a clear differentiation between "authority" and "authoritative." In Hebrew, a person usually is labeled as a *makor yodeah davar* ("a source who knows") or a *makor musmach* ("a source who has been authorized to speak"—that is, an official source). It is interesting that when Israeli officials refuse to go on the record, they usually ask that they be referred to as an official source rather than a knowledgeable one, the former, apparently, in bureaucratic terms being a title indicating higher status.

The story of "Chaim Weizmann" is a very good example of an early sign that the credibility of Israeli military spokesmen was deteriorating—and an indication of the cavalier attitude many Israeli officials still take to the issue of credibility. Chaim Weizmann was, of course, Israel's first president. A leader of the Zionist movement prior to the establishment of the state, his name is as familiar in Israel as George Washington's is in the United States. A thoroughly Ashkenazi, or European, surname, it is, nonetheless, not particularly common in Israel.

I and a group of foreign correspondents were introduced to Chaim

Weizmann on the banks of the Suez Canal in August 1970. This in itself was odd: it is Israeli practice never to release for publication the family names of soldiers, with the notable exceptions of senior general staff officers, official army spokesmen, and the dead. Everyone else in the army is almost invariably referred to only by their first name, and sometimes only by the initial of their first name. The IDF Spokesman's Office, having laid out a bus trip to the Suez Canal zone to celebrate the newly announced cease-fire with the Egyptians, offered Chaim as our interviewee. We arrived after another one of those long, hot, and dusty trips from Tel Aviv to the far edge of the Sinai desert. Chaim was a strapping young lad, his dark skin, curly hair, and facial features and a Hebrew accent betraying his Sephardic or Asian background. Chaim couldn't speak English too well. In fact, all he seemed to know were the words *yes* and *no*. We asked to be able to talk to someone else in the bunker who might know English better, or to talk to Chaim in Hebrew. But our military escort officer said that would not be possible. We argued, but to no avail. When the interview began, we noticed that Chaim seemed to have developed a nervous tic in his abdomen, which seemed to seize up at irregular intervals while we spoke to him. I peered around back of him and found our friendly escort officer punching poor Chaim in the back after every question. One punch for yes, two punches for no. I am sure that Chaim's (or whatever his real name was) displeasure at being put through a behavior modification/ negative-conditioning-toward-journalists session was matched only by our disgust at being subjected to such a performance—and at the long, hot bus trip home that awaited us.

I use this example, rather than some of the more well-publicized later ones, to show that the loss of credibility by Israeli officials is not a recent phenomenon. It has a long history. Subsequent events, like the outright lying that accompanied the Yom Kippur War and the invasion of Lebanon, merely served to confirm the skepticism that had begun to grow in the foreign press much earlier. Chaim may have been telling us the truth, but he was hardly credible. Neither was the escort officer/ handler. The escort officer may have had legitimate concerns that whoever spoke to the press not reveal important tactical information on which the lives of the soldiers depended. But rather than brief a soldier ahead of time, rather than prepare for the trip adequately, rather than be candid about his concerns, he chose what appeared to be the easy way out. It was an opportunistic performance without any concern for the long-term implications of his actions. The very fact that as I write this twenty years later, the incident remains so strong and vivid in my memory, is an indication of the long-term effects that casual and thoughtless opportunism can have.

As can be seen, the system for co-optation had been thoroughly undermined at a very early point in the post-1967 period. Like a termite-infested board, the apparently sound and healthy surface only belied the vacuous interior. The extent of the rot became all too plain to see in October 1973; and yet, even after that disaster, the lessons were not learned.

When the Egyptian army crossed the Suez Canal on October 6, 1973, the Israelis were caught by surprise. The Israeli forces along the canal were reeling. A decision was made at Israeli command headquarters to try to temper the Arabs' euphoria by reporting Israeli "victories" in halting the onslaught. "Unfortunately," says one of those who planned the dissimulation campaign, "the whole thing got out of hand. When the real truth came out, it had a very negative effect on domestic morale." It also had the effect of making the foreign press more skeptical than ever about Israeli veracity.

When the Israelis invaded Lebanon in June 1982, their declared aim was to advance forty kilometers to destroy the Palestinian infrastructure in the southern part of the Land of the Cedars. In fact, Israeli forces were soon at the gates of Beirut—and what little credibility the Israeli military spokesmen still had, vanished. It was only recovered, in part, during the Iraqi war when the army spokesman realized that without timely and absolutely reliable public reports on the damage caused by SCUD missiles, national home-front morale would have collapsed.

At the same time as the system of co-optation was collapsing, so, too, was the system of control. The system of control was based on two pillars: accreditation, the ability to deny access to events; and censorship, the ability to deny transmission of information abroad. Every foreign reporter in Israel is required to register with the Government Press Office and, as part of the procedure, must sign a statement acknowledging that he or she is aware of censorship restrictions.

Military censorship is another inheritance of the British mandate. Regulations promulgated in 1945 permit censors to prevent publication of any report that in the opinion of the censor "might, in his view, harm the defense of the country, public safety, or public order"—as broad a mandate as any professional blue penciller could desire. There is no mechanism for appeal against the censor's decisions under these regulations, except for an appeal to the Supreme Court. Although the censors have claimed that they restrict publication only of material that has a direct bearing on national security, often that term is applied very broadly. Up to the mid-1970s, it was used blatantly to prevent the publication of material that was politically embarrassing.

The primary weapon of enforcement in the immediate post-1967 period was the ability of the censors to deny journalists access to the means of transmission of their material. At that time, every letter or can of film sent to a media office abroad had to bear the censor's stamp before it would be accepted at the airport. Every report submitted to the telex office had to have the stamp as well. One could not book a press call abroad (which meant having to wait only twenty minutes instead of two or three days for a connection) without the telephone operator checking first with the censor. Every correspondent's telephone call was then monitored, and if the material had not been cleared in advance and in toto by the censor, the call would be cut off in the middle.

Although the censors denied it, it was my impression that there was a deliberate attempt on their part to make their presence appear pervasive— to make journalists think twice before even writing something that had to be submitted for censorship. A good example occurred in 1970. My girlfriend and I decided to get married. From her apartment, not mine, we called our parents in Canada and the United States to announce our decision. We told no one else. The next day, I walked into the Government Press Office in Tel Aviv and a colleague came up to me and said, "Congratulations."

"About what?" I asked.

"About your forthcoming marriage," he replied.

"How did you know? We haven't told anybody here yet."

"The censors told me," he answered. Naturally, when I went to query the censors, they denied all knowledge of what had happened.

Several factors led to the eventual breakdown in the censors' power. The first was journalists' growing frustration at some of the inherent inequities in the system. The most blatant was the total power that individual censors had over journalists' material. In some cases, censors who were incompletely acquainted with English would blue-pencil material simply because they had misunderstood its meaning—and no amount of arguing by a native English speaker could change their minds. Individual censors also became known for whether they were easy or tough on the material, and savvy journalists would check to see who was on duty before deciding whether and when to submit their copy. There were also differences in what censors in Jerusalem and Tel Aviv would pass—and so sometimes it was worthwhile to make an intercity trip in order to get material approved.

At times, the censors' rationale for blue-pencilling or for allowing a story to pass was the stuff funny folktales are made of. One true example comes quickly to mind. In 1969, a Palestinian terrorist fired a bazooka from a minaret in South Lebanon, hitting an Israeli school bus near the farming village of Avivim. The bus was destroyed and most of the children in the bus were either killed or wounded. It was an extraordinarily gruesome story to cover, even for an area of the world that has known so much violence. After we had seen the site and interviewed witnesses, I and a couple of colleagues, including a correspondent from Italian television, headed down to Safed, the nearest city with decent communications. We filed our first stories by telephone and then decided to head back up north to see if there were any repercussions. When we got to the site of the massacre, all of the journalists had left and we saw an Israeli foot patrol heading into South Lebanon. At that time, before the large-scale Palestinian infiltrations began, the Lebanese border was relatively open. We followed the patrol at a healthy distance (an Israeli soldier had lost a leg that morning from a land mine explosion near the site of the bus attack). Within minutes, we were in Lebanon. We saw that the Israelis had sent in large numbers of patrols to try to find the perpetrator of the attack, and the Italian television correspondent did a "stand-upper," an on-camera voice report, with the mosque in the background. We rushed back to

Safed and I prepared my story, fully expecting that it would be totally censored. When I read the story over the phone to the censor, I could tell from his voice that he was aghast. Not only was I giving details of Israeli troop movements, which was strictly forbidden, I was revealing an appalling lack of field security on the part of the Israeli army. I was told to wait while the censor consulted with his superiors. Less than twenty minutes later, the censor called me at my hotel and informed me that his office had checked with the military commanders in the north. They had told him that no journalists had been sighted at the time I had mentioned in my story and that no journalist had been permitted to enter Lebanon. Therefore, I could file my story because, he said, "it didn't happen." Neither, I assume, did the television stand-upper that was broadcast in Italy the following night.

There were also differences in who was subject to censorship. Some journalists would travel abroad with stories and send them, asking their editors to make it appear as though the material had come from a different country. Other journalists who did not get bylines in their media outlet could and did send material by carrier pigeons. *Time* magazine, in particular, became renowned for what was called "the Thursday courier"— a person whom most correspondents were convinced would come in on Thursdays to pick up the magazine correspondents' reports in time for the weekend rewrite. The material that appeared in the magazine had been censored out of other journalists' reports, so it could never, of course, be traced back to the magazine's reporters in Israel.

Yet another source of anger at the Israelis' system of control was the inequitable treatment meted out to different classes of reporters by the censors. Theoretically, Israeli censors are required to inform reporters when censorship restrictions were lifted on a particular story that they have attempted to file. They usually neglected to do so with most foreign reporters, and not once in more than two decades was I ever called before the item already had been broadcast or printed in the Israeli media. Another source of tension was the preferred treatment given by the Israeli authorities to those reporters traveling with a visiting VIP. Although solemnly warned that they had to submit their stories to the censor, none of the reporters who accompanied Henry Kissinger on his shuttle missions, for example, ever, to my knowledge, submitted copy to Israeli censorship.

But what really undid the system was the arrival in the late 1970s of direct international dialing. No longer did reporters have to go through a telephone operator. They could call from almost anywhere, except a public telephone—and the calls were virtually untraceable. Many journalists began to ignore the censors entirely. During the war in Lebanon, the process went even further, since those journalists who were covering the story in Beirut were subject to neither the Israeli telephone system nor the Israeli censor. Only local Israeli correspondents[5] and foreign television crews were.[6] For the first time, it was the foreign print and radio correspondents who were in the privileged position, because they were totally free of Israeli restraints. Pre-censorship had to change to post-censorship. However, for post-censorship to work, real sanctions had to be applied—and Israel, because it was so dependent on U.S. goodwill, could not afford to alienate the American media. Aside from preventing transmission of an item from a government-controlled facility, like a radio studio or a satellite station, the only sanction that really was available to the Israeli authorities was the withdrawal of a journalist's press card. Without the card, a journalist, theoretically, could have no access to officials or to official functions. Before the intifada, the only time such a sanction was applied occurred in February 1980, when CBS radio correspondent Dan Raviv flew to Rome and did a voice report on an alleged Israeli nuclear test. Raviv, by reporting the story in his own name and with his own voice, virtually forced the Israeli authorities to act. During the intifada, however, the practice of enforcing censorship and applying sanctions to journalists, both foreign and Israeli, became more widespread. But by this time, the system had become so discredited that the sanctions

---

[5]Moshe Negbi (op. cit.) points out that during this highly controversial war, even Israelis knowingly violated the censor's orders, because some editors suspected that "the censorship was being used not only to conceal information from the papers and the people, but also to hide it from the eyes of major cabinet ministers."

[6]The television crews, even those based in Beirut, were put in a unique position early in the war. The Lebanese satellite station was put out of action during the first week of the fighting, and all television reports had to be sent down to Israel by car and transmitted from there. This led to an anomalous situation in which Israeli facilities were used to transmit pictures taken in PLO positions, including interviews with PLO officials. The Israelis, recognizing that they were in the midst not only of a military war but of a media war as well, demanded that all of the video material taken in Lebanon be subject to censorship. On June 21, the censor refused to approve the broadcast of an ABC interview with Yasir Arafat. ABC sent the material to New York anyway, and the Israelis responded by canceling ABC's satellite privileges for forty-eight hours. ABC, together with CBS and NBC, then launched a public campaign against the Israeli sanctions, but to no avail.

were, as the *Washington Post*'s Glenn Frankel said after he had his credentials lifted in May 1988, "a symbolic slap on the wrist."[7]

None of this means that the relationship between the foreign press corps
and the censors was entirely adversarial. Personal, friendly relations did
crop up. Some of the censors made excellent copy editors, pointing out
confusing sentences written in haste, inevitable typographical mistakes,
or errors in the spelling of Israeli names. In a perverse way, they were
also excellent sources of information. During the Yom Kippur War, for
example, I had been filing almost a dozen times a day since the outbreak
of the fighting and was extremely weary by the time Prime Minister Golda
Meir announced that "an Israeli task force" was operating on the other
side of the Suez Canal. I had one more deadline to make at 2:00 A.M.
and had exhausted all of the hard, factual material I could write about
that day. Instead, I decided to write a small background piece based on
a magazine article I had read years before. In it I speculated on the type
of force Israel might employ on the western bank of the canal. I quoted
from a widely distributed report from London's prestigious International
Institute for Strategic Studies to cover my speculations and submitted the
story by telephone to the censor. After a moment's hurried conversation
on the other side of the phone, I was informed that not only could I not
send the report, I would have to come down to the censor's office and
hand in every copy of what I had written. Otherwise, the police would
be sent to get me. Bingo! In my bleary-eyed desperation to get my file in
so that I could get some sleep, I had hit on the kernel of the Israeli battle
plan for crossing the canal. I would never have known it without the
censor's help. In the following years, including during the intifada, I had
similar experiences. They were, admittedly, rare, but they seemed to come
at crucial moments.

With the breakdown in its system of control, Israel had nothing to put in
its place. Spokesmen, censors, politicians, and much of the public looked
like lost sheep, bereft of their bearings. During the intifada, cars began

[7]"Why the Israelis Lifted My Press Card Last Week," *Washington Post*, 1 May 1988, p. C1.

sporting stickers saying WE ARE AGAINST A HOSTILE PRESS. Anger and resignation had replaced the self-assuredness and even cockiness of years past. Some spokesmen, like Avi Pazner, Prime Minister Yitzchak Shamir's media adviser, vented their anger by making outlandish and unfounded criticisms of television crews, thus hoping to turn the press into a scapegoat for the system's inadequacies and inconsistencies.

Yoram Ettinger, the conservative, Likud-appointed director of the Government Press Office, better reflected the sense of helplessness—over both the conflict with the Palestinians and Israel's relationship with the foreign press—that pervaded the ranks of Israeli spokespersons. "We are dealing," he said resignedly, "with a conflict [with the Palestinians] that is almost existential. . . . The press corps from the West is characterized by being liberal to very liberal on national security issues, being critical to highly critical of U.S. policy throughout the world, a disdain for the use of the military, [being] third world in outlook, and favoring the underdog. The press corps is not neutral." Ettinger asserted that since Israel views national security as essential and the military as the backbone of the country, immediately the country is out of line with journalists' perceptions, and since Israel supports the United States so much, journalists find it convenient to criticize the United States via Israel. As a result, Israel had very little room for maneuver. "If you scold the media," he said, "you are not dealing with a teddy bear, but with a wounded bear that is much more vicious and dangerous."[8]

Others, like Deputy Chief Military Spokesman Raanan Gissin, while recognizing many of the real problems the Israeli system faces, was left to lament, "The only thing we can do is damage control, because the overall picture is unfavorable to the IDF."[9]

Some officials and propagandists have tried to put their own spin on the bankruptcy of their system. Now, more often than not, they use the relative freedom the breakdown has accorded journalists as proof of Israel's inherent press freedom and of the benign nature of the censorship system. But that is hardly a true reflection of their real feelings. With a more

[8]Yoram Ettinger, interview with author, July 1989.
[9]Raanan Gissin, interview with author, June 1989.

honest voice, some officials, like Colonel Gissin, speak wistfully and optimistically of reintroducing the system of gentlemen's agreements. And since the outbreak of the intifada, the army has severely limited access to the West Bank and Gaza and the censors have been trying to reimpose censorship with a broad stroke in those occupied territories.

However, the destruction of the system of control has made even the Israeli press more critical and less accepting of official fiats, lies, explanations, and excuses than they were before. The local Hebrew-language press, which had always jealously guarded its turf, its access, and its prerogatives from foreign interlopers, is being driven by a common cause and common circumstances to challenge the very underpinnings of the system of co-optation and control.

There is no formal alliance between the two groups of journalists and almost no contact between their respective representatives in the Foreign Press Association and the Union of Israeli Journalists. The fields of vision of the two groups are too far apart. The local press, more and more, wants to see itself as a watchdog, a partner to making the country work better, though no longer an arm of the security services.[10] The foreign press, on the other hand, while it may share and even want to protect some of the values many Israelis hold dear, does not believe that it need have any commitment to the Israeli system of governance as such. But, although now working along parallel tracks that never touch, the two bodies do share some similar objectives. And therein lies the challenge to the press in Israel, both local and foreign. For the old system can be rescued and resuscitated only with the acquiescence of the journalists themselves.

The danger that the system for co-opting and controlling the foreign press will be rebuilt is a real one. If the current level of press freedom is to be

---

[10]During the first week of the Iraqi invasion of Kuwait in August 1990, when it was uncertain whether Iraq would attack Israel with missiles and poison gas, Israeli radio aired an extraordinary and highly revealing broadcast in which several leading Israeli editors were interviewed. Still smarting from their failure to inform the public of Arab military preparations prior to the Yom Kippur War, the editors felt obliged to plead with the listeners to believe them that this time they would not let the country's citizens down.

protected and expanded, the journalists themselves will have to take the lead. Too often, short-term journalistic expedience has clouded long-term perspectives. In their heated competition, for example, U.S. television networks often have agreed to accept army-controlled pools, for fear that they might lose the all-important pictures they need. They thus undermine the ongoing battle for free access to news events. Moreover, foreign reporters on short tours of duty often feel little obligation to fight battles for those who will follow them.

There is a recognition, if not a total acceptance, among most foreign correspondents in Israel that nation-states have a right to try to present their side of any question in as favorable a light as possible and to use any legal and fair means to do so. There is also a recognition that countries at war may, at times, have the right to limit journalistic coverage when the lives of people, especially innocent civilians, are at stake. But there is a big difference between using limited means of co-optation and control and using them as a blanket system to stifle questioning, accurate analysis, criticism, and dissent.

The techniques employed by the Israelis for co-optation and control are neither original nor unique. The same measures are at work in free democracies like the United States and Great Britain. The power to control that modern nations can bring to bear on reporters, such as limiting access to events, threats to impose sanctions, and restricting the means to transmit information while it is still timely, are major daily concerns for journalists around the world. Natural forces acting to promote co-optation—isolation and loneliness while on the road, fatigue, ideological and cultural affinities with particular parties in a complex dispute—make the whole issue one that journalists must address if they are to prevent both short-term and long-term negative consequences to their work.

An adversarial relationship between journalists and officials is inevitable in some cases. There is no need to cultivate conflict with officials artificially, as some journalists do in order to make themselves appear independent. It is a factor inherent in any relationship between inquisitors and those seeking to present a particular public agenda. The issue in question is the misuse of the powers of control and co-optation. The task in modern democratic societies is to find some golden mean that reconciles legitimate governmental objectives—some of which may require secrecy—while preserving the public's right to know and its capacity to make rational decisions on the basis of accurate information and cogent, expert, analysis. The problem is becoming even more acute as we enter into an age of increasing international interdependence in which the right to know and the need to know is no longer just a national governmental or bureaucratic prerogative, but an international imperative.

Just as the Israelis were muddling through to failure in their attempts to co-opt and control the press, the Palestinians in the occupied territories were blundering into success. It is doubtful whether any public relations outfit, no matter how experienced and skilled, could have created a media drama as successfully as did the Palestinian youngsters who took to the streets in December 1987. But to understand the scope of this success, and the subsequent failure to capitalize on it, again one must look back into history.

Prior to the Israeli occupation, the Palestinians in the West Bank had been held under the rigid control of the Jordanian army, and the Palestinians living in Gaza were at the mercy of the Egyptian administration there. The only widespread, organized political voice these Palestinians had was that of Ahmed Shukeiry, a corrupt blowhard who was firmly under the thumb of the leaders of the Arab states.

T · H · R · E · E

Blundering into Success

The Arab defeat in 1967 and the Israeli occupation that followed the war provided Palestinian political activists, especially those outside Israeli-controlled territory, with new opportunities and new hopes. Shukeiry was discredited, and a new Palestinian leadership that had been developing for a couple of years began to move to the fore. This leadership coalition, which was based outside the occupied areas, was led by Yasir Arafat, the charismatic head of Al Fatah, its largest constituent party. Within half a year after the Khartoum resolution, and operating under the summit meeting's political mantle and rejectionist program, Arafat was directing a campaign of border crossings by Palestinian saboteurs that was to attract instant media attention. In the West Bank and Gaza, the Palestinian leaders were somnolent—either cowed by the Israelis or controlled by the Jordanians. But in Jordan, the Palestinians seemed to have discovered one of their first authentic voices in Yasir Arafat.

The contrasts, to a journalist, could not have been more striking. I can recall interviewing one of the leading Palestinian figures of the time, Kadri Toukan, a high school principal in the West Bank's most important commercial city, Nablus. The interview took place in his office in mid-1968. I came prepared with a long list of questions, but for the hour I spent with him, I got only one response to any and every question: "Everything will be all right when the Israeli occupation ends." It made no difference whether the subject was economic, social, or political, the answer was the same. That is not the stuff of which interesting journalistic articles and broadcasts are made. The response from many other West Bank leaders of the time was much the same—dull and visionless. There were a few men, like the Ramallah lawyer Azziz Shehadeh, who spoke out boldly for an Israeli-Palestinian settlement, but soon after the Khartoum conference, they were silenced.[1] When I proposed a series of programs on the occupied territories to my editors in mid-1968, they could not have been less interested. The Palestinians in the occupied territories may have had a great deal to say, but they were not about to say it publicly, and until they did, there was little of substance that a journalist could

---

[1]Even after Shehadeh was publicly silenced, he continued to carry on an extensive dialogue with a wide variety of Israelis. He was assassinated by an unknown assailant outside his home on 2 December 1985.

write. These middle-aged Palestinians had lived too long under the watchful gaze of the Jordanian, Egyptian, and now the Israeli security services, and they were not about to take any chances.

By comparison, Yasir Arafat, in his *keffiyeh*, battledress, and permanent three-day beard, was offering verbally colorful and visually striking interviews in his "secret" hiding place in Jordan. He quickly became an icon: the Western media's embodiment of the "new" Palestinian. It was a romantic image—that of an articulate and proud fighter for his nation's rights. Arafat looked different enough to seem exotic, without seeming too frightening. He was to become the Palestinian media foil for Israel's one-eyed, charismatic defense minister, Moshe Dayan. Although he had been responsible for a considerable number of sabotage attacks prior to the 1967 war, Arafat was dismissed by the Israelis as a buffoon, as ineffective and ineffectual as Ahmed Shukeiry had been. They judged him and his actions by their own standards, perceptions, and presumptions, not by those of his constituency. It was not the first mistake the Israelis were to make about him and the PLO.

By early 1968, Arafat was sending almost nightly raiding parties across the Jordan River. Most of the targets were civilian installations. Civilian targets were relatively easy to hit until the Israeli army strengthened its border defenses. And unlike military installations, attacks on civilians, or at least their aftermath, were open to media coverage, thus increasing their international impact. The PLO's leaders did not seem to care whether such attacks created revulsion in the West. They were concerned with something far more important to them: establishing their presence in the Arab world, in the occupied territories, and in the world press. In the fluid political environment that followed the Six-Day War, their primary aim was to establish an international perception that there was an entity that could be called the Palestinian people, and that *their* organization was the only legitimate body acting in the interests of that people. They understood that to achieve their aim, they had to grab and then maintain control of the media stage. An attack on an Israeli border kibbutz was like an unpaid spot advertisement on TV for their cause.

It is difficult today to conceive, but at the time, there were many people in the world, not the least of them Israeli prime minister Golda Meir, who did not believe that there was such a thing as a Palestinian nation. The very fact that the idea is virtually unquestioned today—except by the Israeli far right and its supporters—is a tribute to the PLO's early media successes. In fact, it is safe to say that for more than two decades, the Israeli-Palestinian dispute has been fought as much in the media as on the battlefield. For in the late twentieth century, internationally legitimate sovereignty over land comes not merely by the traditional right of conquest or by the more modern concepts of the right of self-determination and the right of a central government to exercise power within its nation's internationally accepted boundaries. It also arises from the control of the symbols, images, and public roles that justify or rationalize the possession of land. "Liberation" movements not only must be able to organize the faithful, rally the wavering to the cause, provide an alternative vision to the existing order, and fight and even subjugate others as in days past, they also must be able to appropriate the pattern of signs, symbols, and myths of those whom they call "the enemy." Today, the media provide the stage on which those political and social markers can be demonstrated to the world for approval. Without such a stage, no nation and no organization has a hope of gaining international recognition, legitimacy, and support.

To get the audience it needs, a nation or organization first must create a recognized name. The PLO, like many other political movements, lacked the instruments of state that often can guarantee a national government access to the press. The Israelis, for example, could build a road or a school. The PLO could not. The Israelis could open a labor exchange or a health clinic. The PLO could not. In part, to compensate for this inherent political weakness, the PLO staged events that would draw the press, like cross-border raids. These events were militarily insignificant in the long run because the Israelis were able to develop relatively effective countermeasures, but they did have the effect of sucking in the press so that the organization would be given an international platform. It was teaser politics for teaser journalism.

A "teaser" in broadcast journalism is a short, sharp introduction or piece of tape or film that is designed to grab a viewer's or listener's attention and hold it until the real import of a story can be explained. Its use presumes that there will be a follow-up explanation and possibly a conclusion. But in the case of the PLO, there never was a diplomatic follow-up to the teaser of a terrorist attack. The teaser was an end in itself. Journalism, which by then often emphasized short, snappy stories, was particularly susceptible to teaser politics of this sort. Teaser politics gave journalists simple messages expressed in pithy, often extreme sound bites. A broadcast journalist limited to two minutes of air time or a print journalist who had only a six-hundred-word hole to fill could find all of his or her obligations to the time slot or space allocation satisfied by single, violent events of this sort. Increasingly, news reporting, especially in the Middle East, was becoming a kind of theater criticism, with a quick description of the day's plot and a short critique of who had played the roles of "victim," "brave warrior," or "self-sacrificing leader."

It was an Israeli plot idea that went wrong that finally allowed Palestinian fighters to play classical heroic roles and turned the PLO into a media force to be reckoned with. Between February 18 and March 19, 1968, the Palestinians committed thirty-seven acts of sabotage in Israeli-held territory. The Israelis chose to retaliate and to send a dramatic and what was expected to be an indelible message to the PLO to halt the nightly raids. But their misperceptions of what the PLO had become was to cause them to make an enormous blunder. The Israeli military decided to attack a Jordanian village called Karameh, three miles over the Jordan River. The village was one of the PLO's main bases of operations in the area.

Seriously underestimating the nature of their enemy, the Israelis made no attempt to hide their preparations. Convoys of tanks and equipment could be seen snaking through the narrow defile leading up to Jerusalem and thence down to the Jordan Rift. On the morning of March 21, Israeli planes dropped leaflets warning of their impending arrival. Then the Israeli units struck. But unlike previous occasions, when PLO irregulars had fled at the approach of Israeli military formations, this time the Palestinian fighters stood and fought. It took the Israelis fifteen hours of tough fighting to clear the area, and when the dust settled, an estimated 150 Palestinians were dead. But the Israelis also had unprecedented casualties for a raid of this sort—twenty-one soldiers were killed and seventy wounded. The message that Palestinian fighters had stood and fought, not fled, galvanized the Palestinian community both inside and outside the occupied territories as no other single event had ever done before. The Israelis had given the Palestinians an opportunity to demonstrate that they could resist even against overwhelming odds, and the Palestinians had taken it. They had played the "brave warrior" role and had emerged with commendable reviews. It had been bloody theater, but theater nonetheless. And the PLO now commanded the media stage.

After the battle for Karameh, Arafat quickly became a media personality. Western journalists considered it a coup if they could get an interview with him. Many journalists who met him were mesmerized. At a very early stage, Yasir Arafat recognized that he was fighting a three-front war: politically, militarily, and in the press. The PLO leadership had discovered a pot of political gold in the press's attention to their actions, but they did not really know what to do with it. They had been used to playing for local, regional audiences but never before had been presented with a large international stage on which to perform. The main problems the expatriate Palestinians faced were how to play the roles expected of them, when to play them, and before which audience to play them. The refugees in the camps in Lebanon wanted to hear something totally different than what the United States did.

To the Arabs, Arafat needed to present the image of the armed struggler who would never lay down his arms. To the Western world, he needed to present himself as a leader of stature with whom one could parlay. This kind of sophisticated maneuvering, however, requires careful strategizing. But strategies can be developed only once there is a coherent and comprehensive political agenda. The PLO, for numerous reasons, was never able to develop a sophisticated set of plans of this sort. Internal divisions within the PLO meant that long-term strategic planning had to be kept to a minimum. So long as the PLO followed a path of consensus politics to maintain a facade of national unity, no coherent plan of action that went beyond the agreed policy of violent struggle could be adopted. What passed for policy and strategy could not be anything more than the lowest common ideological denominator of the organization's constituent parts.

Political planning within the PLO, therefore, was limited largely to shoring up fragile coalitions and to attempts to gain additional leverage and cash within the Arab world. Yasir Arafat could not offer the West the plot line it was seeking: a negotiated settlement with Israel. Having achieved the presence they sought, the PLO's leaders had reached a dead end.

The Palestinian leadership was caught in a bind. Establishing a presence in the media is not enough to achieve real goals. It merely insures that there will be an audience if someone has something interesting to say or to show—a way of carrying the plot to a higher and more interesting level. The extent of the PLO leaders' plight was probably best exemplified in November 1974, when Arafat showed up at the United Nations General Assembly offering "peace," but with a gun strapped to his hip.

Without a coherent and comprehensive strategy, Arafat tried to do the impossible: play on two separate stages simultaneously, in two different roles, with two different plots. To the Arabs, he portrayed himself as a fighter to the bitter end. To the West, he tried to portray an image of moderation. His message to the West was twofold. The first was political and centered on a proposal that a "secular democratic state" be established in Palestine. It had a nice Western ring to it, and many journalists, unaware of the realities of the Middle East, bought it as a viable idea. The notion of such a state, however, was totally at odds with the Moslem concept of governance and it would have meant the dismantling of Israel— something patently unacceptable to the Jews. The second tack, which also fooled many journalists, was Arafat's attempt to portray himself and Al Fatah as a moderate "good cop" to the more radical "bad cops" within the PLO—men like George Habash, the leader of the Popular Front for the Liberation of Palestine (PFLP).

The first idea died a slow death. But somehow, the second image has remained part of the media's vocabulary. It suits our tendency toward thoughtlessly and often indiscriminately using emotionally charged words and short, descriptive titles for people and organizations. We often fail to take into account all of the implications of using those titles and the demonization or legitimization it gives to those to whom they are awarded. In the press, one frequently reads or sees references to the "moderate" PLO leader Yasir Arafat or the "moderate" Al Fatah. "Moderate" compared to what? It is difficult to consider an organization that murdered eleven Israeli athletes at the 1972 Munich Olympics moderate. It also is difficult to know how a man who was responsible for something like the hijacking of the *Achille Lauro* cruise ship and the subsequent murder of wheelchair-bound Leon Klinghoffer could be called moderate.

At some point, the inherent weaknesses in the PLO's position had to be exposed. That occurred in 1970. The Israelis by then had managed to seal much of the frontier with Jordan. Infiltrators caught by the Israelis usually talked under interrogation and revealed the names of West Bankers who had assisted them, thus weakening the resolve of the Palestinians within the occupied territories to aid the saboteurs. And Israeli agents had begun to thoroughly infiltrate the PLO's infrastructure, both inside the occupied areas and in the Arab states. Meanwhile, as they were to do repeatedly in the future, the PLO's leaders, cocksure of their strength, turned on their hosts.

Possibly frustrated by their growing number of failures to strike at the Israelis, they attempted to take over Jordan. King Hussein, who had seen his country's economic development stopped dead by Israeli retaliatory air raids, especially in the Jordan Valley, had nonetheless been unable to control the Palestinians. He had been a part of the 1967 debacle and could not carry on the armed struggle with Israel, except at even greater risk to Jordan's interests. By contrast, the Palestinians, together with the Egyptians fighting along the Suez Canal, were the banner carriers of the Arab world in the fight against the Zionist enemy. Egypt, however, was bleeding from the Israeli air raids across the Suez Canal and needed a respite to rebuild and regroup.

On June 25, 1970, the United States announced that it was going to begin a new peace initiative. By the end of July, Israel, Jordan, and Egypt had accepted the initiative. Syria, Iraq, and the Palestinians rejected it.[2] The political tide had changed, and the PLO was unable to adapt to the altered circumstances. Faced with this crisis, it no longer could maintain its duplicity. Yasir Arafat declared, "We will continue to fight with all our might," and on July 27, a massive rally by Palestinians opposing the peace initiative was held in Amman. That, however, did not prevent a United States–mediated cease-fire between Israel and Egypt from going into effect on August 7.

In reaction, the PLO launched a campaign to vilify Egypt and to attack Jordanian institutions and soldiers. By late August, the PLO had taken over the refugee camps as well as many of the urban areas in Jordan. PLO officials began talking about "the little king" and how they could unseat him at any time. Oblivious to many of the implications of their actions, the PLO leadership was falling into one of many traps—not the

---

[2]Iraq was considered at this time to be a frontline state because just prior to the Six-Day War it had sent an army brigade to Jordan. Despite Jordanian pleas, Baghdad had refused to recall the military units. They finally were removed after the September 1970 crackdown.

least of which was to justify the argument held out by the Israeli right that "Jordan is Palestine." The threat to the throne was real. Up to that point, King Hussein had been afraid to attack the organization frontally for fear of alienating the other Arab states, upon which Jordan depended for a goodly part of its national income. But the times had changed radically. The king had recovered some political maneuvering room.

On August 30, in a television address, he declared that he would not tolerate any attempt to "undermine the absolute sovereignty of Jordan." Although formally denying that the PLO would be harmed in any way, it was, in effect, a declaration of war. The next day, gunmen attempted to assassinate the king as he drove to the airport to greet his daughter, who was returning from Cairo. It was the second such attempt in three months. Once Hussein's throne was seen to be at immediate risk, he could afford to act, because he understood that Saudi Arabia, which feared instability on its borders more than almost anything else, would be at least tacitly on his side and not intervene.

The first week of September saw an escalation in fighting between PLO irregulars and Jordanian soldiers, many of whom were of Palestinian origin. The country was on the brink of civil war.

Then, on September 9, in a monumental miscalculation, the PFLP hijacked two American and one Swiss airliners. One plane, a Pan Am jumbo jet, was flown to Cairo, where it was blown up almost immediately by the hijackers after they had released the passengers. The other two, including a TWA Boeing 707, were flown to a disused British-built airfield in Jordan called Dawson's Field. An attempt to hijack an Israeli El Al jetliner over England at the same time was foiled when a steward overpowered an armed hijacker. Now, in addition to the tacit support of the Saudis, King Hussein also could count on the open support of the Western nations.[3] As Red Cross officials began negotiations with the hijackers for the release of the hostages, the Jordanian army began a vicious crackdown. On September 11, after evacuating the two jets, together with a British VC-10 that, in the meantime, also had been hijacked to Jordan, the hijackers blew up the three planes. Meanwhile, the fighting had spread

[3]The Israelis, with the tacit support of the United States, partially mobilized their army and positioned those forces along the Jordan River, poised to intervene if so ordered. The forces never were used.

throughout the country. Journalists, pinned down inside Amman's Intercontinental Hotel, were unable to gather material or file their stories because most communications links with the outside world had been severed.

By September 13, the tide of battle was in the balance. In an attempt to rally international support, which was in desperately short supply, Yasir Arafat once again sought to play "good cop" and had the PFLP suspended from the central committee of the PLO for having hijacked the planes. But by this time, things had gone too far. King Hussein had managed a major public relations as well as military coup. His Palestinian soldiers had not deserted in droves, as many had anticipated, but had stood their ground and had fought against the PLO's fighters.

By September 17, the PLO fighters were on the run and the organization's underground radio station was appealing for international assistance. Only Syria responded, sending three armored brigades to invade Jordan in support of the Palestinians. The Syrian forces were bloodied by the Jordanian Legion and withdrew three days later. By September 23, thousands of Palestinians were either dead or wounded. PLO emplacements throughout the country had been shattered and overrun. And the international press corps, which had been the PLO's main conduit to the Western world, was being evacuated after spending almost three weeks holed up in the Intercontinental Hotel's cellars. It was truly the expatriate Palestinians' Black September. The PLO leadership withdrew to Lebanon to lick its wounds, to rebuild its shattered infrastructure, and to repeat the same mistakes again.

They were almost back to square one. Their first task, as they saw it, was to reestablish the PLO as an international presence. That meant beginning another series of raids against Israel and terrorist attacks abroad. Almost any means were considered legitimate so long as they could be accorded media time and international attention. Their actions were almost a parody of Andy Warhol's dictum that anyone can be famous for fifteen minutes. Almost at will, PLO saboteurs and hijackers could suck the world press in to provide a moment for media grandstanding in return for dramatic and usually bloody pictures. It was a trade-off the press accepted unquestioningly. This addiction to publicity and to terrorism as an end in itself made the expatriate leaders lose sight of the need to cultivate the images and myths required to be considered real partners to the international diplomatic process, as well as to maintain their position on the world media stage for periods longer than a two-minute film clip on the nightly news programs.

The move to Beirut had, in many senses, been fortuitous. In particular, Beirut was the home of both the largest foreign press corps in the Middle East and the largest number of Arabic-language newspapers. It made an ideal base for sending selective messages to carefully chosen audiences. But that sort of sophistication seemed to be beyond the ken of the Palestinian leaders. The messages had a sameness and a repetitiveness—broken only by the whip crack of gunshots. Moreover, the reports of attacks on Israel often were fabricated. As a reporter based in Israel, I don't know how many hours I wasted trying to verify claims being reported from Beirut. Within a short time, it had made me and most of my colleagues in Israel predisposed to disbelieving anything the PLO leaders claimed. If the Israelis had a credibility gap, the PLO had a credibility chasm.

The year 1971 saw the start of a rash of real raids across the Israeli-Lebanese border. These acts, however, were having little or no effect on the Israelis. By 1972, the Israelis were consolidating their hold on the occupied territories and even were willing to go so far as to hold municipal elections on the West Bank for the first time. In response, letter bombs were sent to Israeli diplomats abroad. But in order to garner real media attention, the PLO's leaders needed to stage major international events. They chose seemingly soft targets.

On May 8, a Sabena jetliner was hijacked to Israel's Lod Airport, but Israeli commandos rescued the passengers unharmed. Later that month, three Japanese terrorists, acting under the aegis of the PLO, pulled automatic rifles out of their suitcases in Lod Airport and indiscriminately fired at everyone in the customs hall—including a group of pilgrims from Puerto Rico. The terrorists certainly had created media events, but with no apparent end in mind.

The tactic came to its fullest fruition, or deepest nadir, on September 5, 1972, when a group of Palestinian terrorists massacred eleven Israeli athletes at the Munich Olympics before the eyes of more than a billion people around the world. It was the ultimate televised media terrorist event, but it gained them nothing. In fact, by taking their campaign of murder and destruction to otherwise neutral sites, they alienated entire political constituencies. They also lost because the massacre, together with the support and training they gave to other terrorist groups from the Philippines to Northern Ireland, drove the secret services in many countries to work ever more closely with the Israelis. Hoping to avoid some of the political fallout from the events in Munich, Al Fatah tried to dissociate itself from the massacre by labeling the group involved the "Black September" movement. But no one was fooled.

The "publicity is all—damn the real consequences" philosophy and the heady addiction to an ideology based almost solely on "armed struggle" continued through 1973. Palestinian terrorism spread worldwide. The Israeli air attaché was assassinated in Washington. The Israeli embassy in Bangkok was seized briefly. The Israeli embassy in Cyprus was bombed, as were the Israeli airline offices in Athens. An attempt was made to shoot down an Israeli airliner in Rome. And three Soviet Jews were held captive on a train in Austria. But undoubtedly the most senseless act of all was the murder of U.S. and Belgian diplomats in Khartoum in March.

On October 6, however, all of the constants in the Middle East—except for the rejectionist positions of the PLO and a number of radical Arab states—were to change. The Yom Kippur War not only brought more destruction and death, it also precipitated the first real negotiations between Israel and an Arab state since 1950. To the daily background drumbeat of shootings and killings was added a new counterpointed melody. The PLO leadership was forced into the background as Henry Kissinger negotiated two postwar disengagement agreements between Israel and Egypt and one between Israel and Syria. In the altered political climate, the PLO had no effective response. Unwilling to play the new game, it acted like a spoiler, staging a series of bloody one-day media events. In April 1974, eighteen Israelis, including eight children and five women, were killed by terrorists in the northern border town of Kiryat Shmona. In May, twenty Israeli children were killed and seventy wounded in a terrorist attack on a school in another border town, Maalot. The leader of the group responsible for the Maalot attack, Naif Hawatmeh, claimed that he had ordered the assault in order to sabotage Kissinger's mission. A Middle East peace settlement, Hawatmeh declared in Beirut, would mean "the liquidation of the Palestinian cause." But these and many other attacks were out of sync with the new story line Henry Kissinger was promoting—that of negotiated settlements. Forced to choose between "armed struggle" and "negotiated settlement," the world was choosing the Kissinger line.

The violence, for all its brutality and horrendous effects, was becoming banal, a sideshow. After a while, the violence shown on TV newsreels becomes as distant and noninvolving as that on "Miami Vice." When subjected to a daily dose of the same thing, initially people are shocked, even horrified. But they eventually become inured, numbed to the point where they can no longer relate strongly and emotionally to brutality. The psychic cost of becoming involved with the picture is too high for most people, and the neuron circuit breakers, screaming "overload," switch off the ability to feel the pain of others. That lesson was lost on the PLO's leadership then, just as it would when it was Palestinians who were suffering from Israeli brutality after the intifada broke out.

Possibly the thing that stands out most in my mind from this period was the absence of a sense that somewhere, in someone's mind, there was a plan of action intended to lead to something—that there was a planned sequence of events with a long-term purpose behind it. Instead, it was a jumble of death and destruction that had no political meaning or thematic base. There was no agenda. The goal—the replacement of Israel by a Palestinian state—was obvious. But, unlike other revolutionary wars, there seemed to be few clear objectives that deliberately were planned as stepping-stones to that goal. Without a strategic vision to latch onto as a guide, the press corps was left without the thread it needed to tie the individual events together into a coherent picture. Coverage became photo-op journalism taken to its absolute and most grizzly extreme.

It has been argued by some that the journalists working in Beirut during this period were little more than mouthpieces for the PLO leadership, repeating their words uncritically. To a certain degree, that is true—because there was little more to report than what those leaders said about terrorist events or feuds within the PLO or disputes between the PLO and other Arab states. In the dispatches of the time, there was little sense of the daily interplay between the leadership and the constituency that one finds in normal political settings. That is not surprising, because often the penalty for dissent in Palestinian political fora was death—not the sort of environment that encourages open, national debate. And without debate, without cogently argued dissent to report on, analytical writing quickly reaches a dead end.

I have emphasized the Palestinian events taking place outside Israeli-controlled territory because, from the point of view of the journalists working the other side of the fence in Israel and the occupied territories, the story was essentially a reactive one. The Palestinians in the Israeli-occupied territories were quiescent, doing little that was newsworthy other than to launch sporadic terrorist attacks or to obey calls for strikes or demonstrations issued by the expatriate leaders. Despite the declaration at the 1974 Fez summit conference that bestowed upon the PLO the mantle of the "sole legitimate representative of the Palestinian people," a major intra-Arab political achievement, there was little in the way of political movement that could energize journalists working in the occupied territories. In fact, there was utter predictability. We knew that at any particular moment, the PLO leadership would choose rejection and armed violence over negotiation and compromise; the exigencies of Arab world politics over the needs of international diplomacy; and a vision of snatching all of the cake over the possibility of getting at least part of the cake. But most of all, the expatriate leadership would choose to express, and react to, the perceptions and demands of the expatriate Palestinians living in the Arabian Peninsula or the refugee camps of Lebanon, Syria, and Jordan rather than the immediate needs of the Palestinians in the occupied territories.

The years 1975 and 1976, however, were turning points in foreign press coverage of the occupied territories. In April 1975, the civil war between the Palestinians and the Maronite Christians in Lebanon had begun. By July 6, according to the Lebanese newspaper *Al Anwar*, 3,314 people had been killed and 16,441 wounded. The PLO's attention had been refocused from the battle with Israel to the bloodbath taking place in the PLO's backyard.

Inside the occupied territories, major changes were taking place that, in retrospect, were to presage and lead to the intifada. In December 1975, the Israeli government caved in to the demands of the mystic Jewish nationalists belonging to Gush Emmunim and, for the first time, allowed Jewish settlers to live in the district of Samaria inside an army camp. Political life in the occupied territories had entered a new phase. Whereas before, Jewish settlement had been allowed only in the desert wastes of the Sinai, on land that had been Jewish prior to 1948, like Gush Etzion, south of Jerusalem, or in the largely unpopulated Jordan Rift, now Jews were being allowed to live in the Palestinian heartland—in direct competition for land and resources with the indigenous Palestinian population. Finally the journalists' story had entered a new phase.

More important, however, was the Israeli government's decision to go ahead with municipal elections in the West Bank. For the first time, the franchise also was extended to women and all tax-paying males, whether they owned property or not. Under the previous Jordanian regulations, only male property owners had been eligible to cast ballots. This meant that for the first time, the elections would provide a more or less representative local leadership.

While Palestinians in Nablus rioted in March 1976 against the presence of the new Jewish settlers nearby, an even more bitter internal battle was going on within the Palestinian community. The expatriate PLO leadership came out in opposition to the elections, fearing the establishment of an independent local leadership structure beyond its control. The battle between the expatriates and the newly emerging leadership in the West Bank was a bitter one, but in the end, the local leaders won—by threatening that they would go ahead and run for office anyway, without PLO agreement. The Palestinians in the occupied areas had won their first major political battle with the expatriate PLO leadership.

The Israelis hoped that the elections would create a moderate or submissive leadership that would be a viable alternative to the expatriates. That, however, was not to be. It was an election in which the new generation of Palestinians that had matured under Israeli occupation finally was able to express its choice. And a majority of the ballots, especially in the major cities, went to the radicals running under the "National Bloc" label—most of whom supported one faction or another in the PLO.

For journalists, the elections were not merely a story, they created a new focus and new breadth in news coverage. The town halls provided an address where questions could be asked, interviews with legitimately elected officials could be conducted, and new stories could be sought out. As might have been expected, the questions and the stories centered not on sewage or garbage collection, but on national Palestinian issues. In effect, a new set of Palestinian spokesmen had emerged—with a new journalistic audience available to them. To journalists concerned with fairness, the new spokesmen were a means to balance the intensive coverage of Jews and the pronouncements of Jewish officials. Unlike many Israeli officials, the Palestinian leaders were easily accessible, generous with their time, and, most important, quotable. Contrary to the Israeli practice of officials using almost any excuse to speak "off the record," the Palestinians invariably were more than happy to be named as sources.

With the elections, another, new phenomenon arose. The Palestinian leadership in the occupied areas, flush with its success over the PLO expatriates and the Israelis, decided on a very different course of political and social action than previously had been the case. They decided to adopt the model used so successfully by the Zionists before the establishment of the State of Israel. The local leaders decided to concentrate on building institutions that would provide parallel, independent alternatives to the services being provided by the Israelis. That meant expanding the network of institutes of higher learning on the one hand and day-care centers on the other; the establishment of expanded legal services and handicraft centers; and even the creation of an independent press service.

The number of addresses to which journalists could turn expanded enormously. But it was not merely numbers that counted. Of greater significance was the fact that each address, whether it was a union, a human rights organization like Al Haq, or the Council on Higher Education, was a specialist in its own particular field and could provide journalists with the kind of specific information and expertise that previously had been either unavailable or dispersed through a wide variety of sources. As policy-making bodies, these institutions had to make choices. The very act of these Palestinians grappling with alternatives, of weighing one option against another, provided the journalists who sought out these conflicts with the real meat for analytical stories. Unlike the stodgy and unimaginative PLO, the local Palestinian leaders were poised to go beyond teaser politics. In less than two years, a broad-based Palestinian system of press co-optation was established and a real threat to Israeli political control in the West Bank was emerging.

One organization that would have a particularly significant impact on press coverage of the intifada was the Palestine Press Service. The PPS was established in late 1977 by a strong and articulate PLO supporter from the West Bank city of Ramallah, Raymonda Tawil. She had become one of the main contact persons for the foreign press—especially those who had been "parachuted" in from abroad. A parachutist is a reporter sent in for a short period either to cover a breaking story or to produce a special report. Among other things, Tawil would provide contacts with local Palestinians and translations from the Arabic-language newspapers published in East Jerusalem. At that time, she was one of the very few Palestinians in the occupied territories who had regular contacts with the foreign press, who understood its needs and how best to approach it. She had a well-developed talent for putting a Palestinian "spin" on events and projecting the position of the PLO. She chose as her partner Ibrahim Kar'een, a young Palestinian student who was working on his master's degree in English literature at the Hebrew University.

Their format was relatively simple and filled a major hole in the foreign press's news coverage. Twice a day, they issued a bulletin containing a precis of what had been written in the Arabic-language press and a summary of the day's events in the occupied territories. Kar'een claims that by 1979 he had between forty and fifty subscribers. The fifty-dollar-a-month subscriber fee was hardly enough to maintain the organization, and there were suspicions, voiced openly by the Israeli authorities, that the PPS was being funded by the PLO.

To many foreign correspondents, the arrival of the PPS was a godsend. While many knew little or no Hebrew, fewer, if any, knew Arabic. The office in East Jerusalem also became a source of information for Israeli journalists. Over the years, it was to become one of the few genuine meeting places for Palestinians and local and foreign reporters. It also was to become a training ground for Palestinian journalists who were to become stringers for the foreign press. To get around Israeli regulations that all local media outlets be licensed, the PPS listed itself officially as a translation service. In 1978, it applied for a telex to speed its service to subscribers, but the request was denied because the Israeli postal service claimed that it had no lines. In 1985, the service finally got its telex, which not only speeded up transmission but also enabled it to reach the journalists in Tel Aviv, where most of the television networks were located.

The growth in size also led to greater harassment by Israeli censors, who began demanding that everything be submitted to them before transmission to other journalists. This resulted in delays of up to an hour or more. Nonetheless, the PPS had become an invaluable tipster service.

At the outbreak of the intifada, according to Kar'een, about 85 to 90

percent of the foreign journalists were using the service. During the early
stages of the intifada, the PPS offices became what Kar'een describes as
a "salon," where journalists would gather to compare notes and barter
information. Unlike the hierarchical and stratified Israeli system of news
management and distribution, the PPS was professionally egalitarian, providing all journalists who wished to use it with almost equal access to the
material available. Not all of its material was accurate. Ibrahim Kar'een
claims that he was meticulous about verifying the facts he disseminated
and would fire any journalists who made more than two mistakes. However, in an informal poll I took of many of the PPS's subscribers, the
consensus was that until about three months into the intifada, the service
was considered an unreliable source. Then, according to the consensus,
"someone" must have made this criticism known, and the accuracy of
the reports improved immeasurably. So effective was the PPS in disseminating the Palestinian perspective and Palestinian news items that it was
shut down by the Israeli authorities four months after the intifada began.
It continued to operate, however, at a reduced level, with Ibrahim Kar'een
now listing himself as a "stringer."[4]

The year 1976 was a turning point in journalists' coverage of the
occupied territories for other reasons as well. With the expatriate leadership
so involved in the Lebanese Civil War, there were fewer cross-border
attacks or attacks on Israelis abroad. (A notable exception was the hijacking
of an Air France airbus with 247 passengers and 12 crew members to
Entebbe, Uganda. As was the case with the Sabena jet hijacked to Lod
Airport, the Israeli commando raid that led to the release of all but one
of the hostages was an Israeli public relations coup of the first order. News
of the rescue operation totally upstaged the long-planned U.S. bicenten-
nial celebrations of the same day.)

The expatriates' preoccupation with events in Lebanon meant that

---

[4]The decision to shut down the PPS was yet another extraordinary example of Israeli media
myopia. Fortuitously for the Palestinians, the closure of the press service forced most of the
major foreign media organizations to set up independent stringer networks of Palestinian reporters
in the Israeli-occupied territories and to hire Palestinian journalist staffers for the first time. This,
in turn, led to vastly expanded Palestinian access to the world media and routinized the Palestinians' input into foreign journalists' daily files. With the hiring of Palestinian staffers, no
longer was the Palestinian story an irregular sequence of journalistic blips. Now it was an integral
part of each media organization's daily activity

there was more room for local Palestinian initiatives in the occupied territories. With no one to represent them, and with a long list of issues and grievances that had not been addressed, the Palestinians took to the streets. There were demonstrations throughout the summer, especially in Nablus. There was renewed violence in October. And then, beginning on November 22, there was a relatively sustained series of demonstrations, riots, general strikes, and clashes with Israeli troops. With hindsight, this period seems almost like a first rehearsal for the approaching intifada. Another feature of the intifada that was previewed then was the Israeli decision to close the territories to press coverage. On December 14, the Foreign Press Association sent a sharply worded note to the army spokesman announcing that it was breaking off all relations with him to protest restrictions in coverage and increasingly heavy censorship.

The rioting eventually petered out and the story in the occupied territories was supplanted by two momentous events: one, the victory of the Likud in the May 1977 general elections and Menachem Begin's subsequent takeover of the reins of government for the first time, and two, President Sadat's visit to Jerusalem later that year.

The end of the rioting and similar relatively short-lived upswings in violence in the occupied territories in the years to come were to leave long-serving journalists with a highly provocative question that would preoccupy them at the outbreak of the intifada: Could the Palestinians ever sustain their public protests over time? Almost unnoticed at the time was the strengthening of the *Shebiba*, the PLO's youth organization. It was there that the new, young cadres born under Israeli occupation were indoctrinated and organized. The *Shebiba* was to play a pivotal role at the outbreak of the intifada, organizing demonstrations, participating in the rioting, guiding journalists, and answering the question of sustainability.

It is impossible to underestimate the influence that the *Shebiba* had on the intifada. By the time the intifada broke out, approximately 70 percent of the Palestinians in the occupied territories were under the age of twenty-four, and many, especially in the refugee camps, had been members of the organization. By 1981, it was clear that the patterns of deference within the Palestinian community had changed. In previous years, when I had gone to a refugee camp to do a story, I usually would have been escorted to one of the village elders for an interview. By 1981, invariably I was escorted to someone in his late teens who was quite obviously considered the real local leader by the youngsters in the camp.

In the lifetime of each generation, there are only a few periods of time that can be labeled accurately as "seminal"—when events of such magnitude occur that they refashion whole nations' perspectives for years to come. Nineteen seventy-seven was such a year. Menachem Begin and his Likud government came to power, and Egypt's President Sadat arrived in Jerusalem. The Likud's victory in May brought to power a man who was easy to demonize. Menachem Begin's demagogic speaking style and his nationalist ideology encompassing "the whole of the Land of Israel" (including the West Bank and Gaza) were discomfiting to Western ears. His decision, made the day after his election, to increase the number of Jewish settlements in the occupied areas created an immediate, physical, civilian image of the conflict between the Jews and the Palestinians. Up to that point, the conflict had been portrayed in the press largely by focusing on the actions undertaken by such instruments of government as the Israeli army. Now there was a new visual image on which to focus, the mystical nationalist settlers who were being called on to populate the biblical lands of Judea and Samaria. Many of these settlers, "true believers" in their extremist ideology and strident in their language, were American immigrants, thus making them ideal interviewees for the broadcast media. Over time, they were to form the extreme right frame of the press's picture of events in the occupied territories.

A countervailing force, however, was President Sadat's visit to Jerusalem on November 19. Virtually singlehandedly and almost instantaneously, he flipped the story line of violent conflict to its obverse side, "land for peace." As might have been expected, the expatriate PLO leadership opposed the visit. Yasir Arafat, speaking on Syrian radio, labeled it "an abominable action." Significantly, a PLO call for a general strike in the occupied territories on November 21 went largely unheeded. In a matter of days, Sadat had been able to present a new vision to Israelis, Palestinians in the occupied territories, and the rest of the world alike. Although he called the Palestinian problem "the core and crux" of the Middle East problem, the expatriates feared that he would sacrifice their interests for those of Eygpt. Those living in the Israeli-occupied territories were less sure and many were openly willing to give Sadat the benefit of the doubt. His acceptance of Prime Minister Begin's plan for at least limited autonomy for those under Israeli occupation held out the hope that some of the pressing social issues soon would be addressed.

That expectation posed a supreme danger to the PLO's hegemony among Palestinians in the occupied territories. The PLO's primary concern throughout the post-1967 period had been to stifle or to excise any challenge to its organizational dominance. Even those who were supporters of King Hussein, like Bethlehem mayor Elias Freij or Gaza City mayor Rashad a-Shawa, were forced to pay at least public obeisance to the PLO. To prevent the political fissures from widening too much as a result of the hopes engendered by the Sadat visit, the PLO began to employ its extreme form of "prejudice" against Palestinians who dared to seek open compromise with the Israelis. From late 1977 to early 1978, five leading Palestinians in the West Bank who favored dialogue with Israel, including a senior education official and a prominent businessman, were assassinated "for collaboration." Outside the West Bank and Gaza, there was also a series of assassinations for ideological deviance and political dissent. These internecine killings established an important paradigm for Palestinian political conduct under periods of threat to the PLO as an organization; and events arising out of this paradigm of behavior during the intifada were to become important parts of journalists' coverage of the uprising.

Unable and unwilling to respond imaginatively to Sadat's vision and the changed political environment, the PLO became determined to change the story line back to one of violent confrontation. On March 11, 1978, eleven Palestinians came ashore in rubber dinghies in the Israeli nature reserve of Maagan Michael. They killed an American nature photographer, Gail Rubin, and captured a bus. They forced the bus to drive in the direction of Tel Aviv, firing out of the windows as they sped past oncoming cars. By the time the bus was stopped by Israeli security units just outside Tel Aviv, thirty-four Israelis had been killed, and over seventy had been wounded. Nine members of Al Fatah lay dead, and two had been captured. The raid, said a PLO spokesman in Beirut, was designed to frustrate Sadat's "capitulationist designs." It had been the bloodiest Palestinian attack on Israel since 1948. The Israelis responded three days later with a massive attack into southern Lebanon, up to the Litani River. It took two months for the Israelis to withdraw.

Another series of terrorist attacks and bombings in Israel and the occupied territories in subsequent months did not, however, prevent Sadat, Begin, and U.S. president Jimmy Carter from signing the Camp David peace accords on September 17. The PLO, preoccupied with the civil war in Lebanon, was in a period of eclipse. Their raids on Israeli border villages and Israeli counterraids had no effect on the implementation of the main parts of the Camp David accords.

The PLO's political impotence led, in part, to the establishment of one semiunderground political forum in the occupied territories and the strengthening of another. The first, known as the National Guidance Council, was established in 1978. It brought together under one political umbrella a majority of the secular nationalist Palestinian leaders in the occupied territories. It was, in effect, a protolegislature whose members were drawn from the corps of newly elected public officials and the leaders of the rapidly developing institutions in the West Bank. Although its meetings were held out of the public eye, its membership was well known to most West Bankers. The very act of joining the council and being recognized by their peers relegitimized these leaders and made them ever more a focus for foreign journalists' interviews. To counter the influence of the new secular nationalist leaders, the Israelis tried to organize a different forum, called the village leagues. These leagues were based on the traditional leadership of the rural areas, but they never attracted any real support, because they never were viewed by the Palestinians themselves as truly indigenous and broadly representative.

The second real indigenous force centered around the long-established, fundamentalist Moslem Brotherhood. The brotherhood, which preached religious renewal from within rather than armed conflict, was an archenemy of secular nationalists throughout the Arab world. For that reason, its strengthening was welcomed by the Israelis. The brotherhood's base of support lay in the Gaza Strip and in the rural areas of the West Bank. Its members preferred to stay out of the limelight and its activities went almost unnoticed in the foreign press. With its growth, though, came an increase in political sophistication that made it a true competitor to the various secular nationalist parties for Palestinians' loyalties. That competition was to backfire on the Israelis once the intifada broke out. The fundamentalists' organization *HAMAS* ("zeal"), formed almost immediately after the intifada began, heated up the rebellion by taking to the streets to compete with the secular nationalists for control of whole neighborhoods.

The Israelis, preoccupied with their single-minded policy of control in the occupied territories, failed to recognize the true nature of these political developments. Israeli officials still were convinced that if only they could apply enough pressure, the political movements within the occupied territories would wither. I can recall interviewing the main Israeli policymaker in the occupied territories at that time, Colonel Menachem Milson, a professor of Arabic studies at the Hebrew University when not in uniform. His dream, he told me, was to institute an Israeli-run regime in the occupied territories, modeled on the U.S. administration in Japan after World War II, in which he would be able to change everything from school texts to long-term political outlooks.

Among other things, Milson ordered the disbanding of the National Guidance Council in 1981. The next year, the Israelis began to fire most of the mayors who had been elected. Any hopes that West Bankers may have had about being on the verge of achieving some sort of representational government finally were buried. With their primary public voices muzzled, the West Bankers took to the streets in a wave of rioting that was to end only with the Israeli invasion of Lebanon.

Two events at this time were also to have long-term political implications for the future of events in the occupied territories. The first, in March 1980, were bomb attacks on the mayors of Nablus, Ramallah, and El Bireh in the West Bank. As was uncovered later, a Jewish underground made up primarily of settlers in the occupied territories had been created and a precedent for settlers' vigilante attacks on Palestinians had been set.

The second was the Knesset's passage of a law—at Prime Minister Begin's behest—reaffirming the status of Jerusalem. The law made it legally impossible for the Israeli government to change the status of Jerusalem without first securing the abrogation of the law. The vote was largely symbolic. East Jerusalem had been formally annexed to Israel almost immediately after the Six-Day War. Nonetheless, the new law was to have an important effect in shaping Palestinian perceptions. It would leave Palestinians in the occupied territories without even the vague hope of achieving some sort of control over the city in the near future, and it would engender a fear that the Israelis were trying to hive off the Palestinians living in the city from the rest of the population in the occupied territories. Later, this perception was to play an important role in drawing the East Jerusalem Arabs into the intifada. When these East Jerusalem Palestinians did join in the intifada, the effect was to send a powerful signal to journalists that a turning point in the uprising had been reached, and immediately, the press's perceptions and coverage of the story changed as well.

The next year, increasingly heavy shellings by the PLO in Lebanon on Israeli border towns and the assassination of President Sadat on October 6, 1981, finally rediverted press attention away from the peace process and back to armed confrontation, as the PLO had hoped. Even the final Israeli withdrawal from the Sinai Peninsula in April 1982 no longer could arrest the process. The PLO's actions of the period were not so much a war of attrition against the Israelis (although that certainly was part of the intent of the shellings). Theirs was a military campaign against an idea. To an organization as intellectually moribund and byzantine in its internal politics as the PLO, Sadat's vision of a negotiated peace over time was more threatening than Israel's military force. To the Likud government, with its difficulties in reconciling the Sadat vision with its stated ideology of maintaining control over all of the occupied land, the PLO's shellings were a gift, because they succeeded, at least temporarily, in stifling internal dissent in Israel over the future direction of the peace talks. That hiatus, however, was not to last very long.

On June 6, 1982, the Israeli army invaded Lebanon. The war had enormous political repercussions as well as a major effect on journalists' perceptions of the Israeli government. But it also altered the perceptions of Palestinians living in the occupied territories in a very profound way. Israeli defense minister Ariel Sharon did achieve his personal objective of driving the PLO's leadership out of Beirut, but along the way, he set in motion a series of processes that helped lead eventually to the intifada. The first was the creation of a large body of Palestinian martyrs, many of whom were a product of the massacres by Israel's Phalangist allies in the

Sabra and Shatilla refugee camps in Beirut from September 16 to September 18, 1982.

The second was the weakening of the Israeli intelligence apparatus, in part because of the demoralization within the intelligence services that set in after the Sabra and Shatilla massacres, in part because of the killing of twenty *Shabak* agents by a Shiite suicide car bomber in Tyre on November 3, 1983, and in part because human intelligence resources previously used in the occupied territories had to be transferred to Lebanon.

The third factor was the release of 600 convicted Palestinian terrorists to their homes in the occupied territories as part of a massive exchange of 1,150 Palestinian prisoners held by Israel for 3 Israeli soldiers captured during the Lebanese War. These Palestinian prisoners, who had, in effect, been training for leadership while in prison, soon were acting as role models and organizers among the youth in the West Bank and Gaza.

The fourth was the emergence of the Shiite factor. Until the war, the Shiites had been among the most quiescent and downtrodden of the ethnic and confessional groups in Lebanon. During the war, they found not only their voice, but also their military strength. Their constant attacks on Israeli soldiers were the main factor that led the Israelis to withdraw from most of the country. That success, widely broadcast on Israeli, Jordanian, and Syrian television, was to serve as a model for many Palestinians in the occupied territories. Moreover, by letting the Shiite genie out of the bottle, the Israelis set off a chain reaction that would lead to the round of Shiite kidnappings that eventually drove the foreign press corps out of Beirut and made Israel the media capital of the Middle East. Any event that occurred in Israel or the occupied territories from that time on would be magnified in the foreign press.

But the most important factor was the very removal of the PLO's leadership from the scene, creating a political vacuum in the occupied territories. The PLO's long-held insistence that it control the activities of the Palestinians in the West Bank and Gaza had, in many ways, made Israel's job of policing those Palestinians incomparably easier.

In the wake of the war, the PLO was weakened severely by internal strife and thus unable to impose the measure of control on the occupied territories that had been the norm previously. There were revolts within the PLO and even open fighting between the factions supporting and opposing Yasir Arafat. Palestinian moderates were threatened, and one of the leading moderates, Issam Sartawi, was shot dead by agents of Abu Nidal in Portugal in April 1983.

From the beginning of 1983 until the beginning of 1986, there was an upsurge in what Israeli officials judged to be locally organized terrorist attacks. But in addition to hot weapon attacks, which involved guns or grenades, there were also more demonstrations using rocks and tire burning as their primary weapons. Stonings were almost the only means left to the Palestinians for political self-expression, and what they expressed was continually building rage and frustration. They were both the final warning signals and the final rehearsal for the intifada.

The events of the period were not just a rehearsal by Palestinians in the occupied territories. The Israelis, the foreign press, and the PLO also took part. The PLO tried to retake control of the media stage from its new headquarters in Tunisia by such actions as the hijacking of the *Achille Lauro*. The Israelis, following their established pattern, tried to retake control in the occupied territories by adding more military and administrative sanctions to their "iron fist" policy—without trying, at the same time, to resolve the deep social and economic issues that underlay the unrest. The Israeli military restricted press coverage in the West Bank and Gaza. And the foreign journalists practiced techniques to get around the army roadblocks that had been strung out throughout the occupied territories.

One did not have to be a professional seer to realize that a critical mass of unrest had built up in the West Bank and Gaza that could find no outlet. The Levant, an area of the world that cannot tolerate any status quo for very long, was in a state of political gridlock. The only man capable of pushing Sadat's vision forward, Sadat himself, had been removed from the scene by Islamic fundamentalist extremists. Behavior patterns for dealing with the unrest that was building had become well established and rehearsed among all parties. Institutions that were to direct the course of events had become well entrenched. And the foreign press was standing by, waiting to report, ready to become the Palestinians' communications pipeline to the world. In an extraordinarily prescient interview, Shlomo Gazit, the former head of Israeli Military Intelligence and former military governor of the West Bank, stated in the fall of 1985:

"This latest wave of violence may calm down, but things cannot go on like this. I don't know whether it is going to be the summer of '86 or '87 or whenever, but if this situation continues there is going to be a real explosion."[5]

It would take only five more major events over the next two years for the volcano to blow. Each, in its own unique way, was to lead directly to the uprising. The first began on November 26, 1985. Zafir el Masri, a bright and extraordinarily capable young politician, was appointed mayor of Nablus. El Masri came from one of the wealthiest, most respected, and most powerful Palestinian families. His cousin, Tahir el Masri, was the Jordanian foreign minister. Several things set Zafir el Masri apart from the rest of the politicians and would-be politicians in the occupied territories. He was a pragmatist rather than an ideologist. He was a true grassroots politician who had spent the eighteen months prior to his appointment building up a broad constituency among the residents of Nablus. He also had worked hard to get approval from Israel, Jordan, and the PLO. He could speak to the Israelis in their political language, to the Jordanians in theirs, and to the PLO in its particular tongue. He had a long-term political vision based on small, incremental steps. Articulate and careful in his use of language, el Masri had a comfortable and easygoing way with both the Israeli and the foreign press corps. In other words, he had all the makings of a Palestinian Willy Brandt—with a true statesman's ability to reach out beyond the present to the future. For all of these reasons, he was assassinated by Palestinian extremists outside his office on March 2, 1986, exactly three months after his appointment. Although he had belonged to a family with close links to the Hashemite throne, more than ten thousand Palestinians turned out in the streets to give him a nationalist's funeral. The Palestinians in the occupied territories had lost the one man who truly could communicate their problems and their frustrations to the world.

The second major event occurred on the night of June 6–7, 1987. A group of Jewish settlers entered the Dehaishe refugee camp near Bethlehem under cover of darkness. Dehaishe had long been one of the centers of Palestinian activism, and often its youngsters had pelted Israeli cars

---

[5]Thomas L. Friedman, "Palestinian-Israel Fight: Arab Lands Now Spectators," *New York Times*, 3 October 1985, p. A10.

with rocks as they drove by on the main artery leading south from Jerusalem. Once inside the camp, the settlers went on a rampage—smashing windows, denting cars, and attacking any property in sight. As the settlers had intended, the Palestinians throughout the West Bank began to feel physically insecure to a degree they had never felt before.

The third event occurred the following September. The head of the Israeli administration in the West Bank, Brigadier General Ephraim Sneh, resigned his position after a policy dispute with his superiors. He had sought dialogue with the Palestinians. His superiors had insisted on an iron fist. According to Palestinian leaders with whom I spoke, Sneh was unique among Israeli officials in the occupied territories. "He would call me into his office," one Palestinian said, "and tell me to shut the door. He would then ask me what I thought about things and I would reply 'If I tell you, you'll throw me into jail.'

"He would say, 'No one gets thrown in jail for saying anything here.' And then we would start to talk, and I would tell him the truth about everything that was going on—even if he didn't like what I said." With Sneh's departure, the Israelis lost the only high-level official who had succeeded in reaching out to the Palestinians in the occupied territories and gaining their genuine respect. He was virtually Israel's only effective "ear" in the occupied territories. When he quit, Israel lost the only official to whom Palestinians of stature would talk openly.

Two months later, a fourth major event was an Arab summit meeting held in Amman. For the first time, the Palestinian question was not at the forefront of the discussions. The Arab rulers were concerned first and foremost with establishing a unified stand against Iran. Although he met several times with King Hussein, Yasir Arafat was, on the whole, given a decidedly cool reception. To Palestinians in the occupied areas, it seemed as if their issues were being passed by, that no one in the Arab world was interested in their problems of living under occupation.

The fifth event was later that month, on the night of November 25, when two Palestinian terrorists flying motorized hang gliders sped low over South Lebanon. One was downed by the Israelis, but the other landed close to an Israeli army base near the border town of Kiryat Shmona. In a suicide attack, the Palestinian ran into the army camp, firing as he moved. Before he was shot dead, he had killed six soldiers and wounded nine others. In a world where perceptions are often more important in public decision making than is reality, the Israeli army, the symbol and instrument of Israeli control, now was perceived by many in the occupied territories as vulnerable.

In sum, by the time the intifada broke out, the Palestinians had lost their last effective local political public voice. The Israelis had lost their only sensitive ear. Israel had killed the messenger service and Palestinian extremists had killed the most effective messengers. The Palestinian youngsters were infused with a sense of fear and desperation and a belief that they had nothing to lose. No one, not even in the Arab world, seemed to care. And the symbol of Israeli deterrence, the army, no longer was perceived of as the undefeatable monolith it once had been. When the Palestinian youngsters finally took to the streets, they did it in the only way they knew how: theatrically, and before the eyes and ears of the only group that seemed to want to watch and listen and carry their message to the world—the foreign press corps.

There are many postscripts to this story. Two are worth noting at this point. On March 2, 1988, there was a major riot in Nablus as part of the intifada. Much of the stoning took place just outside the locked burial tomb of Zafir el Masri. It was the second anniversary of el Masri's death, but no one among the demonstrators paid the cemetery any heed. He and his style of politics had been forgotten. Not long afterward, Ephraim Sneh sought to bring his unique perceptions to politics when he tried to get on the Labor party's slate for the upcoming elections. Labor party officials, sensing a threat from a newcomer, kept him off the ballot on a technicality.

A Zoom Lens in a Maze Made of Mirrors

Prior to 1967, the vast majority of foreign journalists in Israel were stringers. Many large news outlets had no one at all to represent them. Only a few major organizations, like the *New York Times* and Associated Press (AP), had foreign staffers manning their bureaus. When the war broke out, there was a rush of firemen (parachutists who deal only with breaking stories) into the country, and a mad dash to acquire a local stringer. Andrew Meisels, for example, who had been working for Israeli Radio, got a job as a radio stringer for ABC because he happened to wander into Tel Aviv's Hilton Hotel during the war and met a stranger who turned out to be Amie Collins, in Israel to cover the Six-Day War for ABC-TV. Collins was looking for a radio stringer and Meisels got the job.

To this day, stringers form the backbone of what might be called "second-tier" coverage of the Middle East, serving those media that want independent coverage but are unable or unwilling to spend the money needed to maintain a staffer. Stringers are among the most cost-effective workers in the world. They are paid by the piece, file only as needed, and are given no social-service benefits. But no matter how long they work for their companies, and no matter how high the quality of their reporting, they are inherently distrusted by their employers. Michael Elkins, one of the finest foreign journalists ever to work in Israel, was an example of this. In 1967, he got the scoop of the war: that Israel had destroyed the Egyptian air force and was on its way to a major victory. CBS Radio News, for whom he had worked since 1956, did not want to air his report. When he finally convinced them that he was correct, they did not offer congratulations. His editor told him only, "You'd better be right." Elkins, who went on to do distinguished work for the BBC and *Newsweek*, quit CBS soon afterward.[1]

Stringers work with several disadvantages, no matter where they live. In Israel, where the story is so emotionally laden, the difficulties are magnified. In the post-1967 period, most of the stringers in Israel were Israeli citizens and Jews and therefore were suspected by their editors of bias in favor of the Jewish State. As a result, although many of the stringers were fluent in Hebrew and had extensive contacts throughout Israeli society, they were never as well trusted as a newly arrived staffer who knew neither the language nor the customs nor the way the country operated.

Among other reasons for this syndrome is the fact that, working so far away from their head office, the stringers rarely had the chance to meet their corporate coworkers and to develop their trust. And as stringers around the world have found, often it is almost impossible to interest an editor in a new story—unless a similar report already has appeared on a news wire or on television or has been printed in a newspaper that has a staffer in the same country.

Even when the stringers and the home office editors had met, there were often distinct differences in perception about the nature of a story. That is a common occurrence between field reporters and deskmen, but

---

[1] It is indicative of the nature of the stringer-employer relationship that to this day Elkins remembers the incident with considerable bitterness, while CBS executives continue to boast of the scoop as one of the seminal achievements of its Middle East coverage.

the problem is infinitely magnified when the reporter is not a staffer. A journalist working close to home, or one on staff, for example, is always at an advantage in arguing his case, if only because there are rarely complaints about the expensive telephone costs that such arguments incur. A staffer invariably is viewed as part of a company team. A stringer is not. Free-lancers often are seen as nothing more than hired hands taken on for unavoidable reasons. A staffer abroad is considered his or her organization's area expert and commands respect. The free-lancer often is considered an unfortunate second choice to a real team member and is usually not accorded that kind of treatment.

Sometimes these differences in perceptions can reach absurd heights—or depths. While working as a stringer for the Canadian Broadcasting Corporation, I once had an editor say to me, "Don't tell me what the Israelis say, tell me what I know." It was the kind of comment no deskman would have dared give a staffer, because it would have sent any self-respecting staffer running to senior management to complain. Generally speaking, stringers take their livelihoods in their hands if they appeal to higher authorities.

Another problem affecting the coverage stringers offered was low pay, a factor that persists even today. Many of these reporters must maintain a stable of outlets in order to keep body and soul together. Although the vast majority are energetic reporters, when a major news story breaks, multistring reporters often are hard-pressed to provide adequate coverage for all of their strings. Moreover, since they are not on staff, the stringers rarely are accorded the resources normally made available to staff personnel, such as extensive expense accounts, corporate funds to hire a temporary backup reporter, and the right to commit company funds without prior approval. This severely hampers their ability to react quickly to fast-breaking stories.

Insecurity among the stringers was and remains an endemic and chronic disease. Since the Six-Day War, there have always been young reporters arriving in Israel, eager to make a name for themselves and ready to sell their wares more cheaply in return for the chance of getting their name in print or their voice on the air. The level of insecurity and even paranoia among stringers increased vastly in the post-1967 war period as the story continued to grow and many outlets began first to send firemen on a more regular basis to cover the juiciest and thus most lucrative stories, and then later, to send their own staffers to establish full-time bureaus.

Free-lancers also know that they usually have no institutional protection if they contravene, or are thought to contravene, press-directed laws, like those dealing with censorship. More than staffers, they have to anticipate the judgments of the censors if they are not to waste precious work time in wrangling with the blue pencillers.

The treatment of stringers and the home office's perception of them helps create a self-fulfilling prophecy. Lacking resources, trust, and financial security, stringers tend to go for "safe" and cheap stories. They tend to seek out the easily gathered and colorful stories that are inexpensive to produce, not the challenging but expensive and time-consuming material required for in-depth reports. More important, in order to guarantee that their stories will be used—and thus paid for—they tend to play to their editors' preconceptions and to conventional wisdom rather than producing intellectually challenging but controversial analyses. One radio stringer told me during the opening phases of the intifada, "I go out every morning to the Arab villages around Jerusalem and gather some sound. That's enough to last for the whole day. The rest I pick up off the radio. It's not cost-effective to spend any more time out in the field. . . . I give them [the editors] what they want."

Since most of the reporters in the immediate post-1967 period were local stringers, they tended to congregate in the press room of the Government Press Offices in Tel Aviv and Jerusalem. The offices provided desks, the companionship of friends and colleagues the stringers had known for years and even decades, the latest government press releases, and most of all, for the deadline- and cost-conscious reporters, telephones with free dialing anywhere in the country and easy access to the international operator for overseas calls. No less important, the army spokesman's representative was upstairs or next door, and the censors were immediately at hand to provide the precious stamp that would enable the reporter to send out the daily dispatch. It was the finest hour for the Israeli system of co-optation and control. That finest hour, however, was relatively short-lived.

By mid-1968, the nature of the story and the attitudes toward their jobs of staffers and stringers alike had changed rapidly. As the war of attrition along the Suez Canal dragged on and the Palestinian saboteurs continued their forays across the Jordan River, the story began to develop enough momentum to make it worthwhile for many media outlets to invest more heavily in coverage. Some former stringers were put on staff or were awarded contracts that would guarantee them a minimum annual income. Even those who remained pure stringers benefited. Expense accounts for things like telephone calls or authorized out-of-town trips became more liberal. Jay Bushinsky, who then reported to the *Chicago Daily News* and to Group W radio, was one of the first to benefit. At the time, all of the other stringers were in awe of him. Breaking all tradition, he set up his own office with such unheard of professional luxuries as a staff assistant, a private telex machine, and his own AP wire machine.

As the War of Attrition progressed, news coverage was focusing more and more on events on the frontiers, rather than in centers like Tel Aviv and Jerusalem. This gave staffers with discretionary expense accounts an inherent advantage over free-lancers, because the staffers could react more quickly and seek out stories farther afield. One consequence of this phenomenon was to encourage more media outlets to send staffers so that they could get equivalent coverage of their own.

The installation of the Golem (the simultaneous transmission of government announcements by telephone) also meant that journalists no longer had to be close to the press office at all times to ensure that they would get an army press announcement as soon as it came out. Then came a series of government budget cuts that included a curtailment of services by the Government Press Office. A succession of bureaucratic-minded heads of the press office acquiesced to every cutback in funds. First, the valuable newspaper archive in Tel Aviv, which contained the only depository of news clippings from all of the newspapers in the country, was closed. Soon after, the free telephone service was withdrawn. The result was that all journalists were being forced to become more independent. By 1974, the press rooms, which once had rung with the clatter of typewriters and the chirp of conversation, were almost empty. There was less and less need to come to the press office and almost no need to stay.

At the same time, the continuing growth in the number of stories emanating from the Middle East and the accompanying steep rise in the cost of maintaining firemen in hotels led many media outlets to reconsider their approach to news coverage in the region in general and in Israel in particular. Those able to afford it established bureaus in both Israel and at least one Arab capital, usually Beirut. Those outlets with greater budgetary restraints established only one bureau, usually in Beirut, then the media capital of the Middle East. It was an exciting, cosmopolitan city with excellent communications, food, lodging, and the freest Arabic-language press in the Middle East. It was the media and diplomatic listening post for the entire region. But another factor that led journalists to locate in Beirut was a perception among editors that a reporter living in Lebanon could always legitimately pick material off the wire about Israel or from Israeli radio and rewrite it, or hop over to Israel to cover a breaking story. By contrast, an Israeli-based reporter's usefulness could be affected because he or she might be refused visas to the Arab states merely for having been stationed in Tel Aviv. Beirut also was preferred because the home offices often viewed those serving in Israel for any length of time as somehow tainted: in many organizations, there was an underlying suspicion that these journalists had become contaminated by their contact with the Zionists.

The buildup of the staffer press corps in Beirut did not mean that Israel was neglected entirely. By early 1968, AP had expanded its bureau, United Press International (UPI) had created a full-time bureau, and Reuters had brought in an outside staff reporter to beef up its coverage. Of the major U.S. television networks, NBC was the first to establish a proper office and the other networks soon followed suit.

The following few years were a transitional period in the type of coverage emanating from Israel. Most of the new reporters were largely ignorant of the subtleties of politics in the Middle East. But since so much reporting at the time was events-driven and required little prior background knowledge in order to write cogent if not complete reports, the newcomers could operate on almost an equal footing with long-serving reporters. Moreover, they could rely on a great escape mechanism for media political illiterates: the coverage of personalities. The Middle East was awash with colorful international figures. King Hussein reigned in Jordan. Gamal Abdul Nasser was the undisputed leader of Egypt and one of the three major leaders of the nonaligned movement. Many of Israel's greats still were alive. David Ben-Gurion, arguably the father of his country, remained active and available for interviews. The iron-willed but emotional Golda Meir was prime minister. The charismatic one-eyed Moshe Dayan held down the defense portfolio, and the mellifluous Abba Eban was playing the role of Israel's spokesman to the world.

No less influential in shaping the nature of press coverage during this period was the fact that the whole Middle East question was a highly charged issue in the United States and Europe. Hence, people there who were concerned with the course taken by the Middle East were becoming highly polarized into pro-Israeli and pro-Arab camps. Those who joined one or another of these camps were often less concerned with the quality of press coverage than with whether their particular agenda was being given equal play. Because of this audience pressure, all too often the measure of a journalist's performance was not qualitative, but quantitative and ideological. Those, unfortunately, are still too often the criteria in use today. The danger for the public of a journalist operating in this type of environment was, and is, that it's easy for reporters to get away with painting pictures of the events in this region in bright and often garish primary colors. Even more unfortunate for media consumers seeking depth in reporting was that discussion of the pastels of politics, of nuance and ambiguity—the real contribution long-serving reporters can make—was discouraged by many editors.

During this period, most of the new reporters settled in Tel Aviv. There were spacious houses for rent, reasonably good restaurants and shops, a high-quality American school for their children, a wide variety of cultural activities, and the sea. Being based in Tel Aviv also made sense professionally. The main Government Press Office was in the center of town. Tel Aviv was and is home to most of the Israeli print media. The first editions of the daily newspapers were on the streets an hour before they were available in Jerusalem. The only film studios and processing labs in the country were just outside the city. Most important, Tel Aviv had far superior communications facilities. For example, it was the only place from which wire photos could be sent, and when satellite transmission first was introduced, film material could be transmitted only from Tel Aviv.

Moreover, the Defence Ministry and IDF headquarters, which were providing the bulk of the news copy in the late 1960s and early 1970s, are there; and the real political action at the time always took place in Tel Aviv rather than Jerusalem. The headquarters of the main political parties remain there to this day. Many of the leading politicians live there and commute to Jerusalem only when the Knesset is in session. To this day, almost every minister maintains a separate office in Tel Aviv, where he or she spends a very considerable amount of time. It is still traditional for the politicians of the largest parties to "escape" Jerusalem each Thursday and come to Tel Aviv for the main political meetings of the week.

By contrast, Jerusalem in those days was a backwater with few modern amenities, poor facilities, and little secular cultural life to speak of. It may have been the country's capital, but it was hardly treated as such by the nation's political leaders. The periodic stories that erupted in the West Bank were insufficient to draw most journalists away from the coast on a permanent basis.

In the early 1970s, the situation began to change. Prime Minister Meir made a policy decision to try to induce more foreign journalists to come to Israel. Her rationale was that, since the bulk of the foreign press corps in the Middle East was based in Beirut, Israel was being treated unfairly. She believed that because they did not have full-time correspondents in Israel, news outlets abroad were printing Arab claims and policy statements in reports sent by foreign correspondents in Lebanon but were ignoring or disparaging the Israeli side of the debate. In keeping with the conventional wisdom that the quality of journalism can be measured quantitatively, she wanted what was then thought of as "fairness," meaning equal air time and print space to plead Israel's cause.

By cajoling editors and offering such inducements as better communications facilities, she hoped to induce more media outlets to station correspondents in Israel or to hire Israeli-based stringers. Her intent, and that of all of her successors, was to entice the media—if not to provide outright propaganda for Israel—at least to carry the Israeli version of events *alongside* that of the Arabs. One cannot know if she ever dreamed that the foreign press corps in Israel would eventually be larger than that of Beirut, but that is what finally came to pass. And when that happened, the consequences were far different from what she had intended and reached far beyond anything she could have conceived of. By the time Meir left office in the wake of the 1973 Yom Kippur War, major changes in the nature and composition of the foreign press corps in Israel already were taking place. The war had been a watershed in both Israeli history and in the press coverage of the country.

At its outbreak, press sympathies were largely with Israel. By launching a surprise attack on the holiest day in the Jewish calendar, when most people in Israel were fasting and praying, the Egyptians and the Syrians were looked on as somehow immoral, even by supposedly neutral journalists. There were also high expectations that Israel would deal an immediate counterblow and ravage its enemies for this perfidy. In reality, the Israelis were reeling and needed time to regroup. In an attempt to cope with public and press expectations, and believing that the Egyptians should be denied the encouragement that comes from success, Israeli officials made a conscious decision to tell half-truths and whole lies. Particularly in the early stages of the war, they made claims of military successes that had not happened or were merely temporary, like the bombing of the pontoon bridges the Egyptians had flung across the Suez Canal.

It was the kind of strategic decision that can be made only by a national leader—and then only under extremis. Lying to both the press and the public is an act that should be used only when there is no other alternative—and even then only once in a generation. It is the equivalent of emptying a warehouse full of carefully accumulated and hoarded arms for use in one desperate battle for survival.

When the truth of Israel's initial weakness did become known, there was shock both among reporters and among the general public in Israel. However, while the revelations made the foreign press more skeptical, the lies did not engender outright hostility. There was a recognition among many of the journalists at the time that Israel had been in dire straits, and there was a belief that this was undoubtedly a one-time strategic decision that would not be repeated for decades.

Unfortunately for Israel, the use of lying during the war set a precedent in the minds of those who could not think strategically. As a result, the use of lying as a tactical measure to dissimulate and cover up inadequacies and follies, to avoid dealing with issues, or for simple bureaucratic protection and manipulation began to spread. By the 1980s, when queried about some matter, even low-level officials in charge of the matter routinely would say they didn't know or that they couldn't get the information requested. Like a cancer, the phenomenon spread, reaching its zenith—

but not its end—during the opening phases of the invasion of Lebanon, when even the Israeli cabinet was lied to by Defence Minister Ariel Sharon.

This postwar facile approach of taking the seemingly easy way out was to be one of many turning points in the relationship between Israeli officials and the foreign press. The slow metastasizing of the tumor the war had implanted was not perceptible immediately, but it came at a particularly inauspicious time. Following the Yom Kippur War, more media outlets had decided to expand their operations in Israel. The new crop of journalists who arrived were of a different breed than those who had served in Israel before. Some had come from service in the Soviet Union and Vietnam, where official lying, and thus press suspicion of politicians, was particularly intense. Others in the American press had just weathered the firestorms of the coverage of Vietnam and Watergate in Washington, along with the official lying that had accompanied those events. No statement by a politician, Watergate had taught the U.S. press, should be accepted at face value. Under the new unwritten rules established by the Watergate and Vietnam debacles that many American journalists carried in their heads, there was often a subconscious presumption of guilt until an official could prove his or her innocence.

Another domestic U.S. factor was to affect some journalists' perceptions of the Middle East dispute. The generation of American reporters that began arriving in Israel following the 1973 war had matured during the period of the civil rights struggle in the United States, and as a result, any intercommunal struggle anywhere often was analogized immediately to the profound upheaval that had taken place in the American South. In the backs of the minds of many reporters, the Palestinians in the occupied areas were viewed as the Middle East equivalents of the blacks in the United States.

The perception that the Arab-Israeli dispute was an intercommunal human rights conflict was reinforced by four major events that took place in the years immediately after the Yom Kippur War. In the minds of those who were so predisposed, each built on the other to produce a lasting paradigm that, if not false, was certainly only partially true.

The first major event was the arrival on the scene of Henry Kissinger as a mediator. His extended shuttle missions between Israel and Egypt and Israel and Syria both exhausted journalists and captured their imaginations. The prime legacy of these missions was the altered perception of what the Middle East problem was all about. Until his arrival and his subsequent success in negotiating three disengagement agreements, the Israeli-Arab conflict had been portrayed most often as an intractable military conflict that seemed impervious to political intervention. By the time he left the area, political compromise and negotiated agreements had become the main media stories.

The results were noticeable immediately. Journalists began spending more time in Jerusalem, because that was where Kissinger had been holding all of his talks with the Israelis. Just being in Jerusalem for extended periods had a profound symbolic impact on the foreign journalists. Tel Aviv was the seat of the Defence Ministry and the IDF's General Staff, and its very proximity to where the journalists lived and worked set much of the tone for their coverage. Jerusalem was the seat of government and the center for international, if not domestic, politics. The very act of being in Jerusalem and reporting from the city could not but change the focus of reporting.

When journalists exited the Government Press Office in Tel Aviv, they faced the Defence Ministry–General Staff complex just up the street. When journalists looked out of the windows of the King David Hotel in Jerusalem, where Kissinger stayed, they saw the spotlighted walls of the Old City and the Arab sector of town. As the story became more political in character, more attention was paid to Jerusalem. Within a few years— and particularly after the election of Menachem Begin and his decision to transfer the main Government Press Office to Jerusalem—the bulk of the story and many of the journalists had shifted permanently to that city. Once in Jerusalem, they could not but begin to deal in greater depth with the outstanding political issue nearby—the fate of the Israeli-occupied territories.

No less important was the manner in which Kissinger operated. He presented himself as the writer, director, and star of a show he himself created. He manipulated the press corps that traveled with him in an absolutely astounding and skillful manner. As he shuttled back and forth, he would brief the traveling journalists and leak material under the rubric of "a senior American official," using the resulting press reports as a lever to extract ever more concessions from each side. The picture of the Israelis that emerged was of a government essentially reactive and visionless, with no agenda of its own, intent on niggling over details.

Israeli officials, unskilled in the art of media manipulation and totally in awe of their distinguished guest, were struck dumb by this new approach to the press. Unable or unwilling to respond to Kissinger's media machinations, they allowed the secretary to set both the tone and the substance of the public debate that accompanied the negotiations. While he briefed his private coterie of journalists sometimes twice or even three times a day, the Israelis withdrew. Israeli spokespeople, for the most part, hunkered down and said nothing of value either on or off the record. Both local and foreign reporters in Israel therefore turned ever more often toward Kissinger and his entourage for basic details. Kissinger, however, kept most of his staffers in the background and on a tight rein. Official spokespeople did little except provide schedules and technical details of his movements. As a result, the real briefers were the experienced and meticulous note-taking journalists who accompanied him. He spoke directly to them, giving his impressions and his spin on the course of the negotiations, and they, in turn, spread his version of the events to the public. The traveling press, in effect, had been co-opted as his spokespeople to the world. In an extraordinary and precedent-setting way, the secretary of state had made the journalists traveling with him not merely observers and describers of events, as they had been in the past, but direct participants in the Middle East political process. The traveling press had been turned into an instrument of state. And by not intervening on their own, the Israelis allowed Kissinger to create what amounted to a media monopoly over both the interpretation of the events taking place and the dissemination of information relating to those events.

It was a mistake the Israelis were to repeat often in the years that followed, most notably during the Lebanese War and in the early stages of the intifada. Time and again, the Israelis were to acquiesce passively while others shaped the state's image as a directionless, visionless, agendaless, reactive polity.

The second major event to shape press perceptions was the election of Menachem Begin as prime minister in 1977. Once again, journalists caught in a story line from which they could not escape had been predicting a slim Labor party victory. Even when the exit polls were first broadcast, there was general disbelief. It was not until the small hours of the morning that reality sank in. For the first time in Israeli history, Labor, which had viewed governance as its legitimate patrimony, was out of office. A social revolution, which had been building in Israel for years, finally had surfaced.

Significantly, Begin's first act after his election was both symbolic and substantive. Using the same, well-worn, chauffeur-driven Peugeot sedan with which he had crisscrossed the country in the weeks before his triumph, he drove out to the Jewish encampment near Nablus and promised the settlers there that not only would they be provided with permanent quarters, but many more settlements in the area would follow. By this one statement, Begin helped to propel the human rights paradigm to the fore. If under his annexationist ideology the areas of the West Bank and Gaza were to be nonnegotiable, then the civil, human, and political rights of those living under the occupation could not but become a major public issue. Under these circumstances, only Israel could be responsible for the well-being of these Palestinians. In other words, because of Begin's words and his later deeds, what once had been viewed as an international conflict now would be seen as an intercommunal dispute—to be judged not according to international strategic criteria, as the Israeli government wished, but according to those prevailing in a civil war.

Another effect was to reinforce the "conflict over land" story line. The argument that Israel needed all of the territories purely for self-defense did not wash among most of the representatives of the foreign press. After all, the Labor party had been on record as having been willing to give up large chunks of the occupied territories in return for peace—and Labor had more former generals among its leaders than the Likud did.

The third event was Egyptian president Anwar Sadat's peace initiative. It served to expand and entrench the perceptions and precedents created by the Kissinger shuttles and the Begin election. Sadat reinforced the notion that essentially the dispute was political, that it could be solved only by a political solution arrived at through negotiations and compromise, and that negotiations with no preconditions were possible. Through two declarations, he tied both the conflict-over-land story line and the human rights issue together. In his speech to the Knesset and in his later press conference with Prime Minister Begin, Sadat stated that "this land [the Sinai] is ours," and that the Palestinian problem was "the core and crux" of the Middle East dispute.

Although the eventual agreement included only provisions for limited Palestinian autonomy in the occupied territories, in the public mind, the successful promotion of a resolution of the Palestinian issue became inextricably intertwined with the need to give up land to gain a peace settlement. And this idea held both for annexationists and for territorial compromisers.

Sadat, like Kissinger, was a masterful manipulator of the press. Beginning with his famous interview with Walter Cronkite on November 14, 1977, he made journalists active participants in the political process, using them as a significant part of his overall political strategy. He believed that to secure an agreement, he would have to go over the heads of the Israeli leadership and talk directly to the Israeli people in order to break the "psychological" defenses the Israelis had thrown up over the years. The international and Israeli media were his vehicles.

Sadat's trip to Jerusalem on November 19 was the media event of the decade. Israeli officials estimated that some four thousand journalists from around the world were in attendance. Then, and until the moment he was assassinated, he was able to present himself as a political visionary, while projecting an image of the Israeli leadership as a group of small-minded individuals who niggled over legalistic details and could not relate to the grand goals he had enunciated.

One of the outgrowths of his media campaign was to give journalists a stake in the story and the story line he was creating. Until his famous speech to the Egyptian People's Assembly, in which he declared his desire to go to Jerusalem, many events in the region had been wholly predictable. Even more predictable had been the statements of the various leaders. I used to play a game with my wife. After each major public event, or before each important public speech by an Israeli leader, I would tell her what I thought the leader or spokesperson would say. In many, if not most, cases, I would be able to get the wording almost perfect. In the period immediately after the Sadat visit, that was no longer possible.

By becoming participants in the political action, we reporters also began to have a stake in the success of the peace process. We wanted it to succeed because it had become "our" story—our place in history. It was we who would be able to tell our grandchildren that we were present when history was being made and that we were intimates in a process that changed the world. We were affected when the talks broke down. We also were affected when the Camp David talks in September 1978 succeeded. We would be equally affected when the negotiations on partial autonomy for the Palestinians in the occupied territories collapsed. An indication of our gut commitment to the process was the often-used phrase among journalists during critical points in the negotiating process: "Oh, the Israelis [or the PLO or the Americans] have blown it."

The fourth event that influenced the press's perception that this was an intercommunal dispute over human rights was the entry into the Middle East arena of President Jimmy Carter. It was Carter, more than any leader in the Western world, who was waving the banner of human rights as his personal and political flag. The image he projected was that the peace process, even more than being a political issue, was an ethical and moral one. His introduction of that dimension into Middle East discourse had an important effect that went far beyond the life span of his own one-term presidency. It legitimized discussions about Palestinian *human* rights as an equal item on the political and media agenda with their *political* rights. In an interview in the *New York Times* on August 1, 1979, Carter directly linked the Palestinian cause to the civil rights movement in the United States, thus providing official U.S. government backing to the paradigm.

For a while, the Sadat peace initiative overshadowed and placed in abeyance questions that had arisen in the wake of the Likud's ascendancy to power about the long-term direction Israel would take. Those questions, however, soon resurfaced. In retrospect, although I have emphasized that press attitudes toward Israel underwent a slow and incremental change, if I were forced to point to a single period in which press perceptions of Israel changed forever, it would be the months of August and September in 1979.

On May 25 of that year, the Egyptian defense minister, General Kamal Hassan Ali, and Israel's interior minister, Yosef Burg, had begun talks on implementing the autonomy scheme for the Palestinians living in the occupied territories. The next day, Yasir Arafat, fearful that he was being excluded, declared that he would "crush the triangular alliance of Carter, Begin and Sadat" and "chop off their hands" for ignoring Palestinian rights.

By August, the talks on autonomy had broken down as Israel rejected Egyptian demands that the autonomy plan include the Palestinians living in East Jerusalem and outside the occupied territories, and that the self-governing authority in the occupied territories should have real judicial, executive, and political powers, not merely administrative ones. Whatever the real merits of the positions taken by the two sides, the Israelis were perceived to be standing in the way of the peace process. And to journalists, who had their own stake in the progress of the talks and already were skeptical of Prime Minister Begin's motives, the breakdown was a sign of Israeli intransigence.

At the same time, the PLO had been launching a series of raids into Israel from Lebanon in a deliberate attempt to break up the peace talks. Yasir Arafat enjoyed a distinct but peculiar public relations advantage at this time. He had been discounted as a member of the negotiation process, and his attempt to play the role of spoiler also was discounted as being peripheral to the true course on which the history of the Middle East had embarked. Unlike the dispatches from the peace front, the PLO raids were reported factually (or as factually as could be done under the circumstances). They contained none of the emotional overlay that blanketed the stories about the peace process.

The Israelis were caught in a policy bind. Residents of the northern border area were clamoring for an immediate halt to the disruption in their lives caused by the PLO attacks and for vengeance against the perpetrators. But any major response could not but affect the peace process and give Arafat the political victory he was seeking. The Israelis chose, as they always do when they cannot come up with original strategies and tactics, to fall back on David Ben-Gurion's dictum: "It doesn't matter what the goyim [Gentiles] say, it's what the Jews do."

The Israeli army responded to the PLO's provocations with an extraordinarily heavy artillery barrage on the villages in southern Lebanon. It was the first time that Israel had used artillery in such a massive way in an area inhabited largely by civilians. Although the Palestinians had set up many of their bases in civilian areas, the sheer volume of the Israeli response brought intense criticism from Washington. The Israeli army, which had developed a well-earned reputation for neat, elegant surgical operations, was perceived of as having changed. It appeared that the values and the ethos of the army and of the government that controlled it had altered beyond measure. It seemed as though brutality had taken the place of skill—that the military no longer would use a scalpel when a club would do. The army's heavy use of artillery was viewed by many foreigners in the country as being symbolic of and indicative of an entirely new approach to the Arabs by the Israeli government.

But the event that had the greatest impact—and that has largely been forgotten by journalists since then—was a revelation made in the Knesset on September 14, 1979, by Knesset member Uri Avneri. Avneri revealed that a certain Israeli lieutenant, Daniel Pinto, had tortured and killed four Lebanese during the Litani Operation in March 1978. After the army's incursion into Lebanon was over, Pinto had been tried by a military court, found guilty, and sentenced to twelve years in prison. An appeals court had reduced the sentence to eight years. Avneri charged that the chief of staff, the Likud-appointed General Rafael Eitan, however, had intervened and used his prerogative to reduce the sentence to two years. With good behavior, that meant that Pinto would serve only eighteen months in prison. The military censors had banned the story when Avneri had tried to talk about the affair in a Knesset speech in July. But this time, with journalists in attendance, the story got out. Most Israeli liberals and almost all of those who covered the story were shocked by the revelation. One of Israel's premier national myths—that of the "purity of arms"—had been shattered. Israel under the Likud government was perceived as being truly a different place from what it had been in the past. Not only had the country's leadership changed, the value systems had changed—and the new ones were not values with which Western correspondents could identify.

The cumulative effect of these three events—the breakdown of the peace talks, the artillery barrages into Lebanon, and Uri Avneri's revelations—was the creation of a perception that Israel was suffering from a political and moral malaise. In an act that gave legitimacy to that perception, Foreign Minister Moshe Dayan resigned from the cabinet on October 21. One of the main engineers of the peace agreement with Egypt, Dayan quit over the government's inflexibility on the future of the West Bank and Gaza. The peace process was seen to be dead. Moreover, as if to reinforce the perception that the government as a whole was incompetent and out of control, in November, the Central Bureau of Statistics published figures indicating that inflation had shot up to 116 percent per annum. That same month, Defence Minister Ezer Weizman voted against the government during a no-confidence debate in the Knesset. Several months later, he was drummed out of the Likud for ideological and political deviance.

Another phenomenon that was occurring at the same time was having an effect both on the nature of press coverage and on press perceptions. Many of the new reporters who arrived in Israel during the mid-1970s were expected by their organizations to be regional correspondents. Beginning in 1974, it had become much easier for foreign reporters based in Israel to travel to at least some Arab states. Egypt, Jordan, and Lebanon accepted the use of double passports by journalists, and questions asked at the borders were cursory at best. Turkey, Greece, and Iran (until the rise to power of Ayatollah Khomeini) also were considered to be within the territory a reporter posted to Israel could be expected to cover. This change from being a single-country foreign correspondent to a regional reporter had two main effects.

First, reporters based in Israel now could hear directly from the principals what their positions were on various issues. The correspondent no longer needed to rely on radio stations, wire service reports, or Israeli statements about Jerusalem's interpretation of what the Arab positions were. This, in turn, led to a number of confrontations between reporters who had visited a particular Arab country and Israeli officials who claimed that they knew the positions of those Arab countries. The discrepancies between the reporters' interpretations and those of the Israeli officials were often extremely wide.

I can recall one confrontation between Peter Grose of the *New York Times* and the Israeli Foreign Ministry spokesman that almost broke up one of his briefings. The spokesman kept insisting that, despite the decision of the Fez Arab summit conference in 1974 to grant the PLO the status of sole legitimate representative of the Palestinian people, the Jordanians were still the only spokesmen for the Palestinians. Grose, who had just come back from a trip to Amman, said that he had been told by officials in the king's court that this was not so.[2]

In my own case, I took a trip to Egypt in late 1974 and found, much to my surprise, that Egyptians, from top officials to café regulars, wanted some sort of long-term political settlement with Israel. When I told Israeli officials of my findings, they merely scoffed. It is no surprise, therefore, that they were totally unprepared when President Sadat announced his intention to visit Jerusalem.

The second effect of the change to regional reporters was that those journalists who did travel extensively began to view stories and issues in a regional context. A subject like Israeli-U.S. strategic cooperation, for example, was seen not merely in bilateral terms, but in terms of U.S. interests in the entire eastern Mediterranean or in the Middle East as a whole. In many cases, that meant that the Israeli position or allegation was not necessarily, as Golda Meir had hoped, given equal length with, and juxtaposed alongside, an Arab position or allegation. The Israeli part was integrated into a single story—and the proportion of space devoted to it was a matter of judgment for the individual correspondent. This, in turn, meant that Israel had to compete more than ever before for newspaper space or broadcast time, for the privilege of having its positions relayed to the world by the foreign press stationed in Israel. If the Arabs had more to say that was considered interesting or valid, or if they were doing more that was of interest to journalists, they would get greater attention—even in a story that was being written in Jerusalem.

This may seem sensible to anyone, but it was a point that was missed totally by most Israeli officials. The very idea that they might have to compete with their adversaries on their own home turf was not even considered. When the intifada erupted, they were therefore totally un-

[2]One of the basic rules of spokesmanship is that any spokesperson should try to extract as much information from an interviewer as he or she gives the interviewer. Journalists are an important source of information for bureaucrats. But this talent for listening and extracting, rather than just talking or justifying positions, always has been singularly lacking among Israeli spokes-people.

prepared to react to journalists' coverage of events—other than to blame the messengers for conveying discomfiting news.

While the 1970s had been a turbulent time for Middle Eastern press coverage, the 1980s would see an even greater upheaval and realignment of journalists' perceptions. There were to be wide swings in the nature and subjects of coverage. The decade began inauspiciously with a terrorist campaign of violent co-optation and control against both local and foreign journalists in Lebanon. On February 24, 1980, Selim al Lawzi, the editor of the Lebanese newspaper *Al Hawadess*, was murdered. In June, Dr. Charles Rizk, the head of Tele-Liban, was kidnapped. And on the next day, June 5, Bernd Debusmann, the bureau chief of Reuters in Beirut, was wounded by gunmen. Although journalists had been subjected to threats and occasional violence by the various militias for years, such a concerted violent campaign against the press was unprecedented. Journalists had become fair game in the mayhem that was Lebanon. No reporter who worked in Beirut during this period was unaffected by the violence. It was at the back of their minds as they sat at their desks or teletype machines. It was at the forefront of their minds as they approached one of the innumerable roadblocks thrown up by the gun-toting militiamen—not knowing which press card from which militia to pull out as identification. Pulling out the wrong card at the wrong time could mean death or the possibility of being kidnapped. It was part of their dreams as they slept. It was media control in its most absolute form.

Few outside the media community knew what was going on. Only one article, in the *International Herald Tribune* on August 5, 1980, described the situation. Although the life of the press corps in Beirut in the early 1980s had little if any effect on press coverage of the intifada, it was a harbinger of issues that were unaddressed by journalists but that would come to the fore in a different form when the intifada broke out.

It is rare, if not impossible, for an entire pattern of press behavior to arise suddenly, full-blown. Over time, there are small changes that go unquestioned and unchallenged, and they eventually accumulate into a general mode of behavior. The patterns of behavior that first became evident in Lebanon and that became the focus of criticism later during the intifada are an example, albeit an extreme one.

The first behavioral change for the press grew out of the problem journalists faced in gaining access to stories—and their dependence on those who could give them access. The journalists living in Beirut were subject to the whims of the militias and to their ability to intimidate. The press corps could not afford to alienate the local militias or the PLO because then they either would be denied access to events or briefings or would put themselves in direct personal danger. This could not but affect their coverage.

I am one who believes deeply that the only real defense a journalist has in times of trouble is to increase, not decrease, the amount of information available to the general public. Only in this way can a supportive constituency for free coverage be built. Furthermore, it is incumbent upon journalists to inform their readers, listeners, and viewers of the circumstances under which they are working, so that the public can understand the background to their dispatches. This is not "inside baseball," as some editors allege; it is important factual information the public needs to know. By not exposing the conditions under which they had been working, the journalists were doing both themselves and the public a disservice.

Beyond this, if journalists are to criticize or note restrictions on coverage or censorship in one of the countries within their territory, it is important as well as only fair that they put such restrictions within the context of the treatment they receive in other nations in the region. It is distorting, for example, to note restrictions on coverage by the Israelis while ignoring what may be even more severe restrictions in the countries that are Israel's adversaries.

The situation in Beirut also exacerbated a common journalistic norm, particularly among parachutists. Every major news center has its "journalists' hotel" or, in the case of the stringers in Israel, who were glued to the Government Press Office in the immediate post-1967 period, its press center. Beirut was no different. When the fighting in the city erupted on a large scale, much of the foreign press corps sought shelter in the Commodore Hotel in the Moslem sector of the city. The story of life in that Palestinian-owned hotel is one rich in anecdotes and modern-day legends. From a journalist's point of view, the hotel was ideal. It was central. It was close to the action. It had communications facilities when all of the other lines in the city were out of order. It had good food and drink and its own electrical generator. It was also a place where journalists could meet their peers and make casual conversation with newsmakers or their spokespersons.

Such media centers, for all their indisputable value to the press, lead to two problems of which the public is often unaware. The first is the danger of conventional wisdom. In this sort of incestuous environment, journalists not only share stories, they also tend to reinforce one another's preconceptions and story lines. This, in turn, can lead to a kind of insularity and homogeneity of thought that creates unthinking journalism. Second, by staying on territory held by one party to a dispute, there is an inevitable tendency to play up the point of view of that side—if only because members of that party are closer to hand and in more frequent contact with the journalists. It simply is easier for a broadcaster to go one block for a sound bite for an urgent story than to travel miles for that same six-second clip.

The Israeli invasion of Lebanon in June 1982 brought with it further harbingers of how the press would behave during a period of crisis in the Middle East. Much has been written about the war, but from a press coverage point of view, several phenomena stand out that were precursors of the type of coverage given the intifada. The first, as mentioned before, was the official lying. Dissimulation was used by both the Israelis and the PLO. Any political or warlike atmosphere imbued with a constant stream of lies does more than make journalists skeptical. It creates a syndrome and a dynamic in press coverage that lasts long after the event being covered is over. For the post-Vietnam, post-Watergate generation of journalists, the lying was merely another confirmation of the essential perfidy of politicians. This perception, particularly in the period from June to September, led to a press attitude akin to "a plague on both your houses"; it was a form of neutrality in which detailed analysis and often ordinary common sense were decidedly absent. The phenomenon led many old hands and experienced area specialists into what I term "an escape into professionalism." Emphasis is put on gathering as much information and accurate data as possible without providing the kind of interpretation that ties the many facts together and gives them meaning. For newcomers to the scene, this unbridled cynicism combined with ignorance and a lack of credible sources of information led, in part, to straight misreporting and a willingness to believe or disbelieve almost anything. Additionally, where facts cannot be double-sourced, there was and is another form of escape and self-protection: attribution. In periods of such extreme confusion and uncertainty, there is a tendency by many journalists to file almost any allegation, no matter how seemingly absurd or implausible, so long as it can be attributed to a public figure or public organization.

These relatively widespread, self-protective journalistic reactions to the conditions under which the press was working were encouraged by the Israeli decision to restrict press coverage during the first five days of the invasion. Professional and experienced foreign journalists are often the bane of their hosts. They often uncover information that is unflattering and objectionable to local politicians. But as technically proficient gatherers of information, they also are able to validate local claims and invalidate those of the other party. By not allowing the foreign press corps into Lebanon in the first few days, the Israelis left the field open for their opponents. On June 10, for example, the Palestinian Red Crescent, which was run by Fathi Arafat, Yasir Arafat's brother, released claims that ten thousand people had been killed since the beginning of the war. Those figures were picked up and used by journalists because they could be attributed and because they were the only ones available. As it turned out, the figures were patently false, but until they could be disproved by journalists in the field, they were given wide credence—especially by U.S. television networks.

A direct result of the Israeli refusal to allow coverage was the almost total dependency journalists had on the local radio stations, almost all of which were mouthpieces for one militia or another. Later, during the intifada, the Israeli army spokesman's frequent refusal to answer questions meant that, as in Lebanon, the Israelis denied themselves the right of a timely reply to the Palestinians' allegations.

Yet another sign of things to come during the intifada was the fact that for the first time in the Arab-Israeli dispute, a journalist could cover both sides of the confrontation single-handedly. Many journalists took the opportunity to cross the green-line buffer zone in central Beirut and report from the other side. They could report on events on one side of the green line separating the warring parties one day and the other side the next day. When the intifada broke out, this ability to crisscross lines within minutes—rather than the hours it often took in Beirut—meant that both sides could and would be represented in the same news piece.

A last noteworthy change in the way the Middle East would be covered in the future was the ability of journalists to compare notes about events taking place in widely separated places on the same day and to use all of that material in a single dispatch or broadcast. Of equal importance, those reporters coming from the Israeli side were able to provide a political and social perspective on the events that had been unavailable to the Beirut-based correspondents, and vice versa. There was a considerable amount of bartering of information—and even the sharing of sources. And this, in turn, helped to reinforce the trend toward double-sided coverage.

Coverage of events within Israel also was changing during this period. In June 1981, the Israelis held new elections. It was a campaign marked by unprecedented violence—particularly by Likud supporters against Labor candidates. It looked to observers as though the country was becoming unglued—as though the rules of political behavior had broken down. Nonetheless, despite the violence and an inflation rate that analysts were predicting would reach 180 percent per annum, the Likud increased its share of the overall vote. The social revolution within Israel, with its new value system, had become entrenched.

In the aftermath of the voting, the ultra-Orthodox Agudat Yisrael party was brought into the government by the Likud. Because of the Israeli system of proportional representation and the plethora of parties this system produces, Agudat Yisrael, while small, had enormous leverage within the cabinet. Within months, the party had extracted new laws and regulations that included restrictions on archeological digs, the termination of flights by El Al Airlines on the sabbath, and new restrictions on abortions. The old status quo on religion had been broken and, as with perceptions about the new political value system, Israel's image as a secular state was altered to a measurable degree.

Early 1982 saw the completion of the Israeli withdrawal from the Sinai as part of the peace pact with Egypt. Israeli settlers in the town of Yamit on the Sinai coast dug in and resisted the army's attempts to dislodge them. Eventually the army did take control of the city and raze it, but

Israelis and foreign correspondents alike were left with the deep feeling that the nation had become so polarized that civil war no longer could be discounted if more precious territories like those on the West Bank were involved. The idea of violent resistance by settlers was thus implanted in the minds of correspondents—and it became a focus for coverage when the intifada broke out.

The war in Lebanon and its aftermath also had a significant impact on domestic Israeli politics. The massacres at Sabra and Shatilla horrified Israelis and, together with the resistance of the Shiites and the sense that Lebanon was a quagmire that distorted and demoralized all those who came in contact with it, led to the formation of a popular multipartisan coalition in opposition to the war. Widespread public opposition to government policies is not a new phenomenon in Israel, where public demonstrations are almost a way of life. In fact, public opposition to the Labor government's handling of the situation prior to the outbreak of the Yom Kippur War was one of the causes for the party's ouster from office. But the rift between the government in power and its citizens that arose in the wake of the Lebanese debacle was of unprecedented proportions.

The concept of ethics in governance in Israel was undermined even further after the Kahan Commission report on the massacres at Sabra and Shatilla was published on February 8, 1983. Although no evidence was found to indicate that Israel had either planned or taken an active part in the slaughter, the defense minister, the chief of staff, the director of Military Intelligence, and the local Israeli military commander all were found to have had indirect responsibility for the bloodshed by failing to prevent or halt it.

In most other democracies, Defence Minister Ariel Sharon's political career would have been over. On February 11, Sharon was forced out of his portfolio, but he refused to resign from the Knesset or the cabinet. In fact, on February 20, he was reappointed to the Ministerial Defence Committee. The fundamental democratic concept of ministerial responsibility was dealt a crushing blow, and with it, perceptions of Israeli political morality. The day before Sharon was reappointed, Israeli politics reached a new low when Emil Greunzweig, a member of a Peace Now demonstration being held near the prime minister's office, was killed by a grenade.

There is little doubt that Sharon's refusal to leave the government, together with the national demoralization caused by the Lebanese War, led to Prime Minister Begin's decision to resign on September 15, 1983. An era in Israeli politics had come to an end. On October 10, in a move that had both symbolic and substantive implications, Yitzchak Shamir, the man who had openly opposed the peace agreement with Egypt, was sworn in as prime minister. Soon after, inflation actually reached 160 percent per annum, and Israel's national casino, the stock exchange, collapsed after a run on banking shares.

Much of a foreign reporter's work is crisis coverage. Crises, as viewed by journalists, come in two forms. There are short, sharp, usually surprising incidents, like coups d'etat or natural disasters; and crises built up by a sequence of smaller, but nonetheless noteworthy, incidents over time. The period from June 1982 to 1986 and the intifada were to have elements of both. Crises, by their very nature, distort foreign coverage. Because of the press of daily events, journalists are forced to ignore what otherwise might be significant stories, and correspondents tend to lose continuity in their reports because they have to run from one dramatic event to another. Thus, for example, events in Israel during the early Shamir period were reported less critically than might have been the case otherwise, because incidents occurring in Lebanon and within the PLO at the time were so much more extreme or outrageous.

In Lebanon, 1983 was a year for car bombs and the rise of pro-Iranian militant Shiite fundamentalism. In October, the U.S. Marines' barracks in Beirut were bombed, leaving 260 dead, and shortly thereafter, the Israeli military headquarters in Tyre was bombed, killing 61. Elsewhere, what few rules of societal behavior that were left quickly eroded. Anarchy and the rule of arms had descended almost everywhere.

On February 19, 1984, one of the true moderates within the PLO, Issam Sartawi, announced that he was resigning from the Palestine National Council because he had been refused permission to address it. Sartawi was a favorite interviewee of the foreign press and enjoyed wide popularity in the West. On April 10, 1984, he was shot dead by the notorious Abu Nidal group. That spring, talks between Yasir Arafat and King Hussein on how to approach the latest peace initiative of the United States broke down. In the spring, a rebellion broke out within the PLO

when Yasir Arafat decided to promote two cronies to senior positions after
they had been denounced for retreating during the Israeli invasion. By
June, there was full-scale internecine fighting between pro- and anti-Arafat
factions, and on November 25, after bitter fighting, the pro-Arafat faction
announced that it was evacuating its last stronghold in Lebanon in the
northern port city of Tripoli.

Amid this sense of political disarray, several significant trends began
to emerge that were to lead to, and have a direct impact on, both the
course of and the media coverage of the intifada. As so often happens
during crises, when onrushing, related events take place in different venues, almost every event of this period was treated as a discreet individual
moment rather than as part of a pattern. Thus, many of the most important trends went unrecognized, although most had been under way for
some time. Only as the political malaise grew, however, did they come
to the fore.

The first trend was the emergence of a strong, activist, and well-
organized Islamic fundamentalist movement in the West Bank and Gaza.
The Moslem Brotherhood always had been strong in both areas, but it
acquired fresh momentum in the late 1970s and early 1980s. The Israelis
deliberately chose to ignore the rise of the fundamentalists, in the hope
that this would divide the Palestinians and thus aid in controlling the
secular nationalists. The emerging battle for power was apparent at a
relatively early stage. On May 15, 1983, for example, Bir Zeit University
was ordered closed by the university authorities because of clashes between
secular nationalists and fundamentalists. Lacking an election process and
a legislative body in which to show their relative popular support, the
various nationalist parties and the fundamentalists often would use public
confrontations of this sort to demonstrate their relative strengths. For
anyone who spent time in the field, there was little doubt that the fundamentalists were increasing in number. Nonetheless, the growing power
of the fundamentalists largely was ignored by the foreign press. When the
intifada broke out, the fundamentalists would play a pivotal role in stoking
the fires of the rebellion and the press were to play catch-up.

A second trend was the emergence of a policy within the Israeli
administration in the West Bank and Gaza that was directed more and
more toward harsher control and even less dialogue. This trend developed
at the very moment when Palestinians were becoming increasingly agitated

at the growing pace of Jewish settlement activity in the occupied territories and increasingly suspicious of any and all Israeli activities in their midst. On January 17, 1984, the head of the Israeli civil administration in the West Bank, Brigadier General Shlomo Ilya, resigned because he was halted in his attempts to open a dialogue outside the framework of the Israeli-organized village leagues. This growing tendency to ignore the need for Palestinian input meant that the Israelis were becoming more insular and less aware of some of the major social problems developing within the Palestinian community. This lack of awareness and consequent in-capacity to deal with the issues was one of the major reasons for the outbreak of the intifada and for the civil administration's inability to brief journalists on the nature of the uprising.

The third outgrowth of this period of political confusion and upheaval was a burgeoning conflict within Israel between political expediency and the rule of law. Israeli democracy is a fragile animal. In the early 1980s, a majority of the country's citizens had not grown up in a democracy or in a nation noted for the rule of law. Most had come from Eastern Europe or the Arab states.[3] Even during Israel's formative period, any number of evils were condoned by its political bosses or excused under the wide umbrella of national security. It is one of Israel's great strengths that it did create a strong and independent judiciary. In particular, it created, in the Supreme Court, a High Court of Justice to which its citizens had rapid and relatively easy access for adjudication on matters of public policy. Under a succession of concerned justice ministers, the country also has nurtured an independent-minded corps of professional legal civil serv-ants—usually with a distinguished and respected legal mind as attorney general at its head. As the state matured, it was inevitable that the pro-ponents of political expediency or national security at any cost would come into conflict with these apolitical bodies.

By 1984, the conflict between political and military opportunism, on the one hand, and the rule of law, on the other, had reached new

---

[3]As often happens in states facing regular domestic and international crises and whose populace is ambivalent about the value of democratic institutions, the press becomes the focus of popular frustration and discontent. A 1989 study by Tel Aviv University professor Ephraim Yuchtman-Yaar on Israeli attitudes to public institutions revealed that about half of the Israeli public believes there is too much freedom of the press and more than 60 percent believe that freedom of the press is damaging to national security.

heights. Clear evidence came with the publication of the report of the Karp Committee in February. Judith Karp had been deputy attorney general until April 1982, when she resigned because of a refusal by the government to publish or debate a report she and some colleagues had prepared on the justice system in the occupied territories. Her committee had found that the military authorities had pressured the local police forces to close investigations into murder and other crimes committed against Palestinians, and to release Jewish suspects who had been arrested. The committee also accused the government of taking little or no action in response to Palestinian complaints of harassment.

In another event, in March 1984, twenty-seven people, including two army officers, were arrested for having been part of a Jewish underground that had been responsible for a number of crimes against Palestinians, including the attempted murders of several West Bank mayors. There was an immediate cry from the Israeli right to release the suspects forthwith.

On April 12, another event was to spark off the greatest test of the judicial process in Israeli history. It also became a major international news story, further shaping foreign journalists' perceptions, and indirectly, it was to have a profound effect on press coverage of the intifada.

The incident began when a bus traveling from Tel Aviv to Ashkelon was hijacked by Palestinian terrorists. The bus finally was stopped by an Israeli army roadblock at Rafah at the southern end of the Gaza Strip. After ten hours of negotiations, the bus was stormed by Israeli troops and the passengers were rescued. At first, it appeared to be yet another classic confrontation between terrorists and Israeli paratroopers. Within two days, however, it became a cause célèbre.

After the incident, Israeli authorities claimed that all of the terrorists on board the bus had been killed in a shootout. However, on April 14, the newspaper *Hadashot*, breaking censorship, published a photograph showing a live terrorist being escorted away from the bus. On April 25, another Israeli weekly, *Ha'Olam Hazeh*, published a photograph showing a second terrorist being led away from the bus. On April 27, under pressure, Defence Minister Moshe Arens set up a committee to investigate the incident. The committee, which issued its report on May 28, concluded that the two men had been captured alive and died later as a result of blows. The man blamed was the commander of the paratroopers, Brigadier General Yitzchak Mordechai.

Mordechai, however, refused to play the role of patsy. He had been a fighter all his life and was not about to accept a verdict that would have ruined his military career and public standing. He demanded a full-dress inquiry and was exonerated of any wrongdoing on August 18, 1985. That left the questions: Who did do it? And who had wrongly implicated Mordechai in the first place? The case had all the markings of a coverup.

The case might have died and been forgotten had it not been for Attorney General Yitzchak Zamir, whose office continued to investigate the incident. In February 1986, Zamir made a surprising announcement. He was resigning because of the government's failure to pursue an investigation into the security services. That resignation brought the issue to the fore. Eventually, after great pressure, on May 25, the cabinet, despite the opposition of both Likud leader Yitzchak Shamir and Labor leader Shimon Peres, decided to direct the police to investigate the head of the *Shabak*, Avraham Shalom, on charges of suppressing evidence. On June 25, Shalom and three other *Shabak* colleagues resigned, having been granted immunity by President Chaim Herzog. On July 11, seven more *Shabak* officers, including two lawyers, requested and eventually were given pardons after admitting that they had falsified evidence and had suborned witnesses. On July 14, the cabinet reluctantly agreed to a full-scale police investigation into the *Shabak*.

Zamir and his colleagues had won their battle. But the rapidity with which the pardons were granted cast doubt on the ultimate strength of the judicial process to self-repair by prosecuting and punishing those who had undermined the system.

On December 28, 1986, the new attorney general issued the final report of the investigation. Although no corroborating evidence was found to implicate those at the political level of wrongdoing, the *Shabak* was found to have lied continuously and consistently to the courts in order to secure convictions. It had been able to get away with this lying because under the Israeli system, the security services can present secret evidence to the courts without the plaintiff having the right to see it or question it. The lying that had begun as a matter of strategic necessity during the

Yom Kippur War now had become institutionalized throughout one of the most sensitive organizations in Israel.

New regulations governing the *Shabak's* behavior were proposed and adopted. But among journalists, what had long been skepticism about the veracity of the statements emanating from the security system turned to outright suspicion. By this point, charges of harassment or brutality by Palestinians in the occupied territories no longer were being dismissed or ignored by many journalists, as they had been in the past. And although it would take until the outbreak of the intifada for these charges to become central issues of foreign press coverage, the groundwork had been laid for a change in the foreign press corps' perception of what its central job was. During the intifada, for example, legal issues, like the question of administrative detention without trial, or deportation without the right of appeal, were to become major stories. So, too, were the battles between the Defence Ministry and the judicial system over the use of administrative penalties by the army as a means to circumvent the judicial process. Helping to reinforce this new emphasis on the judicial aspects of the Israeli-Palestinian dispute were several commutations of sentence issued to convicted members of the Jewish underground by President Herzog—himself a lawyer and a former head of Military Intelligence.[4]

Two other major processes under way during the mid-1980s helped shape the nature of press coverage. The first was the indecisive Israeli general elections of 1984 and 1988. These elections, in which neither Labor nor Likud was able to form a coalition government on its own and thus had to cobble together a so-called national unity government (they were actually governments of disunity), had, in addition to their substantive effects, symbolic significance, for they demonstrated that the Israeli people distrusted both major parties and would give neither the right to govern alone. And if the Israeli people were so openly mistrustful of their leaders, could the foreign press corps be any less so?

The politicians did not disappoint their electors or the press and continued to squabble interminably both within their parties and with

---

[4]The three main leaders of the underground, all of whom had been sentenced to life in prison, eventually had their sentences reduced by the president and were released from custody in December 1990. Their release was given wide press coverage, and in many press reports, the grant of freedom was contrasted sharply with the much longer prison terms meted out to Palestinians for lesser offenses.

other parties, seeking any opportunistic moment for quick tactical gain. The Israelis had descended to the PLO's level of lowest-common-denominator consensus politics—and the primary victim was the peace process, to which many in the foreign press corps had become viscerally attached.

The second truly important process began in Beirut and ended in Jerusalem. In 1984 the death knell sounded for the foreign press corps in Beirut. While in the past they had been the focus of irregular threats or even shootings, by 1984 they had become primary targets for violence. Symbolically, the Commodore Hotel's bar, the great gathering place for the foreign press, was trashed by a Shiite militant. More personally, journalists, like many other foreigners in Beirut, became the objects for kidnapping. Finally, then, it was time for the foreign press to get out. Some left the region entirely. Others chose Cyprus or Egypt or Amman as their bases. But many bureaus shifted to Jerusalem.

By 1985, Israel had replaced Beirut as the media capital of the Middle East. What once had been considered an outrageous Israeli dream now had become a reality. With such a heavy concentration of journalists in place, it was inevitable that any event would be given saturation coverage. From the vantage point of the 1990s, it is fascinating to compare the complaints of Israeli officials in the 1970s with those of the 1980s. In the 1970s, officials regularly complained that the Israeli story was not given sufficient prominence. By the time the intifada was well under way, the complaint was that the press was giving Israel disproportionately large coverage.

The changes in the press's perceptions of Israel and of the Middle East as a whole were incremental over two decades. Many of these changes became noticeable only several years after the events that first engendered them had occurred. And, contrary to the complaints of many Israeli apologists that many or most foreign press corps members are inherently anti-Semitic or anti-Israeli, a good number of the attitudes prevalent within the foreign press corps were shaped by the Israelis themselves.

There is little doubt that over this two-decade period, the foreign press corps, on average, became more knowledgeable and more professional. By the 1980s, a posting to Israel was considered very prestigious in any media organization. Such postings often were viewed as rewards for high-quality service and were vigorously sought by some of the world's very best journalists.

One process that cannot be underestimated is the institutional memory the press corps developed during this period. Each bureau chief would pass his or her list of contacts and telephone numbers on to the next. Archives were established that helped good correspondents put events into at least some historical perspective. In many bureaus, further continuity was provided by long-serving locally hired help.

But many problems inherent in foreign coverage in the late twentieth century remained. Two are worth noting at this point. The first is the fact that many journalists continue to be assigned to Israel knowing neither Hebrew nor Arabic, nor the cultures and history from which these languages arise. There is an assumption by editors that in the Middle East, as elsewhere, there is no need to invest in the expense of training journalists adequately to communicate with the people about whom they are assigned to write. Media organizations tend to believe that a journalist always can find people who speak English, or can hire a translator when needed. But that is to ignore the fact that those who speak English *think* in their mother tongue. The words, metaphors, and myths that most accurately express their thoughts are best fashioned in their mother tongue. A reporter's most important tool is an ability to listen, to build trust and knowledge through listening, and to discover through extended conversations the answers to questions he or she does not have the knowledge to ask. Any journalist who cannot ask someone on a street corner "What's up?" or "How are you?" cannot do his or her job adequately.

The second problem in foreign press coverage is an outgrowth of the first. Since too many journalists do not have the language skills to venture far afield, they tend to talk primarily among themselves and to the local English-speaking elites—many of whom are totally isolated from the masses in the particular constituency being investigated. This, in turn, leads journalists to accept and reinforce the conventional wisdom of the local elite, to be caught by surprise because of an inability to trace trends before they surface as major political or social events, and to run in packs when a crisis breaks. It reinforces reliance on familiar types of stories rather than those that may be important but confusing; on events that are easy to describe rather than those that require in-depth knowledge; and on actions that can be analogized to prior experiences or are so exotic as to be shocking or "cute" rather than on those that seem implausible because of our own ignorance of the culture of the people we are covering.

The result, all too often, is entrapment in particular story lines, a distortion of the events being covered, a self-reinforcing overemphasis on the dramatic and the nonverbal aspect of events, and weak, one-sided analysis based on the ruminations and often baseless or self-centered prophecies of the elites rather than on the thoughts and concerns of real, powerful, but English-mute constituencies.

F · I · V · E

Technical
Tic-Tac-Toe

The two decades that followed the 1967 Six-Day War roughly paralleled our entry into the new information age. Vast changes in our technical ability to gather and to transfer information from one part of the world to another have fundamentally altered the nature of news coverage. The Middle East has been a laboratory for experimenting with and introducing many of these technological developments on a broad scale. In fact, technology has been an equal partner with the human participants in shaping the type and structure of news gathering and dissemination.

The primary motivations for introducing many of these technological wonders were convenience, saving time, improving technical quality, and cost. But, although reporters have been intimates to this electronic revolution, often we have failed to consider the real implications of our use of these new tools, especially when they go beyond our immediate selfish considerations and expectations. These implications are especially important and acute when assessing foreign news coverage in general and coverage of the intifada in particular. It is my belief that the intifada, like the Iranian revolution that went before, and the student revolt in China, and the tidal wave of change that overcame Eastern Europe later, are signposts of how these technologies have affected our lives in this global village and will affect them even more in the future.

When I first arrived in Israel in 1967, international communications facilities varied from poor to absolutely rotten. The only voice transmission facilities abroad were radio telephone lines that crackled and hissed and distorted anything you said. If you tried to speak over the background noise by yelling, the lines became even more distorted. The only alternative was to use a special radio transmission line that cost three times the price of a telephone call and had to be ordered—sometimes three days or more in advance—from abroad. That meant that any radio journalist using the facilities either had to agree with his or her superiors in advance when transmission times would be (regardless of the timing or nature of events taking place), or had to exchange a flurry of cables establishing particular broadcast times for breaking stories. And that meant that there were inevitable delays between the time an event took place and the time the world heard about it.

Domestic telephone services were not much better. Lines usually were noisy. Exchanges were overburdened and sometimes it could take hours to get a call through. And only a privileged few actually had telephones. Some Israelis had to wait as long as twelve years to have a telephone installed in their home. Arranging interviews and checking facts often could be a nightmarish experience, and more than once, I would have to drive for a couple of hours to clarify something that could have been done over a phone in a few minutes.

Although telex facilities had arrived, many print reporters still used expensive telegram cables to transmit their dispatches. The correspondents were primarily stringers who did not want to invest in expensive equipment, and their media outlets were reluctant to devote funds to a nonstaffer and to a story whose media life span was still in doubt. Cable-ese was a distinct language all its own that had to be learned. It was designed to cut expenses, but it had a price. All nuance in a report was lost. No unnecessary word was allowed to remain in the copy handed to a telegrapher. One colleague, Sigismund Goren, a stringer for the *New York Daily News*, was restricted to two paragraphs of copy a day—three if there was a major event. A typical cable of the time might read:

QUOTE EYE UNLIABLE ANSWER YOUR QUESTIONS IF CONTINUANCE
UNQUOTE ISRAELI OFFICER SAID GUNRAISING STOP QUOTE SURE
EYE NOT RPT NOT AUTHORIZED ALLOW YOU PIXTAKING IN THIS
MILZONE STOP UNQUOTE GRAPH.[1]

Television coverage had its own problems. The old Auricon and Arriflex cameras were bulky, heavy, and usually could hold only four hundred feet of film—less than fourteen minutes' worth. The intense summer heat and fine-grained dust meant that film and the mechanical parts of cameras easily could be ruined. Since there was no satellite transmission and editing facilities were poor, all film had to be shipped out by air. That meant the film bag had to be taken to the censor for a stamp and then hand-carried to the airport, where it could take as long as an hour to fill out the appropriate customs forms. Since Israel is an end-of-the-line stop for airlines, with few onward transfers, all flights to Europe and North America began early in the morning. Any pictures taken after about 9:00 A.M. usually could not be shipped until the next day. The earliest any piece of film could appear on television in the United States was the day after the event had taken place. Also, the journalists in the field usually had no control over how their material was treated once it got into the hands of editors.

Processing film was extremely expensive, and cost-conscious companies, like the Visnews agency, encouraged their cameramen to "edit inside the camera"—that is, to provide an entire news story by shooting only the essentials on one hundred feet of film. It was the visual equivalent of cable-ese.

---

[1]Translation: " 'I am liable not to answer your questions if you continue in this manner,' an Israeli officer said as he raised his gun. 'You can be sure that I am not authorized to allow you to take photographs in this military zone' (begin new paragraph)."

Major technological changes, however, were not long in coming. Nineteen sixty-nine saw the introduction of an underwater telecommunications cable to Marseilles. That meant that there were far more international lines available, and radio reporters finally could get a decent line that was suitable for at least short reports. (The line quality, while light-years ahead of the old radio-telephone system, was nonetheless quite scratchy, and even short radio documentaries still had to be sent either by airplane or by special line.) Many print reporters also were able to use the new telephone system if their home office had stenographers. European newspapers, in particular, found that it was cheaper to use a telephone and stenographer than to send copy by cable or telex.

The better-quality telephone lines had another important effect. They enabled reporters to discuss a story with their editors in advance and in detail, and to answer any additional queries that might have arisen once the copy was sent. This capacity for feedback was to be one of the most important developments of the new technologies. Eventually, these technologies were to allow immediate feedback between the subjects of news reports and the reporters covering them.

To cope with the inadequacies of the domestic telephone system, journalists eventually were permitted to acquire walkie-talkie systems that covered the country. This was a major boon to camera crews and still photographers, because they could be contacted immediately by their offices about a breaking story. The walkie-talkie system provided a degree of mobility and flexibility that hitherto had been unknown. Until then, anyone out in the field, away from a telephone, could not be contacted.

The walkie-talkie system had its drawbacks, however. It was very expensive and could be hired only by major media organizations with large expense budgets. Thus, it remained available only to a select few. The sound quality was poor. The transceivers often could not be used effectively in hilly areas, where the mountains blocked out transmissions. And the required licenses severely restricted what could or could not be sent on these "open" transmission frequencies.

The third major change was the advent of satellite technology in the mid-1970s. For the first time, a television news report could be broadcast the same day the event had happened. But while this gave greater impact and immediacy to the news film, it also meant that television crews had less time to prepare their reports. All film material had to be at the studios by early evening so that it could be processed and edited in time for the satellite feed that night. Because television technology requires so much time for the gathering and editing of the images, the time available for cogent thought was being compressed. The visual images, already so powerful in their own right, eventually came to dominate the content and substance of television news reports totally.

A fourth technology, introduced in full during President Sadat's visit to Jerusalem, was ENG—electronic news gathering, the use of video cameras rather than film. This technology, with its relatively lightweight cameras, solved many problems for television. After the equipment had been bought, it was cheaper to use, because tape was less expensive than film and because no film processing was required. So it also saved time. The quality of the image was far superior, and anyplace in the world could be a studio. It was far more convenient and safe as well. A cameraman could check the quality of his work before he left the scene of events. There was less chance that the tape itself might break, as film was prone to do. The cameras did not have to be opened and required few mechanical parts, and tape was less susceptible to the ravages of heat.

For a while, these new technologies actually reinforced the Israeli system of press control. When the telephone lines were bad, Israeli censors listening in often could not understand what was being said and so would let some things pass. Unprocessed television film could not be checked before it left the country. Processing film inside Israel usually was avoided because it took time and was expensive. Only material the censors knew in advance dealt with military matters had to be processed locally.

With the new telephone systems, the censors gained an unprecedented ability to intervene in news dissemination. I am afraid that I may have been partially responsible for the introduction of one of the censors' gizmos. At 1:50 P.M. one day, I heard that the Israelis had shot down two Syrian MiG 21 fighters. The army spokesman was scheduled to announce the downing at the top of the hour (to enable Israeli Radio to get the story first). I called my editors at Canadian Broadcasting Corporation (CBC) Radio News to inform them that the story was about to break and to warn them that I might have to broadcast live. We were trying to decide whether to hold the line open to ensure that I would be able to connect with the studio in time when a censor intervened in the conversation and said that I couldn't send anything and that I would have to report to him first. I argued that this was simply a service message to my editors and had nothing to do with the actual transmission of a story. Little did I or the censor know that my editors had begun to record the conversation and the eventual argument. It was broadcast across Canada that night. Soon afterward, the Israelis introduced a new system whereby they could cut off one part of a conversation—the outgoing one—and talk to the reporter without the other party abroad being able to hear. This often left editors bewildered as a conversation was suddenly cut off. In one case, it also led to an enormous telephone bill, because the censors forgot to reset their cut-off button, leaving the overseas line to the radio station open and unusable by anyone else for more than twenty-four hours.

With the arrival of satellite transmission, most news film began to be processed in Israel. For the first time, the censors were able to preview every foot of film before it was sent abroad. When ENG cameras arrived, Army Spokesman's Office escort officers could and did ask to see what the cameramen had shot, even before the cameramen had left the shooting site. Control of images and sound was thus almost complete.

This system of control began to break down when direct international dialing was introduced. Direct dialing meant that journalists could call abroad without having to inform the censors in advance. It originally was introduced to relieve the bottleneck caused by a shortage of international telephone operators in Israel. But with the natural increase in overseas telephone traffic by Israelis, and with the removal of the interface of international operators warning the censors in advance that a press call was about to take place, the censors could no longer cope. The system of control was undermined further when computers with acoustic couplers to transmit information over telephone lines were introduced in the 1980s. Journalists who did not have the budgets to have their own telex machines no longer had to go to the telex office to file printed copy. A relatively cheap modem attached to their increasingly inexpensive word processors made them masters of their own copy. The cacophony of beeps and bops the new machines sent over the telephone lines also was totally unintelligible to anyone without a decoder.

Another technical development changed the nature of access to news for journalists. Small, portable police and army radio band monitors enabled journalists to listen in to the transmissions of the security services anywhere in the field. Journalists, and particularly camera crews and photographers, no longer had to wait for an announcement from the relevant spokesperson to find out if an event had occurred; nor did they have to go out to the site of an event before they could judge its significance. All they had to do was wait by their scanners and listen into the conversations taking place. Such scanners are illegal in Israel unless licensed. Nonetheless, they are widely used by those who know Hebrew and, especially, military slang. During the intifada, the use of scanners was particularly widespread. Some of these devices could "read" as many as four hundred military and police channels. Television crews clubbed together to break the army codes and, as a result, often could arrive at the site of an event before the security forces.

By the time the intifada broke out, the technological revolution was in full force. The technical capability of media organizations, as much as the value of the news story itself, had begun to drive news coverage. During the intifada, that capability was to drive the news events themselves.

When we think about the new information age, we tend to conceive of it mainly in two ways: the vast increases in the speed at which data and images can be processed and distributed, and the quantity of material that can be handled. But that is only part of the story—the mechanical part. Even more important for journalists and media consumers, the new information age has afforded us new means of access to news and a capacity to interact with our audiences in real time.

Besides the scanner, two inventions stand out when we look at the problem of access. The first is the arrival of cellular telephones. These mobile telephones are often of better quality than land line phones. Unlike walkie-talkies, they are not so susceptible to the problems created by hilly terrain. In the case of the intifada, they meant that journalists could remain in constant contact with their offices to receive tips on events that were in progress or were likely to occur, even when the Israelis, as they did for extended periods, cut off the telephone lines in West Bank and Gaza towns and cities. Not only that, journalists who could afford these telephones were able to file directly from the site of events, either by using voice reports or through laptop computers with acoustic couplers. No longer did a journalist have to return to his or her home base in order to send material.[2]

---

[2]During the 1991 Iraqi war, this process of making journalists increasingly independent of the

The second invention was the super-8 video camera. These are light, easy-to-operate, relatively cheap video recorders that produce tapes of high quality. The Palestinians initially used home video cameras for their own purposes. With no access to the state broadcasting system and with Arabic-language newspapers heavily censored by the Israeli authorities, Palestinian activists found in home videocassettes an ideal means of circumventing the restrictions placed on them. When the demonstrations began in Gaza, for example, the events were recorded and the cassettes were hand-carried to the West Bank. There, other activists played the tapes on their home VCRs before a crowd of youngsters, who then took to the streets. At a later stage, cassettes of Moslem preachers appealing to the faithful to demonstrate or strike also became widespread.

When the Israeli army began restricting the movements of camera crews in the occupied territories, the major television networks took the process one step further. They began distributing dozens of these cameras to local Palestinians. The army asserted that it was justified in limiting the movements of the camera crews, because the very presence of cameras encouraged Palestinians to demonstrate and riot. But there was also much that was self-serving in those restrictions. The military did not like the pictures of soldiers beating Arabs that were being broadcast. It did not like the scrutiny to which soldiers and paramilitary border policemen were being subjected. It did not like the presence of outsiders in what were termed "operational environments."

There is a considerable body of evidence that, at least during the first months of the intifada, the presence of a FOREIGN PRESS sign on the side or windshield of a car was enough to prevent soldiers and border police from acting at a particular time in a particular place. Many journalists have told me of seeing soldiers or border police approaching villages, only to turn around when they saw the journalists. The military would then wait until the journalists had left before taking any action.

In an attempt to cope with this problem, the military relapsed into the same mistake it had made during the initial stages of the Lebanese

---

government-controlled public communications system was taken one step further when CNN introduced the use of mobile, direct satellite linkups for telephones. A reporter no longer needed to go through an Israeli telephone exchange. Eventually, the Israelis banned the use of these telephone systems on the grounds that they were not licensed and that they enabled reporters to avoid censorship entirely.

War. Without thinking through some of the broader potential consequences of its decision, the army started preventing journalists from gathering information firsthand. Large areas were declared "closed military
zones." Authorizations to prevent access to journalists were distributed
with abandon to officers in command of roadblocks. Junior lieutenants
were given permission to decide on their own whether to allow journalists
free passage on the roads or into villages.

The distribution of the super-8 cameras was a technical means the
main U.S. television networks had for responding to these restrictions on
access. The networks are proud of the way in which they have managed
to circumvent the army's restrictions. This policy is only one example of
how technology is often introduced to cope with short-term problems—
before the long-term consequences are assessed. The distribution of video
cameras to Palestinian amateurs raises some disturbing questions the networks do not appear to have considered—or if they have, they have chosen
not to respond.

To understand why the policy is questionable, first one must understand the nature of modern television reporting and, especially, the
nature of television coverage of the intifada. Television news is enslaved
to images. If an idea cannot be recorded in the form of an image, it will
rarely, if ever, be given extensive time on a nightly network newscast.[3] In
that sense, the intifada was an ideal television news story. It was exciting
and graphic. It was combat reporting in a new form—rocks against guns,
visual symbols like flags and graffiti pitted against the traditional signs of
military power, like helmets and jeeps. And it had participants wearing
clearly defined uniforms that enabled viewers to distinguish one side from
the other very easily.

What made this form of combat reporting special was the absence
of any front line. Rioting could and did spring up everywhere. One day
it might be in a Gaza refugee camp. The next day it might happen in
Nablus in the West Bank. To capture the all-important images, the television networks were forced to resort to "patrol journalism." It is the kind
of reporting that makes even the television networks themselves uncom-

---

[3]A very notable exception to this rule occurred during the 1991 Iraqi war, when television
journalists in Baghdad could use only telephone hookups.

fortable. In the case of the intifada, it meant sending ten or more camera crews out in the early morning every day to patrol the roads to see if anything was happening. Since the television news reporters could not possibly accompany every crew, they had to rely heavily on the crews for the background information needed for the voice-over commentary. On many stories, the television reporters became picture assemblers rather than information gatherers.

The cameramen, therefore, became the point men for coverage. Many were brilliant at their jobs—daring and brave and willing to put themselves in considerable personal danger. However, cameramen are not trained to be journalists. They are not trained to spend the time needed to talk to subjects at length, nor are they particularly interested in doing so. It is not their job to be investigative or analytical. Their job is to capture the images. When one talks to cameramen, the discussion is not usually about broad ideas, it is about technical problems with equipment and descriptions of scenes and events. Nonetheless, because of the nature of the medium and the exigencies of patrol journalism, the reporters had to rely on their camera crews to an unprecedented degree for even the most basic information about an event. That only served to reinforce the image-driven nature of their reports. And since they often were not eyewitnesses to an event, the reporters had to trust what their camera crews told them. Trust, however, is a product of long, intimate contact between people.

By handing out video cameras to the Palestinians with whom they had not developed this long and intimate professional relationship, television journalists took this process of abdicating personal control over coverage one step further. By distributing the instruments of coverage so widely to only one party to the dispute, the networks could not help but lay the groundwork for the skewing of future news coverage. The camera operators are, after all, local Palestinians with their own—not a professional media—agenda. Unlike professional camera crews (whether locally hired or home-office based), who must work with the networks on a long-term basis if they are to earn their daily bread, there are few sanctions that can be applied to the amateurs to keep them accountable for honesty and fairness. With their newfound tools and entry into media organizations, it was inevitable that at least some Palestinian amateurs would record those scenes that portray Palestinians in a positive light and Israelis in a negative one. Lacking professional press rules of conduct, they were also more likely to record events staged particularly for the camera.

The television networks' response is that they still control the editing and dissemination process and that they have the professional skills to determine what is real and what is staged. It is questionable, though, whether that kind of subjective judgment is enough protection for the viewer, especially with such an emotionally charged story. Even on-air sourcing of who took the pictures is not enough. Tiny letters on a television screen often are ignored by viewers and quick verbal attributions tend to be lost or diminished by the impact of the pictures.

In fact, though, the networks' argument misses or ignores the real point. Television news coverage is based on the manipulation of images. If an image does not exist on film or tape, it cannot be included in the news package. Thus, if a Palestinian amateur with a camera shoots only scenes of an Israeli beating Palestinians and fails to record scenes of a Palestinian provocation that may have come before, there is no way that what was *not* recorded can be recovered. Since television is image oriented, even a mention of provocation in the voice-over cannot have the same impact on viewers as the beating scene. In this way, television differs graphically from print journalism. If a print journalist misses something in a story or misreports an event, the situation can be corrected by printing another explanation or clarification the next day. In television, this cannot be done, because the image is lost forever.

What makes the information revolution unique, however, is the fact it is interactive. When communications satellites first were introduced, foreign correspondents gloried in the speed with which they could transmit their images and messages back to their home-country audiences. But that one-way traffic could not and did not last indefinitely. Today, it is, at a minimum, three-way traffic.

In areas like the Israeli-occupied territories, China, or Eastern Europe, where there are tight government controls on the press or the government has a news dissemination monopoly, people have always sought alternative sources of information. Media organizations like the BBC's International Service, Voice of America (VOA), or Deutsche Welle have long provided alternative sources of information. During the overthrow of the shah in Iran, for example, activities in the country would come to a virtual halt during the BBC newscasts so that people could find out what was happening in other parts of their own country. The same was true during the initial phases of the intifada. The BBC, VOA, and Radio Monte Carlo were the prime sources of information to the Palestinians about what was happening in their own backyard.

During the intifada, however, a new element was added. The arrival of fax machines not only enabled the Palestinians with access to the machines to receive orders from abroad, they enabled Palestinian leaders to find out in real time the impact the rioting was having on others around the world. A newspaper page could be faxed from abroad showing the exact front-page headlines and the pictures being displayed. This had far more impact than a telephone call discussing a television program or a batch of week-old newspaper clippings that arrived by mail. The Israelis eventually realized the impact that fax machines were having and issued an administrative order forbidding anyone in the occupied territories to possess such a machine without a license. Penalties as stiff as six months in prison could be imposed on anyone found with an unlicensed fax. Local stringers in Gaza working for major international media outlets were invariably refused licenses and, in 1989, were ordered by the military authorities to dispose of the fax machines in their possession.[4]

It is impossible to underestimate the affect this feedback mechanism had on local Palestinians. They translated the enormous publicity they were receiving into a perception that they were winning their struggle for the first time. Within hours, rather than days, of an event taking place, they could tell how much impact their actions were having on others around the world. They could receive positive reinforcement that they were influencing international perceptions by their actions—and this helped fuel the intifada and strengthen the resolve of the demonstrators and their leaders. Decision-making time was compressed beyond all recognition. In other words, foreign press coverage, aided by the new technology, now can drive events in foreign countries.

[4]Seri Nusseibeh, who lives in the West Bank, was sentenced to six months of administrative detention during the Iraqi war for allegedly having used his fax to send information to Iraqi agents abroad. He was released from detention after three months.

The Israeli Army Spokesman's Office, lacking even these most basic tools, could not respond in a timely fashion. Events outpaced their reactions by a wide margin. It was only well into the intifada, for example, that the office acquired a satellite dish. Deputy Chief Military Spokesman Raanan Gissin admits, "We were twenty-five to thirty years behind the times in technology."

For Israeli citizens, feedback also was important. The Palestinians did not have access to satellite dishes, but some Israelis did have such access, and what they saw on their screens affected their perceptions of the intifada.[5] At least in the initial phases of the intifada, while Israeli television was showing quiet, curfewed streets, the foreign reports were showing tear gas, violence, and stones. As international satellite networks like CNN grow, feedback mechanisms will take on an even greater role in shaping news events. Foreign journalists are, in effect, becoming local independent journalists for the local population. An information loop is being formed. The journalists send their copy abroad. It is then broadcast or printed in their media organization's country. The packaged story gets fed back to the local population by satellite or fax. That report then shapes the perceptions and actions of the local population—which, in turn, become the subject for the journalist's next report.

This new aspect of journalism raises important questions about press accountability. Correspondents for international services like the BBC and VOA have always been acutely aware of the potential consequences of their reports and the effect those reports may have on local foreign audiences. That is not the case for those media reporters who have only recently entered into this international information loop.

The only real and effective system of accountability in journalism is audience reaction. However, journalists who are parachuted into a foreign news story from their home office or those who are unaware of the changes

[5]Some could get international television news broadcasts via "pirate" or licensed cable services to which they subscribed. At the time of the outbreak of the intifada, segments from the nightly news broadcasts of the three main U.S. commercial television networks were being beamed by satellite to the U.S. armed forces' television network in Europe. These broadcasts easily could be downloaded in Israel. However, the networks eventually demanded that the satellite transmissions be scrambled, and they are no longer available. CNN, as part of its international service, is being transmitted "clear."

Another substitute is the once-a-week summary of the ABC evening newscasts, which the U.S. Cultural Centers in Jerusalem and Tel Aviv show to packed audiences.

the new information age has brought about in foreign news coverage do not recognize the local foreign population as an audience to whom they also must be accountable. Because of this, there is both a lack of awareness and a lack of concern about the influence they have in shaping events. A standard response I received after querying many foreign journalists about this subject was: "What are we to do? Stop reporting? Are we to stop doing our jobs because it may stop someone from demonstrating?"

Foreign correspondents are reluctant to address the implications of this new phenomenon—mainly because they do not have any answers to questions that inevitably would be raised if the subject were discussed publicly. And since journalists always demand answers of others, they are loathe to raise the subject, for fear that then they, too, will be accused of failing to come up with answers and solutions. Referring directly to the intifada, Nicholas Tatro, the former AP bureau chief in Jerusalem, notes: "We made the Iranian revolution, and the Chinese student revolution, and at the end of the day we walked away and left it [the consequences] to the people. That's cynical, but true. No one has realized it yet. They haven't factored it into their game plan."[6]

New advances in technology, like lightweight, portable, umbrella-type satellite antennas that are now in development, undoubtedly will push this trend toward the internationalization of news coverage even further. But, as with so many aspects of the new information age, human beings have lagged far behind in their ability to cope with the realities and challenges this new order is creating. In fact, in some ways, the human part of the system has retrogressed. At a time when the need for foreign area specialists is increasing, the number of reporters who have dedicated their working lives to foreign reporting, who have studied foreign societies in depth, and who are at home in foreign cultures is dropping.

High-speed air travel and many of the new technologies have enabled many media organizations to cut back on the number of foreign bureaus they staff. Instead, more and more, they have come to rely on home-office reporters who are parachuted into a breaking event. Home-based reporters or those based in bureaus far away deluged Israel and the occupied territories after the rioting broke out.

"The most dangerous component of foreign press coverage," says

[6]Nicholas Tatro, conversation with author, July 1990.

ABC's Tel Aviv bureau chief Bill Seamans, "is paratroop journalism. They come with preconceived notions of a story and report stories that fit those preconceptions. They are not here long enough to give them a real perception of events. The flavor of their story, for the most part, is biased and inaccurate. . . . Some guys do not report Israel, they're at war with Israel."[7]

In my experience, it takes a foreign reporter at least six months just to find his or her way about a country comfortably. It takes about eighteen months of hard work before he or she can begin to decipher some of the nuances of a society. With only a few notable exceptions, it takes about twelve to fifteen years of working in different societies, of running up innumerable blind alleys, and of misreading events and making mistakes before a foreign reporter is really competent. Yet, fewer and fewer news organizations are willing to invest in that sort of training and competence. Thus, while the new information age demands greater cross-cultural understanding and competency than ever before, the number of journalists equipped to fill the area specialist's role is dropping. This has led to what might be termed "star journalism," where famous names within a media organization compete to cover the headline stories—whether or not those journalists know anything about the subject.

This, in turn, is leading to a homogenization of foreign coverage and often to superficial reporting, with the same stock pictures being shown on each network and many of the same sorts of stories appearing in print. Because of parachute journalism, less and less print space and air time are devoted to the analysis of all-important institutions and constituencies and of how they affect political and social events. Studying these institutions and constituencies in depth takes time. And it takes money.

The result is predictable. As occurred during the intifada, when a successful formula for attracting reporters or for covering the events is found, events are then crafted by the participants to reinforce those stock images and ensure air time or print space for their agendas.

That is not to say that technology has created a body of reporters who are less skilled or less intelligent than before. It does mean, however, that the more we come to rely on technology, the more we must think

[7]Bill Seamans, interview with author, July 1989.

beyond the immediate benefits it provides. This is true particularly when we assess crises or fast-breaking stories, such as the intifada.

Since television is the medium that is most dependent on technology, it is there that the consequences of the new information age are most apparent. During periods of public chaos, television, because of its image-directed technology, is by far the best medium for conveying the extent of that chaos. There are those who claim that television sets the agenda for all of the other news media, but that is a gross exaggeration. Many factors influence agenda setting, among them wire service reports, exclusive stories, and government statements. What television does do is determine the initial impact a story will have on the public and on other journalists, how much excitement and public emotion the story will generate. This certainly was true during the initial stages of the intifada.

However, television has difficulty during crises in going beyond impact journalism. The very moment after the medium has established that an event is of genuine public concern, the moment when a journalist's primary duty is to make sense of all of the confusing data rushing in, television invariably fails as a useful disseminator of information. Television, because of its dependency on images and technology, is less able to shift gears from descriptive reporting about events to reporting about the ideas behind the events. While faster than any medium in describing scenes vividly, television reporting is also the slowest of all in gathering and editing analytical material.

As a result, having captured a potent image, television tends to repeat that image, or others similar to it, almost indefinitely. Television reporting, with its heavy reliance on tons of equipment and the many individuals needed to run and service that equipment, is cumbersome. Print reporting, by contrast, is more nimble. It can deal with imageless stories. Print reporters, unfettered by the requirement that every story be accompanied by a visual package, need less time to prepare an original, in-depth news story.

Television reporting of the intifada has been subjected to intense criticism for being shallow. Many of the criticisms of individual news stories are valid. Many television news reports did overemphasize the violence. There were a number of false analogies and outright inaccuracies in some of the reports. However, after the crisis period, when the correspondents were given the requisite time to research and prepare in-depth reports and to find appropriate images that could express abstract ideas, the results were no less competent than the dispatches provided by print reporters. Unfortunately for viewers, after a crisis is over, television reporters have difficulty in getting their material on the air, because invariably, a new crisis or political development has arisen in the interim and the new visuals take precedence.

Media news coverage is a marketplace. Those who participate in it behave no differently from farmers who come to town on Thursdays to sell their produce or brokers who work on Wall Street. Each is out to buy, sell, beg, barter, invest, or steal for his or her own defense or gain. There are known and accepted rules of behavior. The bargaining is intense. And the products vary from the sublime to the positively awful. There are laws of supply and demand, analyses of cost effectiveness, and disputes over practitioners' ethics. The only significant differences between the media news market and any other are the currencies and the commodities involved. In the media news marketplace, instead of soybeans, pork bellies, stocks, or money, information is the currency, and news reports are the product.

The intifada created a marketplace that was

S · I · X

The Medium Is a Marketplace

unique. No group of scriptwriters, media manipulators, Hollywood cos-
tumers, or military strategists ever could have combined to plan and
produce an event of this type. It is such an extreme example of the
marketplace at work that it probably is unrepeatable. But precisely because
it is so extreme and because so many factors were at work at the same
time, it provides one of the best cases for studying the interaction between
press coverage, domestic politics, and international relations—and the
public perceptions and policies that that interaction creates and shapes.
The intifada was an example of how groups and individuals, by commission and omission, are drawn or pushed into relationships over which
they have only partial control and whose consequences they can often
neither predict nor direct.

The Palestinian youngsters who entered the marketplace on December 9, 1987, with stones and *keffiyeh* headdresses as their only visible
means of support were, unknowingly, in an unprecedentedly favorable
position to capture the market. Almost everything they needed to monopolize world attention and to present their case was on their side.

To begin with, the intifada erupted at a time when there was a critical
mass of unrest among the Palestinians living in the West Bank and Gaza.
A broad spectrum of social issues ranging from the *mohar* ("bride price")
to employment opportunities had been left unaddressed by the Israelis,
the Jordanians, and the PLO. It was very easy, therefore, for the Palestinian
youngsters to mobilize thousands of rock-throwing participants within days
of the outbreak of rioting. Initially, there was no organizing body involved.
The intifada was a popular uprising of tens of thousands of like minds—
angry, frustrated, and politically disenfranchised youngsters who believed
that they had nothing to lose.

The level of dissatisfaction was so deep and so intense that a vast
majority of these youngsters, whatever their family background, were
able to speak with one voice. Their message was simple, comprehensive,
comprehensible, and coherent: "We hurt because we are being oppressed."
It made no difference where a visitor went in the occupied territories or
to whom he or she spoke. The theme articulated by all of the youngsters
was the same.

This sense of unanimity in adversity was reinforced by the strong visual image—the means to carry their message to television—that the youngsters projected. Without forethought or deliberate intent, but within a day or two of the outbreak of rioting, they were able to capture and hold one of the Jews' and the Western world's most potent political metaphors. Wearing *keffiyehs* that made them look slightly exotic, and jogging shoes, which made identification with them by Western viewers easier, and carrying biblical-type slings previously used to hunt songbirds, they were able to present themselves as modern-day Davids doing battle against the armored Israeli Goliath. It was the symbolic visual equivalent of wresting the adversary's capital from him without a tough fight and within forty-eight hours of the outbreak of war.

Although they undoubtedly never studied the press consciously, the demonstrators quickly learned to play to the media with great skill. When a journalist arrived anywhere in the occupied areas, there was almost invariably an English-speaking or Hebrew-speaking youngster willing to act as translator, guardian, spokesperson, interviewee, and tour guide. Not knowing who was "important" among the newly arrived journalists, the youths accorded every foreign correspondent equal treatment and equal access. Most of the youngsters were polite, courteous, and hospitable to the journalist strangers, in keeping with Arab tradition. Surprisingly, for an area where political passions run so very high, they also were willing to provide names, addresses, and introductions to their secular or religious political opponents, so even the rivals could be interviewed. Initially, all interviewees were willing to have their names used in stories and to speak on the record. It was not until late December 1987, when the Israelis began their mass arrests, that the rioters began covering their faces and demanded that their names not be used in reports. Incidents that the youngsters saw had captured journalists' attention quickly, like rock or firebomb throwing, were repeated for each new press arrival. These incidents, taking place in Israeli-occupied territory, not in Israel proper, fitted perfectly into journalists' political preconceptions and the prevailing story line of "violent conflict over land." It was as though every youngster had been born to be a press officer—with a complete verbal press kit in his head. What gave them even greater influence was their naturalness and naïveté. These were not the cynical and slick news manipulators to whom the press had become accustomed. The youngsters were ordinary, if angry, people struggling to make their point with the rough means of communication at their disposal.

In those early days of the rebellion, the foreign press and the rebels struck a tacit deal. Neither party ever would use the term *deal* openly because of all of the connotations that word has. But, essentially, that is what occurred. Together, they could and would break the Israeli news management monopoly. In return for a good story, the foreign press empowered the Palestinians to act.

One of the outstanding characteristics of the new information age is the degree of access to the world and to international leaders that those who are disenfranchised or who have no control over the means of information dissemination in their own land can acquire with the help of technology and the foreign press. In this new information age, those very technological means that were once the monopoly of elites and oligarchies, and which have been used extensively by them for mass mind control, can and do liberate and empower the masses. That was one of the prime lessons of the intifada, the overthrow of the shah, the student rebellion in China, and the sudden arrival of movements demanding democracy throughout Eastern Europe. The video camera, the VCR, the satellite dish, and the fax machine are no less powerful in their own way than tanks and guns, because both types of weapons have the ability to shape public perceptions. In this sense, foreign journalists become not merely observers and reporters of instability and change, but facilitators and, in some cases, handlers. By their actions in the field, they teach the disenfranchised how to use the new technologies to advantage.

The Palestinian youngsters in the streets were not alone, of course, in maintaining contact with the press or in shaping journalists' perceptions. Many within the Palestinian elite were available for interviews and commentary on what was happening. Among the most prominent were people like Jerusalem newspaper editor Hanna Siniora and Gaza lawyer Fayez Abu Rahmeh, who had been mooted previously as potential negotiators with the Israelis on behalf of the PLO. The very act of interviewing these members of the elite, however, could not but distort reports in some way, since none of the members of the elite had real constituencies behind them. The real constituencies were not in offices in the occupied territories, but in the streets or in the Palestinian diaspora.

As noted in chapter 3, another media connector was the Palestine Press Service. Almost from the first day of the uprising, it was deluging foreign journalists with material. Several young and aggressive Palestinian journalists, like Daoud Kuttab, were available for free-lance assignments or acted as tipsters. In addition, there were self-interested parties that became important sources of data for the press. Those parties can be divided roughly into two groups—foreign humanitarian aid organizations that had worked for a long time with Palestinians, and Palestinian organizations with particular memberships and agendas that gave them access to information.

In the first category, one can put organizations like the United Nations Relief and Works Agency (UNRWA), which runs most of the schools for Palestinian refugees and provides basic foodstuffs. Since UNRWA was most active in the refugee camps, where the majority of demonstrations were taking place, and since it had an independent communications network to transmit information, its officers became both primary and secondary sources of information for foreign journalists. Although UNRWA's officers were decidedly on the side of the Palestinians or were Palestinians themselves, they tended to be treated as neutral observers by journalists.

A second group consisted of Palestinian organizations like Al Haq, which monitored human rights violations, and spokesmen for the various universities. Many of these organizations, like trade unions or professional associations, were shut down by the Israelis during the course of the intifada, but by this time, the individual leaders were known to the press and could be contacted outside the framework of the organization—unless they had been detained by the Israeli authorities.

One of the most interesting personalities was Mubarak Awad, a Jerusalem-born Palestinian who had lived in the United States for many years and had acquired U.S. citizenship. He had returned to Jerusalem a couple of years earlier with the intent of establishing a center to promote Gandhian concepts of civil disobedience as a political tool in the struggle with the Israelis. He had failed to make very much headway, because he was a Christian, he had forgotten much of his Arabic, and his ideas were totally foreign to the vast majority of Palestinians. However, when the intifada erupted, he viewed the civil disorder as a fulfillment of many of his beliefs. Each morning, apparently acting on tips he had received, he would rush out to some village in the West Bank to see what was going on, and some of the press would tag along with him. Despite serious protests from the U.S. government, he eventually was deported by the Israelis.

The Palestinians also had their own internal mass media service. The local Palestinian press, based in East Jerusalem, remained heavily censored and even was unable to print many articles that already had appeared in the Hebrew press. However, two alternatives immediately arose. Soon after the intifada began, Ahmed Jibril's Popular Front for the Liberation of Palestine–General Command (PFLP-GC) began sending instructions to the demonstrators over its radio station, Radio Al Kuds. The station, which mixed news, music, and political and operational messages, was a major hit in the occupied territories. One could hear its broadcasts almost everywhere. The Israelis eventually jammed its broadcasts, lifting the jamming only in mid-1989.

The second means of information dissemination—and by far the most important and potent—was the arrival of regular leaflets printed by the newly emerging underground leadership. The leaflets began to appear in the first week of January 1988. Written under the auspices of the Unified Leadership of the Uprising (UNLU), the leaflets initially were little more than verbiage and compilations of old, worn slogans. That quickly changed, and within three weeks, they adopted a form that was to remain throughout the days of violence. After commenting briefly on events or trends, they would provide instructions for future events like strikes or boycotts. The arrival of the leaflets was undoubtedly one of the two or three main turning points in the history of the uprising. The printed sheets demonstrated that some sort of local underground leadership was in the process of being formed.[1] While they incorporated many of the exhortations being broadcast on Al Fatah's radio station in Baghdad, careful readers could decipher a considerable amount of local input—a confirmation that a locally based leadership was evolving amid the seeming chaos.[2]

---

[1]This evolutionary process among the secular nationalists eventually was cut short by the Israelis and the PLO. The Israelis deported or detained many of those suspected of having taken a hand in writing the leaflets, and the PLO, in keeping with past practice, refused to allow the UNLU to become anything more than what the Palestinians term "a liaison body."

[2]The fastest and easiest way to discover what that input was, was by submitting a story on the

The leaflets also appear to have been drafted, in turn, by representatives of the different groups within the UNLU, and there were always small but significant shifts in phrasing and emphasis from one leaflet to the next. Those attuned to the subtleties could discover the differences in perception and policy between the various groups. When the fundamentalist HAMAS began issuing competitive leaflets of its own, journalists were able to uncover some of the truly basic ideological conflicts going on within the leadership of the Palestinians in the West Bank and Gaza. Most significantly, though, the leaflets, after they began to appear on a regular and timely basis, set the working agendas for Palestinians, the press, and Israeli security authorities alike. Plans for action by all three groups were based largely on the instructions printed on the white sheets of paper.

The leaflets also served to increase and maintain contact between the foreign press and Palestinian journalists. Palestinian journalists inevitably got the leaflets first. (Some Israeli officials charge that some of those Palestinian journalists actually helped to write the documents.) As a result, many Western journalists became dependent on their Palestinian counterparts to translate and to interpret the meaning of some of the more obscure references.

In themselves, the leaflets might not have had very much impact. But they were accompanied by an aggressive campaign of enforcement by the *Shebiba*, the PLO's youth organization. The January 21, 1988, leaflet was the first to call for general strikes. Not all merchants or workers wanted to obey the strike calls. But gangs of youngsters roamed the streets, threatening people who disobeyed the leaflet's instructions. The Israelis responded by alternately forcing shop doors open or by welding them shut, but to no avail. If they could not control the youngsters, the Israelis could not halt the strikes. The old question journalists had asked about whether or not the Palestinians could ever sustain a period of civil disobedience was being answered. By the beginning of February 1988, it was obvious that the intifada was something different from the demonstrations that had come before and that the violence would not end easily.

---

leaflet to the Israeli censors. Those parts that were blue-pencilled out were the work of local Palestinians. The censors cut out those passages on the grounds that "they had not already appeared in the press or on 'terrorist radio.' "

The vast quantity of information emerging from the occupied territories during the first few months of the uprising did not guarantee accurate reporting. Palestinian spokesmen often inflated casualty figures or made outlandish, unsupportable claims. *Time* magazine's Jamil Hamad remembers that when he would call East Jerusalem's Mukassed Hospital, he sometimes would get five different spokesmen with five different casualty reports. Palestinian doctors frequently charged that the Israeli soldiers were using dumdum bullets, which are illegal under international law, but none of the more than fifty journalists I spoke to ever was presented with such a bullet as evidence.

Nonetheless, this tidal wave of information did, in the end, have several lasting effects, one of the most notable being the change in foreign journalists' perceptions of what is or what may be a story. One of the axioms of foreign press coverage of the Palestinians had always been that the credibility of Palestinians' assertions must be suspect. The more outlandish the claims, the more easily they could be dismissed out of hand. A significant turning point came when reporters were able to verify a rumor that had been circulating for more than a week—that on February 5, 1988, Israeli soldiers had partly buried some Palestinians in a trench in a West Bank village. This event, when combined with examples of widespread beatings by Israelis that journalists also had been able to confirm, changed the notion of "impossible" to "improbable" or even "possible." The inherent skepticism remained, but it had, for the first time, been altered to the point where journalists felt professionally obliged to check out all allegations. It was an almost immeasurable victory for the local Palestinians.

As in all media and military offensives, the key to success was timing, and it is doubtful whether the Palestinian youngsters could have chosen a more opportune moment in which to act. Fortuitously for the Palestinians, in early December 1987, a totally unpredictable confluence of events occurred. The odds against such factors being present at the same time in the same place are almost incalculable, but the youths were able to seize on them and turn them to their advantage.

To begin with, the locally based foreign correspondents had been suffering from a severe news drought that had lasted for months. Stringers and contract free-lancers who did not have regional responsibilities but were limited to reporting on Israel had been particularly hard hit. The stringers had suffered a serious drop in income, too, and the contract free-lancers were under extreme pressure from their outlets to produce material. A few even had been forced to renegotiate their contracts at lower rates of pay. This was also a time when many media outlets were undergoing financial restructuring and major cutbacks in funds for coverage and man-power. Thus, even longtime staffers felt under pressure to justify the cost of their existence in a non-news-producing land. In addition, journalists as a group tend to get fidgety and cranky when they do not have work or when they cannot get into print or on the air. Any major event, therefore, could not but attract immediate interest among members of the press.

By this time, the permanent foreign press corps based in Israel was the largest it ever had been. Most of the reporters for the large foreign media outlets were experienced, had been posted to the area for several years, were familiar with much of the historical background, knew the geography, and had relatively efficient, comprehensive news-gathering systems in place, including tipsters, translators, and lists of potential in-terviewees for any occasion.

Moreover, the shipping war in the Persian Gulf, which had attracted both locally based regional correspondents and a large number of para-chutists, was winding down. Both of these groups, therefore, were available immediately for coverage. It was also right before Christmas, when news reporting in general usually begins to slow down in the Western world. So air time and print space were relatively easily available to anyone producing a good news story.

While the Palestinians and the foreign press corps were prepared and even anxious to become involved in and to cover the outbreak of rioting and demonstrations, Israeli officialdom was in disarray. For years, its monopolistic control of the news marketplace had been eroding, but the bureaucrats had done nothing to counteract the phenomenon. When they were hit by the full force of the free market of information created by the uprising, they were totally unprepared. At times, their reactions were almost pathetic. As with so many centralized, inward-looking bureaucratic systems that have existed too long under the protection of a virtual mo-nopoly, Israeli government news management had become fat and com-placent, suffering from woolly thinking and inefficiencies, out of touch with market realities, and attempting to peddle a product that was out-of-date and would not "sell." While the Palestinians in the occupied territories became extraordinarily aggressive marketers for their ideas, Israeli officials, hit by the shock of real competition, retreated into self-pity and abrogated responsibility. Bankruptcy finally had arrived for the old system of co-optation and control.

There were many reasons for this sudden collapse, and they are worth examining in some detail, because they reveal a great deal about the nature of news coverage and news management. The first, and seemingly most obvious, point is that in order to compete, one must be present in the marketplace. The Israelis chose to stand aside. During the initial phase of the uprising, journalists could get no high-level Israeli response to events and thus were forced to depend almost entirely on Palestinian sources— who were more than willing to press their agenda while providing facts.

For example, almost immediately after the rioting began, Defence Minister Yitzchak Rabin chose to go through with a planned visit to Washington. Rabin was the fulcrum of power in the Israeli government. The timing was crucial to the future of the uprising. He not only was in control of the biggest ministry, but as one of the most conservative leaders of the Labor party, he held the balance of power in the evenly divided government. Virtually no decision, and certainly no decision concerning military matters, could be made within the cabinet without his active participation. In the Israeli system of governance, cabinet decision making is not based on preliminary staff work provided by a cabinet secretariat. It begins in earnest with presentations by the relevant ministers. This, when combined with the jealously guarded perquisites laid out in the coalition agreement, meant that the government could not act without Rabin's presence. By absenting himself, Rabin denied the government its primary spokesman on matters dealing with the uprising. Thus, the Israeli government left the marketplace totally open to the Palestinians, permitting the Palestinians to frame the issues and to set the media's agenda, almost without interference. A leading substitute candidate, Foreign Minister Shimon Peres, was on a trip to South America.

The Israeli government, stalemated from within and oblivious to the implications of its behavior, therefore was unable to respond adequately. With no agreed strategic vision to act as a frame for policymakers on major issues—media and otherwise—decisions had to be tactical and made without reference to long-term goals or a national consensus. Reactions from spokesmen like Prime Minister Shamir and the director-general of the Foreign Ministry, Yossi Beilin, were knee-jerk in nature and served only to discredit the Israeli position. Both blamed the PLO for the disturbances—although it was patently obvious to journalists who had been out in the field that even the PLO had been caught by surprise and that, at this early stage, it was unable to play a part.

Had the Israeli army been less secretive and xenophobic, it could have partially filled this void by the use of field news management. It could have allowed journalists, for example, to accompany soldiers on patrol in order to get the Israeli perspective. Eventually, this was done. But by that time, the Palestinians had consolidated their position as the media's agenda setters.

Even when Rabin returned to Israel, the situation remained much the same. There was no cabinet debate on the issue, since Rabin was being given an almost totally free hand. Cabinet communiqués invariably described any discussion on the uprising with the laconic "The Defence Minister reviewed matters in the occupied territories." There was never any mention of a cabinet debate. From a press point of view, the Israeli government had chosen to be a nonplayer. In an active marketplace, nonplayers are ignored. Later, Rabin did make himself available to a wide variety of journalists, but by that time, it was too late. The Palestinians already had captured the market.

The divided government, able to agree on nothing more than the lowest common political denominator of controlling the Palestinians and reestablishing authority in the occupied territories, was incapable of carrying the news story forward. Even Prime Minister Shamir's late-arriving proposals for limited Palestinian home rule were not new and showed no originality. They were viewed as tactical responses, not visionary strategies. With no new information to give, the Israelis could find few buyers.

In the past, when the government had petrified or bumbled, it often had been saved by its monopolistic radio and television services. The broadcast services contained on their staff rosters a number of inquisitive first-class reporters who were sensitive to issues of public concern and had often acted as bridges between the constituency and the often isolated leadership. In researching and preparing their stories, they often had forced the government to speak out on important public issues of the moment. However, at the moment the intifada broke out, the Israel Broadcasting Authority had just suffered through a crippling fifty-two-day strike. The reporters had lost their battle for, among other things, higher pay, and the demoralization created lethargy and desultory reporting. It was in no position to drive home the impact of the events taking place in the occupied territories to the public or the politicians. Moreover, for the previous few years, it had been going through a process of decay, because its director-general, the Likud's Uri Porat, had been systematically trying to expunge the organization of leftists and "leftist tendencies" among reporters. Despite denials from Porat and other senior executives, it was quite obvious to regular listeners and viewers that the IBA's reports had lost much of their bite and that some degree of self-censorship was being exercised. Many reporters had become demoralized. There was little drive among its journalists to involve the politicians and the public in debate. Television coverage, in particular, was soporific. And the otherwise activist print media could not replace the role of television in providing images and creating impact.

Most Israelis, living far from the scene of events and unable to see the coverage of foreign reporters, could not understand why the fuss abroad was so great. Rather than asking questions of their leaders or their broadcast news executives, many Israelis saw foreign press coverage as a conspiracy to blacken Israel's name—or worse, as anti-Semitism. Car window stickers bearing the logo WE OPPOSE THE HOSTILE PRESS began appearing. Rather than reacting to the substance of the press reports, the politicians, sensing that this popular sentiment could be used to divert attention from the realities taking place, began to attack the press.

In competitive marketplaces where information is the primary means of exchange, no party can hope to survive or to promote its interests without access to the currency being used and without a well-conceived marketing strategy. The Israeli news management system had neither. The body charged with day-to-day contacts with the press was the Government Press Office, but it had neither the formal means to gather original information nor the informal means to disseminate it. The government itself was not talking, and the Army Spokesman's Office, the other main source of data, was in disarray. The only information the Government Press Office was capable of disseminating in any quantity were translations from the Hebrew press.

A potential alternative might have been informal, venue spokesmanship. Informal spokesmanship—that which takes place outside the
confines of the office—is as much a part of the job of news managers as
is formal spokesmanship. The much-derided cocktail party is one such
venue for spokesmanship. The Israelis had used informal spokesmanship
in the past. During the Yom Kippur War, for example, the Dan Hotel
in Tel Aviv had been one such venue. Many of the country's leading
officials stayed at the hotel and were available for quick chats as they came
and went. For many years, the restaurants in the Government Press Offices
in Jerusalem and Tel Aviv had served much the same function. Ostensibly,
officials would stop by for a quick drink or a meal, knowing that they
soon would be approached by journalists—and they always had matters
on their agenda to discuss, either on or off the record. By the time the
intifada broke out, there was no such informal Israeli meeting place and
no one seemed to have thought of establishing one. Outside the Knesset
members' dining room, there was no place where journalists knew they
could expect to meet officials on a regular basis without having to go
through cumbersome channels. Nowhere could officials even pretend to
"let down their hair" and discuss issues that went beyond the government's
policy of controlling the Palestinians and reestablishing authority.[3]
Throughout the intifada, Israeli officials were always locked away in their
offices, with parapets and portcullises of spokesmen and secretaries to keep
the press, and especially the foreign press, at bay. The system of news
control through spokesmen was about to backfire.

By contrast, the Palestinians, because they had no official spokesmen,
had to rely almost entirely on informal contact with the press—whether
in the field or at some central location. They had an ideal venue—the
American Colony Hotel in East Jerusalem. The hotel's comfortable surroundings, with its large lobby close to the front door and its well-stocked
bar, was an ideal spot for such meetings. No journalist entering the
building could fail to see who was sitting there, and even parachutists

---

[3]One significant factor in this huge gap in spokesmanship is the fact that most of the restaurants
and pubs frequented by foreign journalists do not serve kosher food. With the major political
parties so dependent on the ultra-Orthodox parties for support in the Knesset, few official
representatives of the mainline parties—even those who do not abide by Jewish dietary restrictions—could afford to be seen in a restaurant serving the pork and shellfish that are forbidden
under Jewish dietary laws.

with no knowledge of the personalities involved could not fail to take note of colleagues gathered around and talking animatedly to a particular figure.

In this rapidly evolving marketplace, the IDF spokesman's office was positioned to intervene aggressively, but it could not and did not do so. The Army Spokesman's Office, although officially subordinate to the General Staff, is essentially an arm of the intelligence services. No IDF spokesman has ever come up through the ranks of the Army Spokesman's Office. Almost all have come out of the Military Intelligence, where secrecy, rather than accessibility, is the byword. There could be no training more antithetical to dealing with the press than the many years the spokesmen had spent in the world of shadows and intrigue. There is an inherent conflict between the Military Intelligence ethos of secrecy and field security and the spokesman's need to operate imaginatively and flexibly in a marketplace of ideas, where competition is the name of the game.

Until the intifada was well under way, the Army Spokesman's Office had no one trained as a journalist or mass communicator on its staff.[4] It was not mandated to gather information on its own and had almost no independent mechanism to do so. If it was not given any information by the intelligence services, it could not act. Therefore, it was structurally, strategically, and motivationally unprepared to deal with a popular uprising like the intifada.

The Army Spokesman's Office had been structured for wartime, where there are clearly delineated front lines and no competition for news gathering and information dissemination within the area behind those lines. During the intifada, however, there were no front lines and there was considerable competition. In addition, there was a warlike volume of information being produced, which the office, with its relatively small and untrained staff, was unprepared to process. The Army Spokesman's Office always has been based on the premise that in any war, it can nationalize and monopolize the sources of information. In this new form of warfare, it could not do so.

Lacking a preplanned alternate strategy, and inflexible in its behavior patterns, it could not and did not adapt to the new circumstances. It did not, for example, do even the most elementary market research, such as

---

[4]It was only in late 1989 that the General Staff decided to appoint a media specialist, Nahman Shai, as IDF spokesman.

sending its officers out into the field just to see what journalists were seeing, to hear what they were hearing, or even to feel the rush of adrenaline they were feeling. Without basic data of this sort, the press officers could neither relate to nor anticipate the kinds of questions and requests for information the office's personnel would be receiving. The officers were isolated behind their desks, lacking both an empathy and an understanding of what the journalists were going through and unable to relate to the people they were mandated to deal with. Press tours were usually highly structured affairs from which the spokespeople learned little or nothing. Most of the officers who were assigned to accompany journalists were on one-day reserve army duty and brought no impressions back to the spokesman's offices after their day in the field was over. And many press trips, even those arranged in advance, simply collapsed because of opposition from the local army field commander who refused to allow journalists onto his turf.

Even when the army's Foreign Press Liaison Office did realize the type of news coverage that was going on, the officers in charge changed neither their overall doctrine nor their daily information-gathering operating procedures. As a result, their credibility, already low, disintegrated almost entirely. Many journalists, myself included, simply stopped calling for information or called merely on a pro forma basis—not expecting to receive a cogent reply in time for deadlines.

Out of the many I could choose, a couple of examples vividly demonstrate the office's rigidity, disarray, and lack of comprehension of foreign journalists' concerns. During the initial, chaotic stages of the intifada, the experienced journalists did what they usually do in such circumstances: rely on description and retreat into professionalism. That means checking every detail and fact that is available (and that we have not actually seen ourselves) for accuracy. It is a mechanism for self-protection, and it becomes almost an obsession. "During those first weeks," says VOA's Charles Weiss, "We were all running around like crazy trying to make sure that we had gotten our figures right. Was it twelve killed or fifteen killed? Were three people wounded in this village or was it six or seven?"[5] The Army Spokesman's Office, however, was singularly ill equipped to answer basic questions of this sort. It never had been ordered to collect information

---

[5]Charles Weiss, interview with author, June 1989.

of this type; nor had it been given the facilities to do so. Those who might have been able to do this work on the spokesman's behalf, like the territorial commands or the civil administration, were unconcerned and uninterested in doing so. The figures released by the army were, at best, partial.

Deputy Chief Military Spokesman Raanan Gissin responds: "We were caught in a dilemma between credibility and speed. We had to check every piece of information before we could release it. . . . We had problems in separating the information from the noise. . . . We didn't have a mandate to issue information about Palestinians . . . [and] we couldn't beat Palestinian information sources."[6] Nonetheless, Gissin is convinced that his office did remain credible, because what it did release was accurate. What he and the Israeli media management hierarchy failed to understand is that partial truth is not considered "truth" by most people. Information, to be credible, must be both accurate and comprehensive. Saying that the army had confirmed that five people were wounded is only partially true if, in fact, eight people were wounded. In self-defense, journalists generally respond to what they believe is partial information by citing the source. But at the back of their minds, a silent process of delegitimizing the source begins to develop—and for a spokesperson, nothing can be more devastating to his or her effectiveness.

Even when accurate information was available, it was not always disseminated. Officials at the Central Bureau of Statistics complained regularly that even they were not being given the statistical material the Defence Ministry was bound to supply to it. The military spokesmen were unable to provide comprehensive background materials because, in part, the Defence Ministry had failed to commission any independent academic analyses of the situation in the occupied territories during the previous decade. What printed background material there was, was either patently propagandistic or totally out-of-date and irrelevant to the events taking place.

Not knowing what to do and locked in their preconceptions, senior army officers abdicated responsibility for trying to develop a coherent press strategy. That meant that junior officers often took upon themselves the responsibilities for deciding media policy. As mentioned before, blan-

[6]Raanan Gissin, interview with author, July 1989.

ket authorizations were given to junior officers at roadblocks permitting them to decide whether to close off an entire area to media coverage. But there are examples in other areas, too. I once called the spokesman for the civil administration in the West Bank, Captain Olivier Rappowicz, and asked for the statistics on the number of Palestinians who had requested permits for family reunions. I had an old number and knew that it needed updating. I called almost every day for more than two weeks, but each time was put off. Finally Rappowicz told me, "I have the figures, but I won't give them to you because I don't think it is in the interests of the state."

The main body mandated by the Israeli government to gather intelligence in the occupied territories is the *Shabak*. As noted, however, the *Shabak* had been devastated by revelations that it had lied continuously to the courts and by the subsequent departure of many of its most senior officials. It also had lost some of its best agents when the Israeli military headquarters in Tyre, Lebanon, had been blown up several years earlier. Morale was low. More important, *Shabak* operatives had been trained primarily for work in counterterrorism. That is a task that involves seeking out and destroying small armed cells by the use of informants, interrogations, and modern forensic science. In the initial stages of the intifada, the *Shabak* was totally unprepared to deal with a mass popular uprising where there were no obvious or even apparent leaders and planners, and where the protagonists' weapons of choice were rocks and firebombs, which leave neither fingerprints nor cartridge casing marks.

The police were similarly ill equipped. Police riot-control measures are based on the concept of patrol and reinforcement. That is, police officers patrol their beats, and when anything happens, they call in the reserves. Like the military, they are direct participants, with their own agenda and reputations to protect. Police officers everywhere tend to avoid publicizing anything that will cast them in a negative light. And in situations of civil disobedience, where there usually are provocations of some sort from both sides, their one-sided reports of events must be suspect. It was not the Israeli police, for example, that publicized the cases in which border police officers put Palestinian youngsters on the hoods of their jeeps to act as live shields from stone throwers. Moreover, clarifying material with the police was particularly difficult for some reporters, because the police spokesman spoke no English.

In some particularly controversial cases, the police were forced to deal openly with issues raised by the press or by Palestinians. Special debriefings of police officers or the appointment of a special investigator were, on occasion, decided on. But by the time these debriefings were over, or the special investigator's report was in, journalists' deadline times had passed; and while the allegations, true or false, may have made the front page, the delayed, considered, verified response usually ended up on the back pages—if it was printed at all. "The hardest thing about covering this story," says the *Toronto Star*'s Gordon Barthos, "is that so many events were actually continuing stories. What you see as truth the first day, changes day by day. And by the time all the facts have come out, the full story may not even get into the paper because people are already bored with it."

Undoubtedly the most valuable information-gathering apparatus the Army Spokesman's Office could have employed was the regional military commands. The major generals commanding these units were in charge of all day-to-day operations within their territories, and all communications and intelligence data flowed through their communications centers. During the intifada, the central and southern commands were the army's field action centers. However, the generals in charge of these commands were loathe to pass on the information they had. Although an Army Spokesman's Office representative was posted to each command headquarters, that representative was, in effect, subordinate to the territorial commander. The IDF spokesman is only a brigadier, while the territorial commander is a major general.

The territorial commanders are among the most powerful men in the Israeli army structure. Each is subordinate only to the chief of staff and each views himself as a potential candidate for the army's top job. Traditionally, each has always used his access to the local media to promote his personal ambitions. Often, these generals have courted favorites among the local press to act as personal publicists and have used the local press to protect themselves from public attack. "They believe that information is power," says one senior Israeli army officer, "and they are not about to let any information out of their control."

Thus, when the IDF spokesman tried to create a single information center to coordinate the flow of data to the press about the intifada, it collapsed within weeks of being established. Three main reasons can be given. The first is that, unbelievable as it may seem, the army itself had no central intelligence-coordinating committee to process the data coming in from the occupied territories. Any coordination was ad hoc, dependent on the willingness of one officer to pick up the telephone and speak to another. In at least one case, in Gaza, a young officer did not pass on information to his command headquarters because he did not want his unit to look bad. The group of soldiers had been involved in scuffles with Palestinians, and the officer did not want to appear as though he and his men were not keeping his area of responsibility quiet.

The second reason is that the territorial commanders were reluctant to provide the center with the information that was to be the center's raison d'être and life's blood. They preferred to decide for themselves what to pass on and whom to pass it to. Says one frustrated senior official in the Defence Ministry: "They [the generals] are convinced that their tactics [of information handling] constitute a [media] strategy."[7]

A third reason for the collapse of the army's information center is that Israeli intelligence-gathering doctrine was inadequate to cope with a popular uprising. In a situation like a wide-scale rebellion, every action, every sound, every unusual sight is a potential source of information. Journalists are trained to look for these kinds of signs. The average soldier is not. As a result, although relatively few in number, television camera crews often were able to scoop the army on major stories, simply because they were much more aggressive in their information gathering.

In a number of documented cases, journalists, and particularly camera crews, were able to reach the scene of an incident long before the army did. These successes led some Israeli political leaders to charge that the press had been told in advance about the incident—and thus were accomplices. In most cases, however, it was simply a matter of quick thinking on the part of the press. A gunshot would be heard in a place like Bethlehem, and a camera crew nearby would rush to the spot—not needing to query superiors first or to get orders. In the village of Beita, where Palestinians assaulted a group of Israeli hikers on April 6, camera

[7]Interview with author, July 1989.

crews had to inform the army of the incident. The NBC crew had decided
to go there after seeing a convoy of Arab ambulances, sirens screaming,
racing down the highway. The convoy went through several army check-
points, but no one had thought of ordering those manning such check-
points to report unusual actions like the sight of a group of ambulances
and television camera crew cars all racing in the same direction.

Personal inadequacies and sheer miscomprehension of news management are nonetheless insufficient to explain all of the generals' actions.
Dealing with the intifada was as unpopular among senior officers in the
army as it was among large segments of the Israeli population. The army
resented being placed in the position of being policemen and of having
to ward off and to control rebellious civilians. A senior Defence Ministry
official noted after the intifada had been under way for eighteen months:
"We are still not organized. There is still a feeling in the army that this
is not our war."

Almost from the onset of the demonstrations, the general staff also
was saying both publicly and privately that the only solution to the uprising
was a political one. The senior officers argued that all they could do was
contain the rioting, not resolve the political and social problems that had
led to it. They were hypersensitive to the possibility that the politicians,
unable or unwilling to resolve the crisis by political means, would lay the
blame for the continued violence on the army. One senior officer told
me, "This is war. But it is the most political war in our history." By
"political," he was referring to both domestic and international politics.

Eventually, the generals' fears were confirmed when people like the
then Trade and Industry Minister Ariel Sharon claimed that he (who had
created the Lebanese debacle) could put down the rioting. Others, particularly those of the Right, kept trying to skewer the army for not acting
more harshly. "We cannot allow the IDF to be dragged into the political
arena," a senior Israeli army officer told me, almost in despair. "The
army is more than just the intifada. It is central to the existence of the
country."

The Israeli army's response to its discomfiture was to begin to close
large areas of the occupied territories to press coverage. The closures began
in January 1988 in Gaza and continued apace. There were many, including Henry Kissinger, who argued that the occupied territories should
have been shut down completely to allow the army a free hand—as the

British did during the recapture of the Falkland Islands and the United States did during the invasion of Grenada. But the situations in Grenada and the Falklands can hardly be compared to those in the Israeli-occupied territories.

To begin with, neither the West Bank nor Gaza is an island. They are geographical entities that are contiguous with Israel. They are the creations of war and politics, not nature. There are no sharp geographical or geological markers that set Jerusalem off from the West Bank, or Ashkelon from the Gaza Strip. The army did attempt to turn large areas of the occupied territories into islands by declaring them closed military zones. Nonetheless, enterprising journalists had little trouble avoiding roadblocks in order to get stories in villages that had been put under siege and curfew by the Israeli army. Unlike Grenada and the Falklands, journalists could not be sequestered permanently on ships. Although many Palestinian towns and villages did have their telephone lines cut off for days and weeks at a time, I suspect that had such cutoffs been massive and extended, large media organizations would have circumvented that problem by the use of some new technology, as they had when they introduced super-8 video cameras.

Second, even with the boycott of Israeli goods and the frequent strikes by Palestinians, the occupied territories remain highly dependent on the Israeli economy, and vice versa. There was daily interaction. Palestinians kept coming to work in Israel and were available for interviews. Israeli- and Palestinian-owned trucks had to bring in supplies to even the most remote villages, and, in a time of need, the drivers also could have been sources of information. Another continuing source of news material was the corps of Israeli army reservists that was rotated regularly through the occupied territories. Almost all of these reservists had stories to tell after their tours of duty, and many, after they came home, felt an almost compulsive need to vent their feelings and describe their experiences.

No less an opening to the flow of information was provided by the Jewish settlers. They needed to get to their jobs in Israel and also were trying to encourage friends and relatives to visit their enclaves. They therefore demanded that the roads be left open. Moreover, they had their own agendas that they wanted covered by the media, and this meant maintaining contact on a regular basis.

Journalists also had access to foreign humanitarian organizations working in the occupied territories, and the press was quite willing to use material from these sources. As can be seen, with so many sources available, it easily would have been possible to construct a collage of events taking place in the occupied territories even if all of those areas had been besieged.

A third distinguishing feature is that most Israelis are deeply proud of the fact that they are the single democracy in the Middle East. Extensive restrictions on the press undoubtedly would have brought protests from civil liberties organizations and led to petitions to the Supreme Court. It is not inconceivable that such protests would have set the stage for a battle the Israeli government has been trying desperately to avoid—a full-scale debate on national values and on the national self-image. Such a debate could not have but polarized the country even more.

And finally, Israel needs the foreign press corps for its own purposes. It remains highly dependent on the United States for economic and political support. Much of that support has been based on congressional premises and perceptions that Israel is a free and democratic state with many of the same values and legal protections for free speech that Americans enjoy. Massive restrictions on the movement of the press and a large-scale campaign for open coverage by U.S. correspondents undoubtedly would have shaken Israel's image in the United States.

Jordan, a minor but significant player in the past, was stunned into inaction by the intifada. It already was suffering from severe domestic problems of its own, including a major economic crisis that had been building for years. Once its leaders recovered their wits and had assessed the situation, they wanted to place as much distance as they could between the events in the territories and the difficulties at home. If the Israelis could not put down the uprising neatly and firmly, Amman wanted no part of the action. The threat of social unrest caused by the country's economic problems, and the threat of Palestinian Islamic fundamentalist and nationalist violence slopping over from the occupied territories, eventually led King Hussein to withdraw from the occupied territories and from the media marketplace.

In any marketplace, when established participants weaken and falter, there always will be light-footed entrepreneurs, looking for toeholds and niches, ready to take the place of slow-moving heavyweights. In the intifada marketplace, it was the Jewish settlers in the occupied territories and their political and ideological allies who eventually took on that role. Initially, their attitude to the media was hostile but passive. They were available to the press for interviews—and individual settlers did provide often angry and dramatic statements that were juxtaposed against those made by the Arab youngsters—but as an organized group, they did not seek out foreign journalists. It was only several months into the uprising that the coalition began launching an aggressive media campaign of its own. With the official Israeli media machine in a shambles, the settlers quickly found a niche.

The settlers already had an extensive infrastructure for dealing with journalists. Most of the settlers' organizations had had years of experience in working with the Israeli media and were well acquainted with the press's needs. Many of the settlers had been raised in the United States and understood the nature of American media outlets. Their message was simple and unambiguous, and their statements easily could be broken up into radio and television sound bites. They produced handbills and press releases, appointed public relations officers, organized demonstrations of their own and trips to their settlements, and, of particular importance, were able and willing to supply English-speaking interviewees. At a later stage, they also joined the new information age by creating their own videos and even a computer game.[8]

Surprisingly, with the exception of a few large-scale demonstrations by the Peace Now organization, there was no equivalent response from the Israeli Left—even though the Left had as large and sophisticated a

[8]The computer game, appropriately titled "Intifada," was an extraordinarily inventive use of the new technologies and a superb example of how modern communications techniques can bypass traditional information conduits and distribution systems. The cost of producing the game, with its simple animation, was relatively cheap. Since Israeli children regularly pirate computer games, they acted as the primary distribution system. Repetitive political messaging was assured at no cost so long as the players' interest remained engaged. The cast of characters was made up of real people, known to the players, and included many of the best-known figures in the Israeli political scene. The game pitted Israelis, armed with such devices as tear gas and rubber bullets, against *keffiyeh*-draped Palestinians throwing rocks and Molotov cocktails. The political message was clear and simple: if the player does not disarm and collect the Palestinians, he or she is killed and, according to a graphic message, becomes "yet another victim of Arab terror."

media infrastructure as did the settlers. As a result of all of their activities, the settlers, although a tiny minority of the Israeli population, often were able to present themselves in the press as the vanguard of a large and rapidly growing constituency.

The PLO, caught by surprise by the uprising, was also a relative latecomer to the marketplace. As incompetent as the Israeli news managers may have been, the PLO officials were even more so, and as many mistakes as the Israelis may have made in dealing with the press, the PLO made even more. While the Palestinians in the occupied territories may have been naive and unschooled in dealing with the media, they were intelligent and quick learners. The PLO chieftains sitting in Tunis showed that they had learned nothing and forgotten nothing during their years of struggle, and were not about to change.

As had happened so often in the past, the first concern of the ex- patriate leaders was to try to reassert control over the residents of the occupied territories. The greatest fear of the expatriate leaders had always been that a local, independent leadership would evolve that would then pose a challenge to their own hegemony. Using threats, they made it plain that they would not tolerate independent political action by local Palestinian leaders or the formation of an indigenous political body that might negotiate with the Israelis. They demanded from the territories' Palestinian occupants a monolithic response that the PLO was their only legitimate representative and that only it could talk on their behalf—even when this was to the detriment of the Palestinians' political objectives.

A significant example of this came in mid-February 1988. The local Palestinians had by then achieved successes beyond their wildest dreams. Media coverage of the intifada, particularly scenes of Israeli soldiers beat- ing Palestinians, had created an atmosphere in Washington that was im- pelling the Reagan administration to act—or at least to appear to be doing something—to halt the bloodshed. For years, the Palestinians had been trying to entice the United States into intervening in the dispute on their behalf. A long-sought window of opportunity finally had been created by the young rock throwers.

In mid-February, the State Department announced that Secretary of State George Shultz would try to meet with a group of local Palestinian leaders during a trip to Israel in early March. After intense negotiations between the U.S. consulate general in Jerusalem and many local Palestinian leaders, the local leaders announced that they would not meet with Shultz—apparently because of pressure from the PLO expatriates. This refusal might have worked to the PLO's advantage had the organization been able to step in immediately with a coherent political strategy of its own that would have drawn media and diplomatic attention. But that was not to be. Internal battles for power within the PLO and the ever-present need to subordinate the needs of the Palestinians in the occupied territories to those of the expatriate constituency precluded any imaginative political move of the sort that would have carried the story and the events ahead to a new plane. From that moment on, the intifada began to die. A month later, media attention began to wane because the story had become repetitive, with no advance in the plot and no conclusion in sight.

The PLO's single-minded drive for control strangled the intifada. Under any other circumstances, the focus of media attention would have changed over time to deal more intensively with the internal political conflicts in the occupied territories that arose out of the opportunities the intifada had created. By quashing public dissent among the secular nationalists, the PLO effectively destroyed the momentum the media story had developed. The story in the occupied territories where the foreign press was concentrated and available failed to rise above the plane of violence. After four or five months, the action story, with its daily deaths and woundings, became abstractions. Numbers replaced faces in the public mind. The story became homogenized, and the human narrative of internal conflict, of having to choose options and priorities, of facing fears and shattered dreams, of exhilaration in renewed success, were all lost. With no political movement, the violence became mere background noise. The Palestinians lost the ability to influence events in Israel and in the United States. The window of opportunity was lost.

The PLO leadership in Tunis, geographically isolated from both the real action and the foreign media coverage of the events, did try to respond by attempting to force its way onto the screen and into the newspapers. But their attempts were pathetic at best and their "successes" momentary and usually counterproductive. The expatriates believed that they had to show the world that they were part of the action and that they could run the show. But what they demonstrated instead were mental impotence, a lack of political imagination, an insensitivity to the reality created by the Palestinians in the occupied territories, and that they had even fewer political goods to sell than did the Israelis.

As in the past, they tried to shift attention away from the occupied areas to sites where they could control events. That in itself was foolish, because the Palestinians in the occupied territories were waging a media war and had the attention of the world's press. Any action that did not push the political story forward (the only arena where the PLO leadership could intervene effectively) only diverted attention away from those who had become media stars. The expatriates' actions were the equivalent of a stage hand stepping before the lights during a highly emotional scene from a play and performing an amateurish song and dance act.

Possibly the best example of this foolishness occurred in early February 1988. The expatriate leaders decided to buy or to charter a boat to bring Palestinian deportees back to Israel. The idea was to try to steal an Israeli political and military symbol by re-creating the 1947 voyage of the *Exodus*—but with Palestinians instead of Jews as the stars of the show. As with so many revivals and remakes of once-successful dramas, this one was destined to flop. To begin with, the idea was unnecessary, because the local Palestinians already had captured the even more powerful Davidic symbol; and the remake of the *Exodus* plot only detracted from the locals' success. Second, it turned attention from the real battle in the occupied territories to Greece and Cyprus, from which the ship was to depart. Third, the negotiations to purchase or to charter a ship took more than two weeks, giving the Israelis plenty of time to react.

Finally, an old, decrepit ferry was found in Cyprus and the PLO announced that it soon would set sail with two hundred deportees, two hundred journalists, and two hundred guests. But on Monday, February 15, a blast under the waterline shook the ship as it was docked at the Cypriot port of Limassol, and the ferry sank. The great media drama ended ignominiously and quickly was forgotten.

Even less comprehensible was the decision to send a terrorist raiding party into Israel's Negev desert from Egypt on March 7. Among other things, the raiding party captured a bus taking workers—almost all women—to their jobs at the Dimona nuclear reactor. After the bus was halted by the police and the army, the terrorists shot one of their hostages.

A special antiterrorist squad stormed aboard, and when the shooting was over, the three terrorists and two more hostages were dead, and eight other hostages were wounded.

The raid had been a reversion to classic, but always unsuccessful, PLO terrorist military and media tactics. More than anything else, the raid demonstrated the organization's intellectual improverishment and how out of touch with reality its leaders were. The local Palestinians had succeeded in attracting world attention precisely because they deliberately had avoided using firearms. They knew that so long as they used only stones or firebombs, their Davidic image could remain intact—and it was that image that was their greatest continuing media resource. The introduction of firearms into the arena by the PLO, when combined with the organization's negative response to Secretary Shultz's proposals for negotiations, was a gift to the Israelis. Israel could discount the PLO once again as nothing more than a bunch of terrorists intent on Israel's destruction and certainly no reasonable partner to any talks.

In the kind of multidimensional, multifront war that was the intifada, the local Palestinians had captured both the media front and the symbolic front. The Israeli army was indisputably the superior military power. The only front open to the PLO was the political one. But rather than play to the Israelis' political weaknesses created by that society's deep divisions, the PLO—by staging the raid and thus reintroducing the subject of terrorism, which the Israelis had manipulated so well in the past—had played right into the Israelis' strengths.

Fortunately for Yasir Arafat, he had an ally in Defence Minister Rabin. The Israeli military began arresting anyone who appeared to have emerged as a genuine grassroots leader during the chaotic first weeks of the rebellion. Attempts by local leaders to establish autonomous "liberated" villages run almost entirely by and for the local residents, were crushed by the army. These villages and similar "neighborhood committees" in the larger cities and towns had been hothouses for independent political experiment—where the political wheel was being reinvented almost daily. This two-pronged attack on the local Palestinian leadership by the Israelis and the PLO was to have enormous consequences for the course of the intifada.

In my experience, "complete," satisfying news stories tend to go through six separate phases. A full description, understanding, and documentation of each stage is the prerequisite for passing into the next one. Initially, stories usually are *events-driven*. Foreseen and unforeseen occurrences create public interest and questions. The media consumer is drawn in as a spectator. If the events have created enough interest, the story becomes *topic-driven*. Journalists try to put the events into some overall context and to explore their background and details of the events. Once there is sufficient detail, journalists usually decide whether they and their audiences have a stake in the outcome of the scenario, and the news then becomes *interest-driven*. By this point, the audience becomes a part of the process, not merely an idle bystander. After the audience's interests are explored in depth, the other possible partners and actors are examined for their motives and interests. The summation of all of these interests is then put into a single common frame, and the story becomes *issue-driven*. Options and priorities are examined for their implications. Accurate framing of the issues then usually leads to public and media demands for solutions, and the story becomes *resolution-driven*. The public and the media become active participants in the process. The final phase, *anniversary-* or *memorial-driven* stories, comes after solutions are found and implemented, and there is a search for the lessons that can be derived from the decision-making process.

The speed of passage through each phase of the cycle varies from story to story and from culture to culture. Each story requires a different amount of knowledge and experience on the part of the actors involved. But if the drama is to maintain its momentum, those involved must appear to strive to take it to its next phase. Their very struggle is an intimate part of the story. If this perception of struggle is not present, public interest is lost. Pacing is crucial.

The intifada died as a strong, continuing story because it never got beyond the second phase. The Palestinians in the Israeli-occupied territories could not or would not press the story beyond the events-driven violence and their explanation of what led to it. It was at this critical moment that they broke with the early Zionist model they had copied successfully up to that time. The Zionists living in British mandatory Palestine, although they were a decided minority of the world's Jews and were heavily dependent on world Jewry for funds, were willing nonetheless to ignore entreaties for caution and much of the political advice voiced in the Jewish diaspora. They were unwilling to allow their fate to be decided by those living abroad. The Palestinians in the occupied territories were unwilling to go it alone and remained tied to false hopes that their interests would take prime place in the PLO's agenda.

The PLO's expatriate leadership would not allow its interests to be compromised in any way by the Palestinians in the occupied territories. It was unwilling to address Israeli interests in a substantive and meaningful way and thus lay out issues for public debate. The press became tired of waiting for the next phase to begin, and its interest shifted elsewhere— to stories with greater public appeal.

No marketplace can survive for long on a single product, and such was the case with the intifada. The media marketplace is no different from any other. As Henry Kissinger and Anwar Sadat demonstrated vividly, the market demands a constant stream of new ideas and new concepts to maintain momentum. The spangles of continued violence can keep international interest only for so long. For media consumers, watching or reading about violence is a kind of behavioral training that eventually inures us to the real human suffering involved. We degenerate from being interested bystanders to being voyeurs. The PLO's inability to extricate itself from its old and bankrupt presumptions was the death knell for the intifada. The eventual tacit acceptance of Israel's right to exist extracted by the United States from Yasir Arafat that autumn with such obvious difficulty was too little, too late. By the fall of 1988, one year after it began, the fate of the intifada had been decided.

The Palestinians in the occupied territories had blundered into a great media victory. The Israelis had blundered into a great media defeat. And by their own selfishness and ineptitude, the PLO leaders had saved the Israelis from a disaster. The violence in the Israeli occupied territories continued and even intensified as the months passed. But it was no longer an intifada—a shake-up. The violence—more and more of it directed toward other Palestinians—became an outlet for rage that Israel and the PLO had tacitly, but nonetheless effectively, conspired to reintroduce monopolistic controls and to create a new political status quo in the occupied territories.

Visions of Reality

Few media events in recent history, and certainly few foreign media events, have been as heavily scrutinized and criticized as was the press's coverage of the intifada. Television in particular was singled out by pro-Israeli media watchers for what became a torrent of public wrath. The sense in a majority of these allegations was that Israel somehow had been "had" deliberately by this medium—or at the very least, had been treated unfairly. Unbridled emotional charges of bias and distortion abounded, and there were even suggestions that anti-Semitism or anti-Zionism underlay all of the reporting on television.

Many Israelis, especially those on the political right, who preferred to ignore the basic social, political, and economic reasons for the uprising, even went so far as to claim that television was directly responsible for much of the rioting that swept the occupied territories. As early as December 23, 1987, less than two weeks after television coverage of the intifada had begun, Avi Pazner, Prime Minister Yitzchak Shamir's press adviser, castigated the American television networks for their performance. After the United States had condemned Israel for using excessive force to quell the riots, Pazner stated, "It just proved that the United States does not exactly understand the situation here. Maybe the impact of all the television reporting led some people to interpret the situation incorrectly."[1] Two days later, he was more virulent. In a front-page interview with the *Washington Post's* Glenn Frankel, he inveighed against what he termed "deliberately distorted and one-sided" reporting and accused television in particular of "blatant bias." Pazner, who had not been out in the field to see for himself what was going on, soon was joined in his condemnations by a host of Likud politicians whose only connection with the occupied territories were visits to Jewish settlements, and by a large number of Jewish critics in the United States who were safely ensconced seven thousand miles away from the scene of events.

Ill equipped and ill prepared to handle a mass uprising, many Israeli officials quickly took up Pazner's clarion call as an outlet for their frustrations. By the end of December, for example, the Israeli army began restricting the movement of foreign television camera crews in the occupied territories, believing that the very presence of these crews incited disturbances.

From the outset, little hard evidence was brought forth to substantiate the allegations made against television. With hindsight, it is quite evident that much of the criticism was knee-jerk in nature, a reaction to the unpleasant images television news teams had brought into American living rooms. A careful study of the nightly newscasts in the United States proves fairly conclusively that there was no universal, overt anti-Semitism or anti-Zionism in the coverage by those American television reporters who had been posted permanently to Israel. To be sure, there were reportorial excesses and errors, and personal impressions did become a very important part of their coverage. But to err is human; and it is impossible to demand and vastly unfair to ask anyone confronting a powerful news event to be

---

[1]Thomas L. Friedman, "Israeli Rebuts U.S. Charges That It Used Excessive Force," *New York Times*, 24 December 1987, p A6.

neutral and to sterilize his or her own moral beliefs. Reporters would be less than human if they did not give vent to disbelief when a government official is lying blatantly, or outrage at the sight of a man being beaten almost senseless while his hands are tied behind his back.

Nonetheless, a detailed analysis of the evidence also points to one irrevocable conclusion: that there is considerable and legitimate justification for the disquietude many American television viewers felt about what they were seeing on their screens, even if they could not articulate the cause of their anger in anything but a press-bashing diatribe.

Television certainly was not responsible for the outbreak of the violence. The television news divisions did, however, become active participants in shaping public perceptions of the conflict and even of some of the events that ensued. They did so not on the basis of the merits of the claims of the two sides, but as a result of the ruling conventional wisdom among the medium's practitioners of what television news ought to be. If there was a "blatant bias," it was one in favor of what television believes it can and ought to do—free of any restraints it does not choose to take upon itself.

A quick look at the historical record of the early stages of press coverage of the uprising is very revealing. The wire services treated the first reports of rioting with considerable caution and certainly did not blow them out of proportion. The permanent reporters for the *New York Times* and the *Washington Post*, arguably the two most influential newspapers in the United States, were out of the country, and their editors initially relegated the isolated bouts of violence in Gaza and the West Bank to the back pages. By this time, commercial radio, the broadcast medium's equivalent of tabloid journalism, had become almost irrelevant as a vehicle for influencing the activities and perceptions of government policymakers. Nevertheless, by December 16, only one week after the demonstrations had begun and only five days after television had begun to cover the story, White House officials felt compelled to condemn the Israelis' use of force.[2] Almost singlehandedly, television had forced the events in the occupied territories to the forefront of the international political agenda and the news agenda of all of the other journalistic media. The reaction of my own foreign editor probably was representative of the reaction of most

[2]ABC News, 16 December 1987.

U.S. television viewers. On December 17, he called me up and asked, "Do you know what I saw on television last night?" I, of course, had not seen the U.S. television broadcasts, but his tone of voice, filled with amazement and shock, was indicative of the impact the pictures from the field had had in Washington. Television news understood that it had achieved a notable level of power, and it began to use that influence without regard to the consequences to any of the other parties involved.

Thereafter, and for months to come, television would play a major role in shaping U.S. government and public attitudes toward the conflict. As a shaper and not merely a recorder of events, television news wielded very considerable power, not the least of which was its ability to impel Secretary of State George Shultz to try a series of abortive missions to the Middle East. However, unlike those governmental institutions that are constitutionally assigned the role of making public policy, television took no operational responsibility for the events it helped set in motion and it was accountable to no one for the results. For that reason, its actions and its guiding ethos deserve special scrutiny.

Television's performance during the intifada was not an isolated event. It was merely an extended and documentable case in point of how it regularly uses its enormous influence. Like computer hackers, many television news practitioners are enthralled by the technical possibilities of the medium and the artifices available to the image manipulator, but they are oblivious to the moral and political implications of such manipulation. Others, as Peter Jennings, for example, demonstrated during the intifada, are both aware of the implications and use the medium to pursue personal political agendas.

Therefore, the most disturbing questions raised by television's participation in the uprising have implications that go far beyond the narrow confines of the rebellion itself. They penetrate to the heart of fundamental issues about the nature of modern public policy making in democratic societies and how, to a remarkable degree, our perceptions of the world around us can and are being manipulated. The questions are unsettling, but some of the answers are positively frightening.

Television draws its power to shape perceptions from its ability to manipulate images. Beginning with our prehistoric forefathers, images, whether cave paintings, frescoes, or splashes of colored oils on canvas, have had a unique hold over humankind. We build museums to enshrine and protect them; and generations of supplicants have stood in awe of their beauty and the messages they have transmitted across the centuries. Each period in human history has been accompanied by a refinement in the production of images and in their producers' understanding of how to create them so that they will have the greatest impact possible on those who view their work. The uses of form, color, light, and shape have been the subject of intense study for centuries.

Television in general, and television news in particular, draws on this rich legacy in almost all aspects of its daily work. The technical, but not necessarily the moral, lessons taught by Rembrandt, Turner, and Picasso permeate television's daily fare. However, with the advent of new and ever more sophisticated technologies, television has been able to elevate the craft of manipulating images to a previously inconceivable level. In so doing, it has created a means for mass subliminal communication that it now uses regularly to help set the American political agenda. How it created this tool and what it did with it during the intifada is my focus here.

It is unfortunate that social scientists in academia stopped investigating the subject of subliminal messaging in the 1960s. Their justification then was that they could find no causal relationship between the message and subsequent actions by test subjects. Subliminal messaging became a sort of academic black hole. In the meantime, though, television news practitioners and commercial advertising "spin doctors" have made major strides in manipulating images, with all too little public discussion of both the techniques and the implications involved. The failure to pursue this line of investigation is all the more surprising because those who depend on image manipulation for their careers and livelihood, like U.S. presidential candidates and their handlers, have talked quite openly about how they set out to alter public perceptions. Intentionally or not, consciously or not, television journalists have absorbed and adopted many of these techniques in their day-to-day work.

The modern craft of written journalism has always been accompanied by images, whether they were line drawings or lithographs commissioned to illustrate articles, potent caricatures that skewered politicians, or evocative photographs that could tell an entire story in one snapshot. These images, skilled in execution as they may have been, were static. Their creators could control only the space within the frame of the image. Television has the ability to magnify this message-sending power geometrically by controlling time—time as we perceive it to be, and the amount of time we are allowed to consider, absorb, and analyze each individual image as it is projected into our homes.

In a medium where, as Dan Rather puts it, "yesterday is ancient history and last week is forever,"[3] television's coverage of the intifada was an anomaly. It lasted for months and, for a foreign story in which the United States was only a supporting actor, produced an almost unprecedentedly large number of reports. News reports from Israel and the occupied territories were broadcast nightly in an almost unceasing stream. The intifada is therefore a unique opportunity to see how television, over time, uses the power at its disposal.

During the early stages of the intifada, television combined many of the special circumstances inherent in this particular uprising with the medium's ability to control perceptions of space and time in order to create an extraordinarily sophisticated and subtle language of images, one not even George Orwell prophesied. These "moving hieroglyphics" might best be described as "imagespeak." Through imagespeak, U.S. television was subliminally able to form and shape public perceptions about events and personalities in the Israeli-occupied territories and to influence the Reagan administration's policies in the Middle East.

Intifada imagespeak as a visual language was created from scratch within a remarkably short period of time—less than seven weeks. No less remarkable is the fact that each of the three main U.S. commercial television networks independently adopted virtually the same elements of "grammar" and the same "lexicon" of images at roughly the same point in time as the language evolved. The stages in the development of intifada imagespeak, as well as its format, form, and rules, can therefore be quite clearly defined.

Television news, as practiced today, is essentially a story-telling medium, with each report or chapter in an ongoing saga fashioned as a miniepic, complete with its own beginning, middle, and end. To cope

[3]Dan Rather, remarks delivered at the Joan Shorenstein Barone Center, Harvard University, January 1990.

with the limited amount of air time available to tell the tale and with the requirement that each episode be self-contained and self-sustaining, story lines invariably are kept simple. When possible, in order to grab viewers' attention, the events described are dramatic or emotionally charged. Protagonists, usually "victims"[4] or "movers and shakers," have to be easily identifiable to the audience. Moreover, each element or scene within the report must serve a specific purpose, either to move the story line along or to highlight a specific character trait. Images and sounds must be striking. Message-sending efficiency is the name of the game.

Intifada imagespeak met all of these criteria and in its most advanced form was an extraordinarily efficient story-telling device that operated on various levels of the viewers' conscious and subconscious at the same time. As with any language, to understand why it was so successful, one has to break it down into its constituent parts. Many of these constituent elements already were present when the uprising took place, and hence out of the immediate control of the storytellers. Others were the result of circumstances inherent in the dynamic of the rebellion. Still others, however, certainly were deliberate television-made creations—the combined work of television crews, reporters, editors, and producers.

The first element was the visual background to the scenes. Some television critics tend to ignore the impact background has. They see it as a video version of a stage tableau, filling in the empty spaces behind the actors. At least in the case of the intifada, nothing could be further from the truth. The backdrop to the rioting acted as a kind of sculpture with its own strong message-sending power. Most of the events described in the early television reports took place in the refugee camps, with their narrow alleyways and sharp, angular buildings. Unrelenting angularity, as we have learned from the cubists, has become an almost universal Western symbol for despair. The sharp-cornered buildings in the camps perfectly matched one of the major early themes of press coverage of the intifada: the anarchy and the sense of utter despair of the youngsters living in the camps.

No less important was the apparent texture of the buildings. The

---

[4]One fascinating study demonstrated that on the local newscasts of three network-owned television stations in New York City, human helplessness was a point of focus in 71.4 percent of the time devoted to news. See Grace Ferrari Levine, "Learned Helplessness in Local TV News," *Journalism Quarterly* 63 (1986):12–18.

surfaces of the homes in the refugee camps were all flat, devoid of the softness and the contrast between light and shadow that stucco or stone imparts. Invariably, when the living conditions of Jews and Palestinians were contrasted in television news pieces, the texture of the surroundings—hard-surfaced Arab-owned buildings surrounded by sun-baked streets, and soft-surfaced Jewish-owned buildings encircled by gently curving plants and lawns—was given considerable prominence.

Also, Palestinian buildings frequently fronted on narrow streets, creating a natural visual frame around the protagonists and the scenes where action was taking place. This frame, in turn, tended to narrow the area of a viewer's direct interest to the center portion of the screen where the confrontations between the Israeli soldiers and the demonstrators were occurring. In keeping with the requirement that visual images be as efficient as possible, the center of the frame invariably was filled with dramatic action of some sort.

Troops chasing the Palestinians into the distance became a well-used set-up shot for NBC. Similar shots of soldiers running or jeeps careening through the streets became common fare on the other networks. When shots were taken in narrow alleyways rather than on open streets, the frame, naturally, was wider and the center of action smaller. The smaller center of action, in turn, magnified the visual intensity of the confrontation, because the center of action was all the more contained and more concentrated.

The narrow streets influenced image production in other ways as well. Camera crews, fearful for their own lives from direct hits or ricocheted shots fired by Israeli soldiers, naturally stood behind the soldiers. The soldiers and their activities, because they were in the foreground, then became the focus of viewer interest. The Palestinians in the distance were more blurred, smaller, and less colorful. The Palestinian youngsters were less recognizable as individuals. Their activities were less apparent. Less viewer attention was focused on them. And so they appeared less dangerous or threatening than the Israeli soldiers occupying the foreground. Their stones flying past at high speed and at a distance were barely caught by the camera. The camera shots of Israeli soldiers in the foreground firing tear gas canisters with long, slow, white, arching, gaseous curves in the sky, especially when accompanied by the crack of the tear gas gun being fired, inevitably became far more prominent and far more aggressive looking. Unlike the rock throwing, the long, white curve of the tear gas canisters also enabled viewers to absorb the impact of the scene. And because the soldiers were being photographed from behind or in middle distance, only their actions, not their emotions of fear or anger, could be recorded. They thus became objects rather than individuals motivated by some sort of human feeling.

Medium and foreground shots of Palestinians could be taken only during periods when the Israelis did not intervene and the camera crew could position itself out of range of the flying stones or slingshots; or if the camera crew by chance was suddenly caught unawares by a flanking movement by one of the parties and found itself in the crossfire; or if the Israelis captured a Palestinian or beat him within range of the camera lens. Under those circumstances, the camera usually was facing them head-on or at a slight angle, and thus the Palestinians' emotions, as seen in their facial expressions and body motions, were very strongly conveyed.

This visual and thematic contrast between the large Israeli soldier and the smaller Palestinian was compounded by a phenomenon of which every amateur photographer in the Middle East is aware. Shots taken between the hours of 10:00 A.M. and 2:00 P.M. tend to be bleached by the intense sun as it moves almost directly overhead. A typical day of rioting would begin at about 7:30 A.M., when the youngsters would gather to work themselves up for their day's activities. By about nine, the chants would begin, and by ten or eleven o'clock, the first confrontations would take place. The effect of the hour of the confrontation on the message of the image was potent. The buildings that formed the frame were bleached of whatever color they had, making them look like a mere jumble of concrete and cement, therefore adding to the sense of despair and waste-land. More than that, however, pictures of the Palestinian activists in the distance also were bleached. The strong green and deep-blue colors of the Israeli army and police uniforms made the viewer's eye focus even more on the activities of the Israelis. Metaphorically, the orderly uniforms and the heavy equipment the soldiers carried, when contrasted with the often indistinct and mixed colors of the Palestinians' lightweight civilian clothing, served to emphasize the David and Goliath story line.

Technicalities such as these may not seem important, but they were used to considerable effect by the reporters and editors as they fashioned their reports. One striking example was a "Special Assignment" piece

done by Bill Blakemore of ABC.[5] The report contrasted the living conditions in the Khan Yunis refugee camp and a nearby Jewish settlement.
All of the shots in the camp were taken between ten and two o'clock. The
pictures in the camp, without exception, were all bleached and bare of
color, emphasizing the sense of desperation the refugees felt. By contrast,
all of the shots taken at the Jewish settlement were done after three in the
afternoon. The set-up shots of the settlement are full of rich orange,
brown, and green hues. The scenes inside the greenhouses were of brightly
colored flowers and deep-red tomatoes. The sidelight of the sun at this
hour made each home seem distinct, private, and secure. One did not
have to listen to the reporter, look at the contrast between the blank-faced
Palestinians and the smiling, rope-skipping Jewish children, or listen to
the hard-line political statements of the settlers and their disdain for the
Arabs to get the point of the report. The simple use of color said everything.
And for the color-blind, the texture of the surfaces of the surrounding
environment in the refugee camp (flat, hard cement walls, steps, and
street gutters) and the Jewish settlement (lush, open, grassy spaces, textured
walkways, and stucco houses) drove home the same message.

The elements that go into manipulating perceptions of space, while
used by the television news teams, were not entirely within their control.
The press did not choose when the Palestinians would march or throw
stones, nor did it significantly influence when the Israelis would coun-
terattack. It had no control over the effects of the sun or the construction
techniques and planning of the refugee camps. Television crews did not
create the open sewers on which they often focused, or the overcrowding
caused by rapid population growth. One of the most powerful and affecting
images from the early stages of the uprising, a shot of a Palestinian with
his hands tied behind his back being driven around Gaza on the bumper
of a command car because the soldiers inside hoped that he would shield
them from stone throwers, was not concocted by the television crews.[6]
Visual manipulation of space was confined largely to choosing and using
recorded images of the natural or manmade phenomena that already were
present, and to camera angles, traveling shots, pan shots, and other standard filmmaking techniques. Some of these basic techniques were used

[5]Bill Blakemore, ABC News, 14 January 1988.
[6]CBS Evening News, 14 December 1987.

to great effect as part of the language of imagespeak, but they were, in rhetorical terms, the equivalent of the bon mot or the well-chosen turn of phrase. Charges leveled by some Israeli officials that some camera crews actually staged events never have been substantiated.

What made many of the naturally found images so powerful in a finished report was, as in the case of the Blakemore piece, television's ability to control and to use elements of time to stunning effect. For if the elements of spatial control are the "letters" that make up imagespeak and the final single-frame pictures are the "words," then the use of time is its "grammar." Time provides the essential past, present, and future tenses of verbs, determines what is a subject and what is a predicate, and enables people to use linguistic devices like parallelism.

U.S. television first began covering the Palestinian uprising in depth on December 11, 1987, three days after the violence had begun. Only NBC got the time frame right. Dan Rather described it as the "fourth straight day of violence in the occupied territories," and Peter Jennings used the phrase "week of violence." Overall, these may be minor journalistic mistakes, but they had the effect of giving viewers the impression that what they were seeing was a story that already had been under way for a greater length of time than was the case. More to the point, the factual sloppiness was indicative of how fast and free television would play with the elements of time in support of its own agenda.

The primary element in this agenda is television news's belief that it must craft its reports as dramatic miniepics. As a medium, it is intoxicated with drama, and drama implies movement through both time and space. The manipulation of time is the glue that binds the individual images together, provides the essential element of change on which drama depends, and gives the entire story its shape and form. Most viewers are aware of the gross forms of time control—things like slow motion and freeze-frame stop action. But time control is used in many other ways as well.

Time control can be divided into three constituent parts: pacing, timing, and sequencing. Sequencing is the order in which individual scenes or events are portrayed. Timing involves deciding where an action sequence will be cut and the particular millisecond at which there will be a cut from one scene to another. Pacing is the length of time given to each shot or scene, both in absolute terms and in relation to other camera shots and other scenes.

Television news's concepts of pacing, timing, and sequencing have altered dramatically in the past decade and a half, largely through the influence of that most relentlessly efficient of all image manipulators, commercial advertising. In television commercial advertising, maybe more than in any other field of endeavor, time is money. Each second of air time can cost an advertiser thousands of dollars. Therefore, each image, each scene, each sequence of scenes must provide a measurable payoff to the person or organization putting up the money. As with its embracing of new technologies without forethought or analysis of the particular technology's long-term implications, so television news chose to adopt many of the techniques of commercial advertising without considering the journalistic implications of using commercial mass-marketing techniques. Many of those techniques and the rationale that lies behind them, if not antithetical to the traditional journalistic ethos, are at least askew with concepts of journalistic balance and fair play for the audience.

The Israelis, with their obsolete television technologies, with no experience in U.S.-style television commercials and no comprehension of the internal politics of the U.S. television networks, could not understand the ethos, the rationale, the techniques used, or the intent behind the reports. All Israeli officials could do in their ignorance was to cry *gevalt* and raise the hoary specter of bias and anti-Semitism as a war club against all television reporters. The Palestinians, who were stunned by their media coup, were equally ignorant and therefore didn't know how to capitalize on their success. The range of images they provided was so limited and eventually each core image was so overused, that in journalistic terms, these pictures ultimately became the video equivalent of, and as interesting as, Yasir Arafat's verbal clichés.

Undoubtedly, the most important change in the concept of time control in recent years has been the switch to ever shorter scenes and shots. Whereas in the 1970s, a single shot might last as long as twelve seconds or more and a statement by someone might be given up to a minute, today, a shot rarely exceeds five seconds and a sound bite is considered long if it goes on for more than twelve seconds. The technique was borrowed from commercial advertising and the intent behind this change was to speed up the pace of the report so that more shots and more visual information could be provided in the time allotted. The effect of this technique, however, is to deprive the audience of the time it needs to analyze the information it is receiving. There is enough time to absorb the impact of the visual message on a gut level but no time to question its meaning before a new shot is introduced.

To ensure that the intended message was being absorbed, television news adopted another technique from commercial advertising: repetition. Television also can control the number of times a viewer will see a particular shot or scene. Because today each scene is shorter, the same types of scenes with the same message can be repeated often in the same news report. In the case of the intifada coverage, the identical scenes (or ones very similar to them) were repeated in report after report, night after night. Contrary to the opinion of some academic analysts, repetition is not filler. It is an integral part of an overall concept of news presentation. Among other things, it reinforces the central theme of the news report and provides continuity between reports in the serial drama that is the essence of television reporting of a long-running event.

If one uses December 15, 1987—the night before the first criticism of Israel by White House officials, but before the major newspapers had begun to headline the uprising—as an example, one can see the following results. The ABC report from Gaza lasted a total of two minutes and twenty-three seconds. Of that, approximately half of the time—one minute and ten seconds—was given over to shots of violence. Nineteen separate shots of violence were shown, each averaging just over three seconds. On CBS, Dan Rather did a voiceover of satellite footage. In seventeen seconds, five separate shots of violence were shown. The NBC report lasted a total of three minutes and thirty-two seconds, of which one minute and thirty-seven seconds was given over to twenty separate shots of violence. Whatever the interviewers or the reporters said, the visual message was one of uncontrolled violence and anarchy. The result, as Peter Jennings reported the next night: "The White House has been unusually critical of Israel for the continued violence."

Yet another effect of this change in pacing and sequencing, and possibly one of the most dangerous in terms of viewer comprehension, is the compression of time and geography. Since scenes are relatively short, more shots from more places can be introduced into a single report. This can intensify the impression that a large number of events are taking place at the same time in a relatively small geographic area. The intifada was a widespread popular rebellion, but even at its height in the early weeks, no more than sixteen separate, significant violent clashes were taking place in a single day—out of a total of hundreds of towns and villages.[7] The concentration by television news on the most dramatic scenes of violence and the reporters' ability to show such scenes from three or four different locations gave the impression that, although in reality the events were taking place at often widely separated locations and at very different times of the day, the rioting was happening everywhere and that it was happening at the same time. When time and space bearings are withdrawn in a report such as this, the result is viewer disorientation—a further obstacle in the path of an audience's ability to comprehend what is going on, to put the events being shown into some sort of context, and to consider the implications of the images being shown.

A true victim of this kind of reportage is historical time—that is, how a particular event or image stands in relationship to a similar event or image that has preceded it. The network news teams did do several large historical pieces, especially around the time of Israel's Independence Day in April 1988, and there were references to history when themes like the future of the Gaza Strip, rather than a particular event, were being described. However, the individual events described daily rarely were put into a historical context. A good example occurred on December 24. All three networks did stories on Christmas under the uprising. CBS did two thematic stories that night, one a "situationer" on the West Bank and the other a story on U.S. reaction to the events in the occupied territories. The first piece required no historical context. The second made reference to how Israel had acquired the occupied territories as well as to the results of the Arab summit meeting the previous November. By contrast, ABC and NBC concentrated on the events of the day and made special note of the security precautions that had been put in place in Bethlehem. There were shots of helicopters flying overhead, body searches, and lots of soldiers. ABC's Dean Reynolds concluded, "It was that kind of Christmas," and NBC's Martin Fletcher noted that "Bethlehem looked like an armed camp." The impression viewers were left with was one of a new

---

[7]This information was collated from my own notes at the time.

situation in which the holy town had been somehow violated. The fact is, since the very beginning of the Israeli occupation, security in Bethlehem on Christmas Eve has always been very intense. The presence of metal detectors and large numbers of soldiers and border police is by no means unusual.

But words and grammatical rules do not a sophisticated, subtle language make. No efficient Western language is complete without its treasury of symbols and metaphors: the kinds of words, phrases, and sentences that can conjure up a wealth of meaning and understanding in a very limited period of time. And here, once again, television's control of time played a crucial role.

The use of symbolic language works only if those symbols relate to an audience's previous experiences. That is, the audience must be able to draw on a personal fount of knowledge to make sense of the symbol. And it takes time to build up that memory bank. Repetition of like or similar images, both within individual pieces and in reports broadcast over time, are crucial to this process. Repetition, in this sense, is not unlike schoolteachers' review sessions with students.

By Christmas 1987 and the arrival of the winter rains, the uprising had begun to wane somewhat. The Israelis had reacted with a series of tough measures, and the Palestinians were unsure what to do next and whether they could sustain the rebellion much longer. However, since the television networks already had geared up for the coverage, and since the period between Christmas and New Year is always accompanied by a drought of news from Western countries, it was inevitable that the stream of reports—on television, on radio, and in print—from the Israeli-occupied territories would continue unabated for at least ten days. This time delay in winding down the story had three immediate effects. One, it gave the Palestinians time to assess their situation and to plan future moves. Two, it gave all journalists a motive to keep active until the next major event occurred. And three, most important for the future of imagespeak, it enabled the television networks to continue building up the lexicon of images that soon would form the basis for intifada imagespeak's symbolic language. Oblivious to the broader implications of their actions, the Israelis extended and nurtured this critical gestation period by creating two major news stories. On December 27, they began holding trials for

Palestinians arrested during the rioting, and at the New Year, they decided on their policy of deporting Palestinians suspected of being ringleaders of the uprising. Both of these stories were to produce some of the most important images used in imagespeak.

The construction of the language and of its lexicon began in the very first days of the conflict, when both full reports and "outs" (tape that had not been used in reports) began to be squirreled away in the archives at the television news bureaus. In a long-running story like the intifada, the "outs" are often as important as the material that is used immediately. In that sense, they are not unlike a print reporter's notes. Not everything can find a place in a particular day's story. But if the material is inherently good, it can be pulled out later, when its use is more appropriate.

Initially, most of the images used in intifada-related news stories were illustrative, designed to complement the reporter's voice report. Almost immediately, they were supplemented by individual symbolic images that have widespread currency in Western nations. Shots of children with upstretched arms making a "V" sign with their fingers (a classic Western symbol of defiance) or open sewers (symbolic of poverty and downtrodden-ness) were commonly used in the early days of coverage of the rebellion.[8]

To these were soon added a series of oft-repeated images—tires burning in the middle of the road, shooting and stone throwing, the waving of Palestinian flags—symbolically meaning anarchy, conflict, and independence. Such simple, easily understood visual messages, what might be called standard imagespeak, form the core of most television reporting and were by no means unique to the intifada. During the uprising in East Germany two years later, the images of people dancing on the Berlin Wall and the wall being breached would play the same sort of symbolic role.

What was special about the intifada was that eventually, the networks were able to assemble and use a whole library of particularly evocative images that ultimately were elevated to the level of icons and emblems. Icons, as I use the term, are symbolic representations of themes and events.

[8]See, for example, CBS Evening News, 14 December 1987.

Emblems are images used to represent an idea that has no recognizable image of its own, or events that could not be captured by the camera because it was not there or because the event had not happened yet.

The development and use of such sophisticated techniques as icons and emblems that were unique to the intifada itself, and not merely part of the library of established Western representational images, was an extraordinary achievement. It was made possible only because the uprising's coverage went on long enough and the visually recordable activities of the main protagonists became so predictable. It was this development, in turn, that gave intifada imagespeak its true potency as a subliminal message-sending vehicle, and when developed in its advanced form, actually gave the television networks the ability to alter American policy toward the Israeli-Palestinian dispute.

Intifada imagespeak, as a language unto itself, appeared in its first primitive form on December 29, 1987. For the first time, NBC began what would become a regular occurrence: using file footage in place of material gathered that day without identifying it as such. It was a shot of a Molotov cocktail being thrown and the waving of a Palestinian flag (symbolic of the conflict and the Palestinian youngsters' independence) that had been used in a report the previous day. ABC adopted the practice of dropping the file footage identification a few days later, and CBS soon joined in. By dropping the identification, the networks were giving the image in question a sense of timelessness and a symbolic value that went far beyond its use as an illustration. The use of unidentified file footage by the networks has been ascribed by some critics to laziness on the part of reporters and tape editors, and by some news executives, to simple, innocent carelessness. But even if there was occasional carelessness or laziness—and I believe that these rationalizations cover only a small percentage of the numerous cases in point—the fact is that unidentified file footage images did become one of the main vehicles for the subliminal imaging that was such a formidable and fundamental part of intifada imagespeak.

I have called imagespeak "moving hieroglyphics," and in fact, the development of intifada imagespeak bears a striking resemblance to the historical development of Egyptian hieroglyphics. In the beginning, there were illustrative, easily identifiable images. Each image was a careful, literal representation of what was found in nature. In the case of television, illustrative images play a great number of roles. They are used to set a scene and give a definition of time and place. They illustrate points made in the reporter's text and highlight a particular point in what otherwise may be a confusing mass of data (freeze-frame and slow-motion techniques are particularly effective in this regard). They can be used to provide new information or reinforce the message of images presented before. And they can be used to send a covert message.

Over time, however, some images can and do take on a symbolic, not just a literal, meaning. This means that images can be strung together like words to form phrases, sentences, or full paragraphs. A good early example of this was a piece done by ABC's Dean Reynolds on January 4, 1988. It was about the Israeli government's defiant reaction to criticism of its decision to deport a group of Palestinians. The report began with a series of shots, each of which already had taken on a definite symbolic meaning. The piece opened with a shot of (1) burning tires and (2) stone throwers, then cut to (3) a boy waving and making a "V" sign, and then to (4) a road strewn with stones. The next shot was of (5) soldiers running down a street after a group of Palestinians and, finally, a shot of (6) a weeping woman. The reporter's text was almost superfluous. The images easily could be deciphered into: (1) the Palestinian uprising is still raging and (2) the Palestinian youngsters have not been cowed; (3) they remain defiant (4) in this war-torn wasteland (5) despite all of the efforts of the Israeli military; but (6) there are victims and there is pain.

As NBC's Martin Fletcher succinctly put it in a January 2, 1988, news report: "The image is the message. . . . Violence by Israeli soldiers against Palestinian youths, women, and children. It doesn't tell all the story, but it's what the camera focuses on."

One of the more fascinating aspects in the development of intifada imagespeak occurred when there was a conflict between the literal meaning of an image and its traditional Western symbolic meaning. Initially, for example, weeping Palestinian women were used to symbolize pain, peasant perseverance in the face of adversity, and that all-important television dramatic figure, the victim. But very soon into the intifada, the reporters found that women were taking a very active role, building roadblocks, breaking up stones for the boys to hurl, and even engaging in stone throwing themselves. They had become movers and shakers. For a while, in late December and early January, the television reports were using images of women in both symbolic roles[9] and even combining them in a single report.[10] But in a medium that lives off clear stereotypes and hates ambiguity, the two contradictory roles could not be represented by one image for long without turning into an absurdity. By January 8, Palestinian women had been most clearly categorized as movers and shakers.[11]

A new symbolic victim was required. The traditional Palestinian candidates for the role were unavailable. Children didn't fit the bill. They were rioting. The elderly couldn't be used, since they were not doing anything and nothing visual was being done to them. Those Palestinians killed by Israeli soldiers already had been elevated by their peers to the rank of martyr. The Palestinian laborers who had been working at menial jobs in Israel, and who earlier were prime candidates for the role of victim,[12] were obeying the calls for general strikes or even were being beaten by other Palestinians for trying to go to work in Israel.[13]

Fortunately for the networks, the Israelis rescued them again and handed them a new victim on a plate. In late January and early February, in an attempt to break a commercial strike called by the uprising's leaders, Israeli soldiers began smashing open the shutters of shops whose owners had refused to reopen under Israeli military orders.[14] It was one of the greatest reversals in the modern history of Western symbolic imagery. Established, financially secure middle-class men replaced peasant women as the symbol of the victim.

A similar, equally incredible reversal occurred on the Israeli side. In their search for fairness and parallelism, the networks needed an equally potent Israeli victim. Among the Israelis, there was as great a shortage of suitable candidates as there had been among the Palestinians, and ap-

---

[9]For example, on 5 January 1988, CBS and NBC portrayed women as movers and shakers for throwing rocks at Israeli soldiers, while ABC portrayed a crying woman as a victim.
[10]See CBS, 22 December 1987; and ABC, 31 December 1987.
[11]See ABC, January 8, 10, and 13, 1988; NBC, 9 January 1988; and CBS, 12 January 1988.
[12]See NBC, 18 December 1987; and ABC, 7 January 1988.
[13]ABC, 11 January 1988.
[14]The merchants' strike, first mentioned by NBC on January 14, became the subject of innumerable reports. The first reports on the Israelis using force to break open the shutters of the stores were on CBS and ABC on 17 January 1988.

parently by default, it was the young conscript soldiers who were chosen. They were portrayed as victims of their own government's policy.[15]

Another variant, usually found in background or special reports, compared and equated the actions of the Zionists of today to those of their former British colonial masters. In these reports, Israeli soldiers replaced British Tommies as the symbol of colonial overlords, and the Palestinians replaced the Jews as the downtrodden in search of independence and self-determination.

Yet another variant involved what might be termed "symbolic revisionism." In this case, the intended and previously accepted meaning of a particular image was "revised" by the reporter. What had been thought previously to be a "positive" image was cast in a "negative" light, or an image previously associated with a unique time and place was made to stand for a totally different time, place, and circumstance. This was a favored technique of ABC's Bill Blakemore, for example. In each of the pieces he did in January 1988, he took a classic Israeli symbol and either debunked its traditional meaning or used it to create a visual false analogy. His January 14 report comparing the living conditions of Israeli settlers with those of the refugees in Khan Yunis inverted Israel's classic symbol of "greening the desert" from a positive to a negative one. His "Special Assignment" report on January 21 turned yet another classic symbol, the forests Israelis had planted in the Galilee over the years, into a negative by highlighting the presence of the ruins of the Arab houses destroyed in the 1948 war of independence beneath the canopy of pines and in nearby fields. Symbolically, this meant that Israel's "redemption of the land" was predicated on the destruction of Arab villages and the dislocation of Arabs from their homes. It is perfectly legitimate and important for journalists and historians to review history in a cold light and to debunk myths or to add a codicil of truth to a symbol. The land used by the settlers might have been employed otherwise to reduce overcrowding in the refugee camps and even to provide some of the refugees with the means to make a living as farmers. Israel did bulldoze a considerable number of Arab villages in the early years of the state and refused to let Arabs return to others from which they had fled. This is not unlike reminding people

---

[15]The first portrayals of soldiers as victims occurred on ABC, 4 January 1988; NBC, 20 January 1988; and CBS, 29 January 1988.

that the so-called taming of the American West and the creation of the mythical, archetypal rugged individualist was done at the cost of tens of thousands of native American lives; that the "Last Spike," the completion of the Canadian Pacific Railroad, symbolizing the unification of the country, its territorial integrity, and its independence, was accomplished only by giving away millions of acres of land to foreign investors; or that the Magna Carta, Britain's symbol of individual freedom, applied primarily to the barons and left the majority of the commoners chained to medieval law and tradition, without what we today would call human rights. Nonetheless, when each piece a journalist does centers in some way or another around the debunking of a highly emotive and accepted symbol used constantly by a nation's citizens, one must question whether the intent was not to delegitimize the entity for which these symbols collectively stood—in this case, the State of Israel.

A January 29 piece by Blakemore went one step further in historical revisionism and symbolic-image inversion. It began with an interview with a holocaust survivor who stated, "I understand their [the Palestinians'] sufferings and I don't think they should suffer." The sound bite represented the emotions and convictions of many Israelis and many holocaust survivors. It was, however, recorded in front of the memorial to the holocaust at Jerusalem's Yad Vashem, where the murder of six million Jews is recorded in grizzly detail. The symbolic implication of the scene as recorded was that the suffering of the Jews during the holocaust and the suffering of the Palestinians under the Israeli occupation were comparable, even equatable, experiences.

Audiences for the evening television newscasts, tired from a long workday and preoccupied with eating or preparing dinner, do not devote their full attention to what is being shown. It is the rare viewer who records the news on a VCR for replay at a more convenient time. As a result, viewers absorb what is being shown but tend not to question what is being presented by the networks as fact. There is even less time or incentive to dissect the symbolic messages of the images being displayed. Thus, once again, time control of the hour at which the reports are aired also influences audience reaction to the images they are being shown.

Once images, and particularly symbolic images, become predominant in television news reports, a reversal in the nature of reporting takes place. When images are primarily illustrative, they serve and supplement the reporter's text. When they become the primary message senders, the reporter's text begins to become subservient to the images. And it is at this point that the reporter begins to lose control of the news report to the camera crew that produces the image, to the producers who collate the images, and to the tape editors who assemble them. A very good example of this loss of control occurred on January 4, 1988, when Peter Jennings, sitting in New York, narrated an entire piece about Israeli soldiers out on patrol in Gaza that day.

As the power to control the final product passes out of the hands of the reporters to the technical image manipulators and the "desk jockeys," several new phenomena take place. The first might be called the short-handing of the visual language, and its development is important particularly when the news item is a narrative. A single image can come to represent the entire story line, so that the basic thread of the narrative need not be repeated over and over again at length each time the storyteller or the audience takes a break. Initially, for example, television needed three images—a tire burning, an Israeli soldier firing a gun, and a Palestinian throwing stones—to represent the concept of conflict. By January 1988, it needed only a single icon, only one of those three images, to represent the same idea. Thus, for example, CBS correspondent Bob Simon's stand-upper on January 5, 1988—in which he said that the Israelis' plans for putting down the rebellion were "not going according to plan"—was done in front of a burning tire on a street. No other image was needed to accompany his text, and even the text was superfluous to the image-driven narrative.

The second phenomenon might be called layering. Images are created by camera crews and chosen by editors so that they will be multi-layered and act on the conscious and unconscious mind of the viewer at the same time. Layered images are the most potent form of visual subliminal message sending. The January 4 ABC piece on the Israeli foot patrol, for example, had a particularly evocative and multilayered shot. It was a traveling shot taken by the cameraman as the patrol was walking down a quiet Gaza street. It focused on a soldier whose gun was dangling from his shoulder. One of the phenomena of filmmaking is that three-dimensional scenes are flattened onto a two-dimensional surface. The loss of depth perception can distort the record of what actually took place. The angle chosen by the ABC cameraman was such that the end of the barrel of the gun appeared to be pointing at a Palestinian boy, when in fact, the gun was directed elsewhere. The overt message: young Israeli soldier out on patrol. The covert, subliminal message: Palestinians under the gun. This device and even this same piece of footage taken from the archive was used in several later ABC reports.

Layering was prevalent particularly in emblematic shots—pictures that were used to represent ideas or events for which no footage was available. For example, when Israel decided to implement its policy of deporting Palestinian activists, no shots were available to illustrate the idea. Those scheduled for deportation were behind bars and out of sight, and since the event had not yet taken place, there was no actual event footage that could be used. To compensate, all three networks dug into their archives and chose similar footage to use as an emblem. It was taken on December 28, 1987, in Nablus, when the Israelis began their trials of Palestinian rioters. ABC, for example, on January 12 and 13, chose a layered shot of a blindfolded, handcuffed Palestinian. The covert, subliminal message: Palestinians (and especially those chosen for deportation) are helpless before Israeli military and bureaucratic power.

A third phenomenon that may occur when reporters lose the power to control the final product is that they become so overpowered by the images they are dealing with that they begin to use false analogies in their text, they try to compete with the power of the images by creating text that is a verbal caricature of the picture, or they simply end up talking gibberish.

Although all of the television reporters fell into one or more of these traps at one time or another—each, for example, compared the violence to "the Wild West"—CBS reporters seem to have been the most susceptible to all three. Bob Simon, for example, excelled in the use of false analogies. To take but a few instances: on December 23, he described the barbed-wire fence that was created in the wake of the Israeli-Egyptian peace agreement and that separates Egypt from the Gaza Strip as "the Palestinian Berlin Wall." On January 10, in noting the presence of Israeli armored personnel carriers in Gaza, he stated that "Gaza is beginning to look like the Golan Heights." And in a description of a clash in Gaza on January 15, he claimed, "It looked like Beirut."

Simon also produced a considerable amount of verbal caricature. For example, in a piece done on January 20 that was full of some of the most potent images produced during the early stages of the intifada, he described the scene of an Israeli policeman firing tear gas as "curfew by canister—gas the whole neighborhood." A camera shot of a merchant's shutter being pulled off its hinges by an Israeli jeep was labeled "Israel's open-door policy." An ice-cream seller in Ramallah who was forced to open his shop in winter even though no one in the city buys ice cream at that time of year was called "the Good Humor man." Refugee camps in Gaza under curfew, jammed with people being kept indoors or on their roofs or balconies, were described as "ghost camps." And over a shot of women hurrying across a field during a break in the curfew to get fresh vegetables, he described the scene as "women fleeing across fields to find food. That, too, is Israeli strategy. Keep them home. Keep them hungry."

A CBS parachutist, Martha Teichner, apparently absolutely overwhelmed by the images she was seeing and dealing with, came up with what was probably the most inane stand-up commentary of the entire intifada coverage. In a January 29 piece on confrontations between young Israeli soldiers and Palestinians their own age, she intoned in a very serious and profound-sounding voice that these "boy soldiers" were the "common denominator in this equation of unease—wild cards in a very dangerous game of chance." Whatever all of those words mean.

Every language, even one made up primarily of images, requires some form of punctuation. In the case of imagespeak, the job of punctuation is done by sound. Two decades ago, the sound that was gathered as part of picture taking usually was called "ambient sound" or "wild sound." Today, that sound has been well tamed and forms an integral part of imagespeak. A gunshot at the beginning of a new scene represents a new paragraph, the amplified roar of a truck motor in the midst of a scene can indicate a semicolon, and a crashing door is invariably an exclamation point.

By the second half of January, almost all of the elements of imagespeak were in place and, through repetition, had been tested for use on a regular basis. It was then that entire stories could be told in a single camera shot, a single news piece, or in a brief wrap-up or backgrounder prepared in the New York or Washington studios. Efficient and powerful subliminal messaging not only was available as a vehicle in support of television's agenda, it came to be used on an almost daily basis.

There are many people who still contend that the reporter's verbal message is as strong a message-sending vehicle as are the images. Among a majority of television news practitioners I have spoken to, however, the belief is exactly the opposite. Virtually all point to the by now almost apocryphal story of Lesley Stahl's October 1984 critical look at how Ronald Reagan used photo-ops to plaster over some of the discomfiting and politically damaging aspects of his first presidential term. Stahl used a series of tape clips to prove her point and called this image manipulation "brilliant." She then braced herself for what she believed would be a highly critical reaction from the White House. Instead, as she told Hedrick Smith, a White House official called her and said, "Great piece . . . Lesley, when you're showing four and a half minutes of great pictures of Ronald Reagan, no one listens to what you say. Don't you know that the pictures are overriding your message? The public sees those pictures and they block your message. They didn't even hear what you said. So, in our minds, it was a four-and-a-half-minute free ad for the Ronald Reagan campaign for reelection."[16]

On its own, each of the elements of imagespeak is a strong message-sending tool. But in a story-telling medium like television news, it is the whole package that counts. The following three examples are cases in point of different types of packages. In each, the package is crafted so that the reporter's text is totally subordinated to the subliminal messages of the images. In the first example, the pictures closely match the tenor of the voiceover. In the second and third cases, the images, as packaged into a whole, actually contradict both the verbal message of the reporter and the images on the screen when viewed individually. Both reports are extraordinary examples of reportorial flimflam and subliminal messaging.

The first is an example of packaging inside the camera. It is a superb example of what some television people call "learned production values"— that is, how to increase the impact on an audience of a naturally occurring

[16]Hedrick Smith, *The Power Game: How Washington Works* (New York: Random House, 1988), 412–14.

event through the use of learned filmmaking techniques. By the end of January 1988, intifada imagespeak was well established and those working in the field knew exactly the types of images to record to send the desired message. And they could do so as instinctively and smoothly as a skilled and practiced orator. The opening scene of Dean Reynolds's January 29 report on ABC consists of one pan shot. The camera focuses first on a Palestinian flag (Palestinians are still demanding independence). It then pans to burning tires (the rebellion is still alight), and stones being thrown (the conflict is still raging), and finally, to a by now familiar shot of an Israeli soldier's gun pointing as a Palestinian walks by it at eye level (the Palestinians are under the gun). Or, as Peter Jennings succinctly put it in his studio introduction—for those who may not have been watching earlier and needed help in deciphering the images—"Despite punishment, the Palestinians are very resilient." In a single camera shot lasting only 5.2 seconds, which never could have been staged, four established and recognizable symbolic images, each rich with its own set of connotations, are presented to the viewer. That is true dramatic terseness and visual efficiency.

The second example, one of field packaging by a reporter, takes the use of learned production values one step further, into the editing room. It is also an example of the legacy of former CBS news executive Van Gordon Sauter, who coined the now-infamous term *infotainment* to describe his vision of what television news should be. Sauter explained that what he was looking for was "something that evokes an emotional response. When I go back there to the fishbowl [the newsroom], I tell them, goddam it, we've got to touch people. They've got to feel a *relationship* with us. A lot of stories have inherent drama, but others have to be done in a way that will bring out an emotional response."[17] This concept of creating drama artificially, the willingness to use any available artifice in the service of story-telling, continues to pervade much of CBS's news coverage and has had a major impact on the other networks as well. The intifada was an inherently dramatic event that naturally evoked an emotional response from the viewer. But the following report by CBS's Bob Simon on January 19, 1988, illustrates how Sauter's concept of news presentation can become an end in itself, and how some television reporters use the techniques

---

[17]Ron Rosenbaum, "The Man Who Married Dan Rather," *Esquire*, November 1982, p. 60.

of dramatic magnification even when the events themselves have all the natural drama a reporter could hope for.

The report begins with a tight camera shot of an Israeli army sniper aiming his large and specialized weapon. It then cuts to a sequence of three shots showing (1) Israeli soldiers bashing open a shop door in Ramallah with a sledgehammer, (2) an Israeli soldier with a rifle bashing open the glass door of a shop, and (3) a group of soldiers running down the street. Simon explains that "for the past six weeks, the picture seemed crystal clear—Israeli occupiers, Palestinian victims." The theme and the dramatic element of violent conflict and victimization, and the identities of the protagonists, are quickly established.

The scene then shifts to an Israeli funeral with mourners crying. "But tell that to the family of Shlomo Takal" (killed on a Gaza street just prior to the outbreak of the intifada), Simon says. A new symbol has been introduced—the Israeli victim.

Simon then interviews Azriel Barak and his wife at a memorial to their son and daughter-in-law, who were killed in the West Bank in 1979. Barak says that the members of his family were killed "because they were Jews" and adds, "we are victimized."

The scene now shifts to an interview with a Palestinian whose daughter was killed by an Israeli soldier while she was hanging up wash in her home. The bereaved father says, "I am a victim, too." A woman is shown crying and the man adds, "They killed her for nothing." Parallel situations have been established now. Simon comments, "Israelis and Palestinians both define themselves as victims—and victims don't compromise." Up to this point, a certain balance appears to have been established, one that shows that not everything in the Arab-Israeli conflict is black and white. But television, for dramatic reasons, abhors ambiguity and, as Sauter explained, demands an emotional response from the viewer. With whom should the viewer identify? In a sense, Simon has created a dramatic competition for the audience's empathy and loyalty.

A new victim is introduced in the form of Bassam Shaka, the former mayor of Nablus who had his legs blown off in 1980 by a bomb planted by members of a far-right Jewish underground terrorist group. Archival footage shows Shaka walking through Nablus and then lying in a hospital bed with the stumps of his legs above the sheets. At no time does Simon note that Shaka was wounded by civilians or that those responsible were caught, tried, convicted, and jailed for their crime. Shaka tells the camera, "He wanted to kill me."

Suddenly, the scene cuts to a soldier, similar in almost all respects to the one whom we saw at the very beginning of the piece, as he fires his gun. The sound track has a sharp report. It is a clever, climactic, but highly deceiving dramatic artifice. This one camera shot, lasting four seconds, is thoroughly disorienting to the viewer, but the viewer is given no time to react or question before the next scene appears. There is time and geographic compression: 1980 and 1988, and a hospital and a street. The viewer is left with the impression that Israeli soldiers tried to kill Shaka—or at least Palestinians—and that despite their assertions, the Israelis are not really legitimate victims.

The report abruptly shifts back to Azriel Barak, who says, "Does anyone want to kill anyone? You are forced to do that," and to the Arab whose daughter was killed, who says, "I love her more than anything. I lost her just like that! Why?" In these paired-off sound bites, the Israeli admits to being a killer, while the Palestinian is shown as a true victim whose only crime was love for his daughter. The effect comes not from the individual sound bites themselves, but from their juxtaposition and their position within the context of the whole package.

The piece ends with a series of shots including a helicopter shot of the city, green fields, Arabs, and a Jew kissing the Western Wall, while Simon "answers" the Palestinian's question with the simple, classic story line. There is no ambiguity left, no question of Israeli defense concerns or Palestinian generational gaps, which have no readily identifiable symbolic image. Everything can be tied to the story line, for which there are images. Moreover, the named aggressor cannot talk back. "For the land," Simon declaims. "That's why people die here. For the land which through their perspectives of persecution, Israelis and Palestinians claim as their own. Two compelling exclusive claims for one piece of land." The report ends with a warm long shot of the sun setting over a mosque.

As can be seen, this report conforms to all of the conventional wisdom of television news reporting. Each segment is accurate in the details presented and there are no factual errors or lies. Yet, as a package, and only when viewed as a package, the report carries a very strong subliminal message that, upon careful analysis, clearly is at odds with the overt theme that there are victims on both sides.

The third case in point, a package produced by ABC's New York home office studio and anchorman, is probably the most egregious example of subliminal messaging to have been created in the early weeks of the intifada. The package was aired on ABC on January 18, 1988, and lasted approximately seven minutes and ten seconds—an extraordinary length for a weekday night television news broadcast that, without commercials, runs only twenty-two minutes. It is so complex and uses so many tools of image manipulation and packaging that to analyze it, one must look at it virtually shot by shot. The basic theme was a comparison between Israel and South Africa. ABC was certainly not the first media outlet to discuss the subject. It had been a matter for public discussion and mention in the print media for some time, and NBC, in a Chris Wallace piece from Washington on January 14, also had made note of it. Israeli officials and Jewish media watchers in the United States were aghast, angry that such a comparison should even be suggested. However, by the time ABC broadcast its package, the subject had become part of the public debate and a clear and objective comparative analysis was a legitimate and responsible journalistic endeavor. What anchor Peter Jennings did with the component parts of the package is another matter.

The package began with a Jennings studio introduction about curfews being lifted in the West Bank and food and fuel being allowed into Gaza, followed by a graphic showing Israeli and U.S. flags and the headline ISRAEL'S IMAGE. Jennings ended his introduction with: "Israelis are concerned about their international image."

The introduction was followed by a report from John McWethy in Washington that began with a series of pictures of violence in the occupied territories, while McWethy stated, "Israel has a public relations problem as night after night, pictures like these are broadcast around the world." Then there were camera shots of tear-gas canisters being fired and a Palestinian boy throwing stones—intifada imagespeak's equivalent of the word *conflict*. Next came a sound bite by Yossi Beilin, the director-general of the Israeli Foreign Ministry, who was in Washington on a trip to counter what the Israelis perceived of as unfair news coverage from the occupied territories. Beilin said: "We have to expose . . . the real context so that it's not just a picture of an innocent boy throwing a stone or a soldier with a rifle being shown, but also the context of this problem." Undoubtedly, since this was the standard government line at the time and he was a government spokesman, Beilin was referring to the intifada either in the context of the Arab-Israeli dispute as a whole or in the context of overall Israeli-Palestinian relations. McWethy, however, used the expression as a means to introduce the real subject of the package, the comparison between Israel and South Africa.

"Troubling," McWethy commented, "are recent comparisons of the situation there [that is, in the Israeli-occupied territories] and the one in South Africa." And McWethy noted that recently the Israeli embassy in Washington had drawn up a working paper to refute the comparisons. Another sound bite of Beilin followed in which he said, "Israel is an open democracy—the only one in the Middle East." This was undoubtedly part of the subject Beilin had been referring to when he mentioned "context," but the statement was totally irrelevant to the theme of Israel and South Africa, and it made Beilin seem weak and unable or unwilling to deal with the subject. Next came a sound bite from the head of the Conference of Presidents of Major Jewish Organizations in the United States, the umbrella body for organized Jewry in America. The president, Morris Abrams, stated, "There is absolutely no comparison whatsoever between the problems of Israel and the problems of South Africa." But Abrams was not given the opportunity to say why he believed this to be true.

Instead, after McWethy did his sign-off, Jennings, acting as the supposedly neutral mediator between the viewer and the subject matter being aired, interjected from his anchor position in the studio, "The Israeli and South African governments do have one thing undeniably in common. They both rule over large populations which have inferior status." From the outset, Jennings thus establishes that the story is to be about victims and identifies their geographical location. There then follows a packaged piece in which reports from Dean Reynolds in Israel and Jim Hickey in South Africa are intercut around a series of human rights themes. A graphic showing the Israeli and South African flags provides the unifying studio image of the subject and implies that there are at least superficial similarities. As each theme is raised, the Israeli report is placed first and the South African second.

Jennings: "How does each deal with unrest?"

THE SCENE BEGINS WITH A CAMERA SHOT FROM INSIDE AN ISRAELI COMMAND
CAR AS IT MOVES DOWN A ROAD. ONCE AGAIN, THERE IS THE SYMBOLIC
IMAGE OF AN ISRAELI SOLDIER POINTING A GUN AT A PALESTINIAN BOY.

Reynolds: "The West Bank and Gaza are under military occupation
and the Israeli army is in complete control."

THERE FOLLOWS A CAMERA SHOT OF AN ISRAELI SOLDIER WALKING DOWN
A STREET AND MAKING BRIEF EYE CONTACT WITH A PALESTINIAN WOMAN
DRESSED IN BLACK.

Reynolds: "Young army conscripts and reservists with little or no riot
control training are employed to maintain law and order."

FOUR SOLDIERS SPIN AROUND ON A ROAD, FIRING THEIR RIFLES, AP-
PARENTLY AT RANDOM. (THIS KIND OF CAMERA SHOT HAD BEEN USED FAIRLY
FREQUENTLY THE PREVIOUS TWO WEEKS AND HAD TAKEN ON THE SYMBOLIC
MEANING: THE ARMY IS NOT QUITE UNDER CONTROL.)

Reynolds: "Live ammunition can be used in life-threatening situations."

THE SCENE IS OF A NARROW STREET. ONE SOLDIER IS SEEN RUNNING
UP IT AS ANOTHER SOLDIER DARTS OUT FROM BEHIND A CORNER AND FIRES
HIS GUN AS TWO PALESTINIANS THROW ROCKS AND RUN AWAY.

Reynolds: "But rubber bullets and tear gas are the preferred deter-
rents."

THE SCENE SWITCHES TO SOUTH AFRICAN POLICE IN RIOT GEAR MARCHING
IN SINGLE FILE WITH THEIR GUN BARRELS POINTING UP.

Hickey: "In South Africa, security forces . . ."

A GROUP OF FIVE POLICE OFFICERS ARE SHOWN FIRING TEAR GAS ON A
PAVED STREET.

Hickey: " . . . have nearly unlimited power . . ."

A GROUP OF POLICE OFFICERS ON A SIDEWALK FIRE SUBMACHINE GUNS
AND SHOTGUNS IN THE AIR.

Hickey: ". . . granted by various . . ."

A CROWD OF BLACKS FLEES FROM A CLOUD OF TEAR GAS.

Hickey: ". . . state of emergency laws."

A POLICE OFFICER BEATS A MAN WHO HAS BEEN DETAINED.

Hickey: "Recently, unrest has been reduced to minimal levels."

A TELEVISION CREW IS PURSUED BY A POLICE OFFICER.

Hickey: "Riot-trained black and white policemen . . ."

ARMORED PERSONNEL CARRIERS WITH SOLDIERS.

Hickey: ". . . are backed up by soldiers, many of them conscripts."

SOLDIERS FIRING FIELD GUNS.

Hickey: "Tear gas, rubber bullets, and live ammunition . . ."

A SOLDIER RUNS ONTO SOMEONE'S FRONT YARD AND FIRES A SHOTGUN ACROSS THE STREET.

Hickey: ". . . are often used to maintain order."

The text in each of these segments more or less matches the images that were chosen, and the symbolic, thematic images, which form the visual core of each segment—soldiers or police officers with their equipment, and soldiers or police officers firing their guns—are quite similar.

A GRAPHIC WITH THE TWO FLAGS AND A PICTURE OF A PALESTINIAN REFUGEE CAMP IS SHOWN, WITH THE HEADLINE "LIVING CONDITIONS."

Jennings: "Are there comparisons between the way most Palestinians and South African blacks live?"

AERIAL SHOT OF A WEST BANK CITY.

Reynolds: "Most West Bank Palestinians live in towns and villages."

SHOT OF AN ISRAELI SOLDIER WALKING DOWN A STREET CROWDED WITH ARABS AND WITH OPEN SHOPS.

Reynolds: "Life has improved under the Israelis."

AERIAL SHOT OF A REFUGEE CAMP.

Reynolds: "A majority in Gaza live in refugee camps."

PALESTINIAN CHILDREN PLAYING IN AN UNPAVED STREET WITH WASH ON THE LINE.

Reynolds: "Conditions are bad, but some services have improved . . ."

SHOT OF A WOMAN TAKING BREAD OUT OF A *TABOUN*, A TRADITIONAL AND WIDELY USED EARTHEN OVEN.

Reynolds: ". . . since the Israeli occupation."

A TRAVELING SHOT FROM A CAR OF A SOUTH AFRICAN SLUM WITH THE WASH HANGING ON THE LINE.

Hickey: "Blacks in South Africa are required by law to live in segregated townships."

CHILDREN AND ADULTS WALKING ON AN UNPAVED STREET.

Hickey: "Most are huge, crime-ridden ghettos."

A FRONT-END LOADER LIFTS A LARGE CONCRETE PIPE.

Hickey: "Although the government has embarked on a limited program to upgrade living conditions."

Once again, while there is a considerable difference in the reporters' texts, there is a striking similarity in the central thematic images—in this case, the slums and the laundry hanging in the streets.

GRAPHIC OF THE TWO FLAGS AND THE HEADLINE "FREEDOM OF MOVEMENT."

Jennings: "If you are a Palestinian or South African black, how much freedom do you have to move about?"

AN ISRAELI SOLDIER CHECKING PALESTINIANS' IDENTITY CARDS IN GAZA.

Reynolds: "Palestinians in the occupied territories must carry identity cards and have . . ."

A VAN WITH GAZA LICENSE PLATES IS LOOKED AT BY TWO SOLDIERS.

Reynolds: ". . . special license plates so their cars can be more easily spotted. They can travel freely through the territories . . ."

AN ISRAELI MILITARY CHECKPOST WITH A WATCHTOWER, A COMMAND CAR, AND CIVILIAN CARS AND TRUCKS.

Reynolds: ". . . and can go to Israel, too, but are not supposed to stay overnight."

CLOSE-UP OF AN OPEN SOUTH AFRICAN PASSBOOK ON A DESK WITH THE CAMERA ZOOMING OUT TO INCLUDE A WOMAN WRITING IN THE PASSBOOK.
Hickey: "South Africa recently did away with the apartheid law requiring blacks to carry special passbooks."
BLACKS GETTING ON A TRAIN.
Hickey: "Blacks may now travel relatively freely within the country."
SHOT OF BLACK PEASANTS HOEING A FIELD.
Hickey: "Blacks living in the so-called tribal homelands may now have South African citizenship, once denied them."

The reporter in Israel does not mention that Israelis, too, are required to carry identity cards at all times. More important, though, while the reporters' texts diverge quite markedly, the central thematic image this time, of the identity card and the passbook, remain virtually identical, despite the fact that the South Africans already have abolished passbooks.

A GRAPHIC OF THE TWO FLAGS AND A PAIR OF SCALES IS PROJECTED WITH THE HEADLINE "POLITICAL FREEDOM."

Jennings: "In Israel or South Africa, if you run up against the authorities, what rights do you have?"

A PALESTINIAN DETAINEE WALKING DOWN A STREET WHILE HANDCUFFED TO A SOLDIER.
Reynolds: "In general, Palestinians can be detained for six months without trial."
TWO PALESTINIANS ARE ESCORTED BY THREE ISRAELI POLICE OFFICERS. ONE PALESTINIAN IS HELD BY THE SCRUFF OF HIS NECK AND THE OTHER BY HIS UPPER ARM.

Reynolds: "During the current unrest, about two thousand have been arrested."

A GROUP OF PALESTINIANS SITTING DOWN IN A COURTROOM.

Reynolds: "They are subject to military, not civilian, courts—as such, . . ."

SHOT OF A LAWYER AND CLIENT TOGETHER.

Reynolds: ". . . [they] have no right to appeal convictions."

THREE SOLDIERS WITH A BLACK DETAINEE. THE BLACK IS YANKED ALONG THE STREET BY THE ARRESTING OFFICERS.

Hickey: "Political dissidents of all races in South Africa can . . ."

CHURCH MINISTERS BEING ARRESTED AND HELD BY THE ARM.

Hickey: ". . . be detained indefinitely without charge under the state of emergency."

A BLACK WOMAN IS DRAGGED ALONG A STREET BY TWO POLICE OFFICERS, WHO SCUFFLE WITH THE WOMAN. ONE POLICE OFFICER EVENTUALLY PUNCHES HER.

Hickey: "Human rights groups say that thirty thousand have been arrested in the past two and a half years. Courts which overturned security legislation are often overruled by the government."

By now, there is a clear pattern in the packaging. No matter what each reporter says, the central thematic image of the segments—for example, detainees being dragged around by the scruff of the neck—will be virtually identical.

A GRAPHIC WITH A BALLOT BOX AND A CHECK MARK ON A PIECE OF PAPER REPRESENTING A BALLOT IS SHOWN, WITH THE HEADLINE "ELECTORAL REP-RESENTATION."

———

Jennings: "Both Israel and South Africa have parliamentary governments, but who has the vote?"

SHOT OF A CROWD OF ARABS WALKING DOWN A STREET.

Reynolds: "The 1.4 million Palestinians in the occupied territories have no vote, . . ."

A TIGHT SHOT OF A MAN WEARING A *KEFFIYEH*—THE TRADITIONAL ARAB HEADDRESS.

Reynolds: ". . . no say in Israeli politics."

A MAN COMING OUT FROM BEHIND A VOTING SCREEN PUTS HIS BALLOT IN THE BOX.

Reynolds: "Seven hundred and fifty thousand Arabs who live in Israel itself are full citizens with voting rights, . . ."

SHOT OF TOUFIK TOUBI, AN ARAB MEMBER OF KNESSET, SITTING IN HIS KNESSET SEAT.

Reynolds: ". . . and elected representatives, . . ."

CAMERA SHOT OF HANDS BEING RAISED IN A KNESSET VOTE.

Reynolds: ". . . but not enough to really affect Israeli politics."

WHITES LINED UP TO VOTE, PUTTING THEIR BALLOTS IN THE BOX.

Hickey: "In South Africa, blacks have no voting rights in national elections, . . ."

SHOT OF THE INSIDE OF PARLIAMENT, WITH PEOPLE STANDING AS THE MACE IS BROUGHT IN.

Hickey: ". . . no representation in Parliament."

SHOT OF A BLACK TOWN COUNCIL MEETING.

Hickey: "Black town councils have limited authority, . . ."

BLACK COUNCIL MEMBERS REMAIN SEATED WHILE A WHITE IN THE CENTER, WITH A ROBE AND CHAIN OF OFFICE, RISES.

Hickey: ". . . but the real power is in the hands of white administrators."

By now it is abundantly clear that, in fact, two different stories are being told—a visual story and a verbal story. The overt story is in the words; the covert story, in the pictures. The overt story highlights considerable differences between Israel and South Africa. The covert story, however, shows the two countries to have great similarities.

A GRAPHIC OF THE TWO FLAGS AND A TELEVISION CAMERA, WITH THE HEADLINE "PRESS FREEDOM."

Jennings: "And is the press free to cover and report unrest and confrontation?"

CAMERA SHOT OF PALESTINIANS IN THE STREET THROWING ROCKS AND WAVING A PALESTINIAN FLAG.
    Reynolds: "Access to trouble spots is officially open, . . ."
    A SOLDIER PUTS HIS HAND UP TO COVER A TELEVISION CAMERA'S LENS (AN ESTABLISHED ICON FOR PRESS CENSORSHIP).
    Reynolds: ". . . but many have been arbitrarily closed by local commanders."
    POLICE GRAB A STILL PHOTOGRAPHER AND BEAT HIM WITH A CLUB AS HE TRIES TO RUN AWAY.
    Reynolds: "There are attempts to intimidate journalists."
    THE LOGO OF MABAT, THE MAIN EVENING NEWSCAST IN ISRAEL.
    Reynolds: "Israeli television is not under strict government control, . . ."
    AN ANNOUNCER READS THE NEWS WITH A GRAPHIC OF THE WEST BANK BEHIND HIM.
    Reynolds: ". . . but practices self-censorship, . . ."
    A SHOT OF SOLDIERS WALKING DOWN A QUIET JERUSALEM STREET.
    Reynolds: ". . . and presents a less aggressive and detailed picture of events."

SHOT OF NEWSPAPER PRESSES RUNNING WITH BLACK PRESSMEN NEARBY.
    Hickey: "South Africa also blames the media for its negative image abroad and has . . ."
    BLACK JOURNALIST WORKING AT A COMPUTER SCREEN.

Hickey: ". . . some of the toughest press restrictions in the Western world."

NEWSPAPER HEADLINE THAT READS: "THE STAR, JANUARY 9, NEW CURBS ON SA MEDIA."

Hickey: "Access to areas of unrest is forbidden."

POLICEMAN ESCORTS A CAMERAMAN AND A SOUNDMAN AWAY.

Hickey: "So is coverage of most political protests and boycotts."

TELEVISION LOGO OF TV 1 NEWS.

Hickey: "What South Africans themselves are shown of political dissent . . ."

ANNOUNCER WITH A GRAPHIC BEHIND HIM HEADLINED "STATE OF EMER- GENCY."

Hickey: ". . . on state-controlled television is a watered-down version of events."

The crucial word in Jim Hickey's text in this segment is in his first sentence: *also.* In other words, Hickey must have known in advance the substance of Dean Reynolds's report from Israel. One can therefore deduce that these are not two separate pieces that have been spliced together for the viewers' convenience. Hickey's report appears to have been tailored to match what Reynolds had said and done.

Hickey's stand-upper: "South Africa, historically, has circled the wagons and gotten even tougher when faced with domestic and international pressure. That behavior adds another dimension to South African–Israeli relations. The two countries share, among other things, military tech- nology. South Africa also shares with Israel a feeling of isolation."

Two things are noteworthy about this stand-upper. The first is that the pattern of Reynolds reporting first and Hickey second has been broken. Generally speaking, a stand-upper that is closest to scenes of action is the one most remembered by the audience. The second is that up to now, all of the subjects under discussion have related to civil or human rights issues. Hickey's introduction of the issue of military cooperation breaks the parallelism of the piece, and the jarring effect of the break rams home the subliminal covert message that has been there all along.

Reynolds's stand-upper: "The Israelis are insulted by comparisons of their country with South Africa's apartheid regime. They say that whatever similarities may exist are not their doing, but the result of living with enemies who would drive them into the sea if they could."

Reynolds's stand-upper is weak in the sense that it does not respond to the issue of military cooperation and also provides none of the arguments that the Israelis try to use to rebut the allegation that they are like white South Africans.

Each of these reports—with the exception of the last comments on military relations—when spliced back together to create two separate wholes, are sober, responsible pieces of television news reporting. Each provides the viewer with a considerable amount of background information on civil and human rights problems in the Israeli-occupied territories and in South Africa. They are by no means complete descriptions of the situation, and they lack both a historical perspective and a more general overall context, but within the confines of the air time available, they do provide a significant amount of data. However, when juxtaposed by Peter Jennings, the final effect is considerably different from that which occurs when the reports are viewed separately.

In an unscientific but very revealing experiment, I asked about three dozen friends and acquaintances in the United States and Israel to view this package. First I played the studio-produced package—showing only the images, not the sound. After each segment, I asked them whether, as a result only of what they saw, they would have to draw the conclusion that Israel and South Africa were alike in that particular respect, or different. Without exception, each viewer came to the conclusion that the two countries were very similar. I then played the tape again, using only the sound track and no images, again stopping at the end of each segment to ask the same question. To their astonishment, each viewer came to the conclusion that, based only on what was *said*, the two countries were very different. After a break, I then played the package again, with both the sound and the images, and asked them which they remembered more. The answer, again unanimous, was that they could remember the images more clearly than the words. Imagespeak speaks to people. With packages such as these being broadcast, Israeli officials had a right to be concerned about what was happening to their country's image internationally.

Both of these latter packages are extreme examples of the use of intifada imagespeak. They are, however, also indicative of the potential for perceptual manipulation contained in the artifices of television news production. Therefore, they are warning flags whose message should not be ignored or forgotten.

Intifada imagespeak was a particularly potent example of television's ability to manipulate images in a variety of ways in order to send subliminal messages. But on February 1, 1988, just as this language was at the height of its power, its development suddenly stopped dead and never was revived. The story of why this happened is, as they say in television, "to be continued."

E · I · G · H · T

Whence Words?

Free, democratic societies, in their own self-interest, permit the press to operate in a wide variety of areas. Among others, these areas include describing events, acting as a public watchdog over government officials, and raising issues for public debate. Not all media outlets are willing to take on all of these tasks, but one of the major assumptions of a competitive information marketplace is that someone, somewhere, will fill any open niche. Within this marketplace, television, radio, weekly newsmagazines, daily newspapers, and wire services act as the information equivalent of department stores. Specialist magazines and journals are the boutiques.

Most Americans today choose to buy their information in these media department stores. In order to exert some form of organizational control over their minions, most of these media outlets operate on the basis of routines that have been established well in advance. There are house rules for gathering material, house styles for writing, and long- and short-term institutional budgets that are often the determining factor on how, and in how much depth, a story will be covered. In the broadcast media, there are also in-house concepts of how to gather and use images and sound. As one journalist acquaintance put it, "No matter what comes across my desk, it's just another day at the office."

If the organizational and bureaucratic task of news outlets really is to "routinize the unexpected,"[1] then the coverage of crises—be they natural or man-made—is the ultimate test of any news organization. There is an almost existential tension between a news organization's need for routine and the requirement that it cover crisis situations, for routines are based largely on past experience and crises are, by definition, events that were unforeseen or events for which the news organization did not prepare.

By any definition, the intifada was a crisis. It came unexpectedly. It had a major impact on many people and on public perceptions. It swept away much of the conventional political and journalistic wisdom of the time. It required everyone directly involved to use more material and intrinsic resources than usual and to adapt quickly to changed circumstances.

The success or failure of each media outlet's plan during the intifada was not, and could not have been, the product of some momentary action or stroke of brilliance on the part of an editor or reporter. Daily tactics could be varied to meet unanticipated needs and circumstances, but strategies can arise naturally only out of routine practices with which everyone in the organization is familiar and out of policies that had been agreed on and adopted long before the uprising took place. The intifada, therefore, was not merely a test of an individual reporter's skill, determination, and integrity. In many ways, it was a public trial of each news organization's long-term corporate strategy.

In a fast-breaking, crisis-oriented story like the intifada, journalistic success is predicated on resources, access, sources, and trust between the reporter in the field and his or her supervisors. All four factors must be present prior to the outbreak of a crisis, because once the balloon goes

---

[1] Gaye Tuchman, *Making News: A Study in the Construction of Reality* (New York: Free Press, 1978).

up, there is usually little or no time to acquire these prerequisites. Of the four factors, the long-term commitment of resources is the key element. It is also the only element that is not, at least partially, within the field reporter's area of responsibility.

The Palestinian uprising was an example of a story that could not be covered adequately without an organization's willingness to commit considerable resources, both long term and short term. It was the kind of event where the quantity of resources available began to be more important than the quality of resources. Merely by looking at resource allocation, it is possible to tell which organizations were serious about original foreign news coverage and which were not.

The most obvious short-term material resource was money. Unlike most fast-breaking stories, this one took place largely outside Jerusalem, the national capital, or Tel Aviv, where much of the press was stationed. Reporters who had come to rely primarily on unpaid sources, carefully cultivated over time, as a substitute in the face of organizational budgetary restrictions, no longer could compete. The standard "golden Rolodex" of government officials, members of the Palestinian elite, intelligence analysts, and academics often simply did not know what was going on. Virtually none of these standard sources ever had spoken to the youngsters who were leading the uprising in the streets. The traditional sources could offer conjecture and quotes, but they were in no position to know what really was happening. Reporters had to get out into the field, had to get to tiny villages they had never visited before. One short-term immediate resource, thus, was the money to hire cars. Since car windshields constantly were being broken by stone throwers, rental cars became a necessity, not a luxury.

But short-term money allocation was not everything. Being able to finance parachutists with large expense accounts—another short-term resource—did not necessarily make for better or even adequate coverage of the intifada. The short-term allocation of supplementary budgets could not overcome long-term structural problems within news organizations. In some cases, throwing money around only served to reveal how hopelessly inadequate some organizations' strategic planning had been and how lacking those organizations were in an overall guiding philosophy. And in fact, although the Middle East had been a major international story for more than twenty years, most news organizations demonstrated an appalling lack of strategic depth in their ability to cover the intifada. I met one BBC parachutist, for example, who was so raw that he could not recognize Jerusalem's Teddy Kollek—unquestionably one of the most famous mayors in the world and one of the leading figures in Israel's political hierarchy.

In general, long-term decisions on resource allocation are made on the basis of the priorities an organization sets for itself, its internal bureaucratic structure, and its appreciation of what it takes to do the job adequately. To me, one of the more disturbing phenomena of modern American journalism has been the diminution of the understanding by media organizations of foreign reporting as a profession unto itself—or at least as a specialty that requires particular training. One can see this most readily by looking at each media outlet's long-term resource allocation for things like in-house training. Often, employers do not give reporters the opportunity to study, in advance, the language and culture of the countries to which they are to be posted. And once in the country, reporters are not given the material, technical, or psychological backup they need. As a result, rifts between field reporters and home editors are common. Too many foreign editors today, for example, have never even served for extended periods in the field or have had only one posting to one particular country or region. They often do not have a clue about the conditions under which reporters have to work while living in an alien culture, and they are unable to question a reporter so that the nuances of the story will be highlighted. Nonetheless, it is they who usually are responsible for setting organizational strategies.

When it comes to subeditors, it is even more exceptional to find one who has been sent out into the field to get a feeling for what the reporter is doing. Subeditors are the print equivalent of television technicians— concerned more with issues of style, format, and impact, and less with content. But without an understanding of the content, they cannot know the questions to ask of the reporter or cut the material to size under deadline pressures without losing the richness provided by nuance. More than one foreign reporter has looked in horror at the way his or her copy has been mangled by a subeditor who did not have the means to comprehend what the reporter was writing.

One of the disasters of modern journalism is that youngsters graduating from journalism schools are put on the desk to edit copy without ever having worked as full-time reporters. They are promoted within the organization and often reach senior positions without ever having covered a story themselves. This, in part, explains the often wide discrepancy between the headlines written on the desk and the actual report from the field. It also goes a long way toward explaining why distortions, caused by ignorance and a lack of understanding of the subtleties of the political language used in foreign cultures, creep into edited stories. In part, it helps explain why American-based media outlets are so dependent on the U.S. State Department for guidance on foreign events—and thus, why the American press is manipulated so often by State.[2]

Each of the major American media outlets in Israel had a record of long-term resource allocation. Each, for example, had established a full-time bureau in Israel, with all of the expense that that entailed. Television's use of the resources at its disposal was remarkably uniform throughout the three major commercial networks. When it came to the intifada, each blanketed the occupied territories with camera crews in the expectation that at least one of these crews would come up with the all-important dramatic images that could be used that night.

The very opposite was true for the Associated Press and for three of the major U.S. newspapers—the *New York Times*, the *Washington Post*, and the *Los Angeles Times*. Among these four, there was often a great consensus of view of what was a major story, but there was also an extraordinary diversity in approach and conception of how the material should be handled and presented.

Television's takeover as the prime medium for mass foreign news distribution appears to have left the print media in a state of considerable confusion as to what their audiences want, how the material should be presented, and what the readership's real needs are. Numerous public opinion studies have shown that approximately two-thirds of the American public say that their main source of news is television. This phenomenon has left the print media unsure of what their public mandate is or should be, and during the early period of the intifada, this led to a great deal of experimentation—to the benefit of readers who had access to all three newspapers. In fact, the first six months of coverage of the intifada by these newspapers is virtually a textbook and catalogue of all of the styles

[2]This subject will get greater treatment in chapter 9.

and writing techniques available to modern print journalists. But variety and competition is probably not the full answer to audiences' real needs.

The intifada proved that television is a remarkably effective medium in alerting people to the existence of a crisis. But as was demonstrated again during later events, like the San Francisco earthquake and the collapse of the Berlin Wall, it does not do very well in handling the detail of crises. This is because detail often interferes with drama, and detail includes ideas and concepts for which there are often no images. The standard analytical package of facts, depth, background, understanding, and trend projection is one of the largest and most important press niches that television's juggernaut journalism has left in its wake. It is the painstakingly assembled detail behind an event, the placement of that detail in its historical and current context, and the analysis of that detail that creates public understanding and allows for cogent public policy-making. This is the area where print can, if it wishes, excel and come into its own during periods of upheaval.

The remarkable similarities in the coverage of the intifada by the three main U.S. commercial networks led many Jewish and Israeli media critics to accuse the networks of conspiracy in their coverage of the Israeli-Palestinian dispute. The constant emphasis on violence, the similarity of images, and the use of many of the same interviewees (some of whom were highly critical of the government) were put forward as evidence that television as a whole was anti-Israeli.

The television reporters and producers responded that they were just telling the story of what was out there in the field, that Israel was blaming the messenger.[3] As in so many highly emotional and polarized situations, there was at least a grain of truth—and sometimes much more—in the positions of both sides.

There is no evidence of collusion or conspiracy by the television networks. The answer to the similarities in their coverage is more prosaic. It lies in television's perception of what its standard operating routine

[3]See, for example, the interview with the president of NBC News, Lawrence K. Grossman, in Glenn Frankel's "Israelis Criticize Coverage," *Washington Post*, 26 December 1987 p. A25. Referring to the criticism of the foreign press by Prime Minister Shamir's spokesman, Avi Pazner, Grossman stated, "He's talking through his hat as usual because he seems to make a practice of blaming the messenger for Israel's problems. We didn't cause the riots—the rioters were in places the cameras weren't, as well as where they were."

should be—no matter what the event may be. Unfortunately for viewers who seek depth and not merely entertainment, this routine is based on a deadening, dulling lack of vision of what television news can and should be. The sameness in the product is the result of a formulaic approach to the assembly and production of material—common to all of the major commercial networks—that goes far beyond the restraints and expectations of "house style."

In conversations I have had with top tape and film editors over the years, one thing always stood out. When asked why they chose one image over another, or why they cut it in a particular way or at a particular moment, the answer was invariably the same. "Because it works," they would say, or "Because it tells the story." When I suggested a different image or cut, the editors would not give a long, detailed explanation of why or how the image they wanted to use was better, or was more effective, or would "get" a person. Even had they wanted to, most of them could not express in words why they were doing what they were doing. Their's is not a world of words. Instead, years of training and in-house critiques by their superiors have given them a gut feeling about what "works" and what doesn't—and, more important, what is routinely acceptable and what is not. As they pulled out and assembled the images, they were not trying to press a particular political position. The very opposite was true. Their handling of the tape was usually totally apolitical. Whatever their personal political beliefs, their loyalty at the tape machine or the film editing table was not to one side or another in a political dispute. It was to the story and to the drama contained within it.

Tape assembly and editing is a craft. Although some technical aspects are taught in schools of journalism and filmmaking, the craft is really mastered only after many years of apprenticeship. During this apprenticeship, tape editors and producers learn not only the technical skills they need, but also what is expected of them in terms of storytelling by *all* of the commercial networks. These lessons are reinforced constantly as the years go by, and the ability to implement them to the full is the basis for promotions and higher-paying new jobs.

There were decided differences in the personal styles of the three main U.S. television reporters. ABC's Dean Reynolds took a relatively cool and sober approach. NBC's Martin Fletcher was more reflective. CBS's Bob Simon was more colorful and dramatic. The different networks gave varying amounts of air time to the story, and some of the artifices—like the use of historical documentary footage or the juxtaposition of contrasting images and sounds—differed. But one can still talk of "U.S. television news coverage" as a single whole, because underlying the stylistic and personal differences of the reporters was a homogeneity of conception of what news is, which images should be gathered, and how they should be assembled.[4]

In this sense, the networks are noncompetitive, and this sameness is only furthered by the relentless ratings game and, more recently, by the corporate takeovers of the networks and their emphasis on the bottom line. None of this encourages diversity in conception. Rather, it has the opposite effect. Many concepts—like longer sound bites that allow interviewees to present a cogent argument—are discouraged, while any new idea or technical concept that does not engender the wrath of audiences or member stations is adopted immediately by the other networks.[5] It is not unlike the phenomenon of a hit TV entertainment show bringing in its wake a series of clones. Sameness is a kind of "protection in numbers" for intellectually risk-averse organizations. With the acquisition of the networks by large, broad-based conglomerates for whom broadcasting is but one more "product," and with individual station owners becoming more restive and independent, the central concern of network managers often has been to prevent network disintegration. This new reality has made experimentation and large breaks with conventional television wisdom anathema.

During the intifada, however, this sameness also meant that many of the images presented on the evening newscasts were, in fact, tame by

---

[4]This phenomenon is hardly new and had been noted by both critics and television insiders long before the intifada or the big corporate takeovers. See, for example, James B. Lemert, "Content Duplication by the Networks in Competing Evening Newscasts," *Journalism Quarterly* 51 (1972):240–42; Joseph S. Fowler and Stuart Showalter, "Evening Network News Selection: A Confirmation of News Judgement," *Journalism Quarterly* 51 (1972):712–15; Joe S. Foote and Michael E. Steele, "Degree of Conformity in Lead Stories in Early Evening Network TV Newscasts," *Journalism Quarterly* 63 (1986):19; and Av Westin, *Newswatch: How TV Decides the News* (New York: Simon and Schuster, 1983). The phenomenon has, however, been exacerbated in recent years by the shake-ups in the network news divisions, the firing of large numbers of personnel, the emphasis on the news divisions as corporate profit centers, and the increasing power of the network anchor stars.
[5]Here I differentiate between program niches that are original, like "Nightline," and the overall concept of what television news reporting should be.

comparison with what actually was happening in the field. In that sense, there is much irony in the complaints of Israeli spokesmen like Avi Pazner. On December 24, he told an AP reporter that the foreign media was "presenting a distorted picture" of the clashes. Referring specifically to television, he said, "What has happened to us was an injustice, I would say intentional."[6] If anything, however, the images presented on U.S. commercial television during the first few weeks of the uprising understated and underplayed what actually was occurring. In keeping with the standard television practice of not reporting on incidents for which there are no images, TV did not tell the story, for example, of Israeli helicopters dropping tear gas into Gaza's Shifa hospital on the first day of rioting. And in keeping with the conventional television wisdom of not showing blood and gore during the dinner hour, camera shots of wounds, at least initially, were relatively rare—and those that were shown were certainly not the kind that would make most viewers queasy as they ate their supper. Not one of the networks showed the scenes I saw in the long, crowded wards at the Shifa hospital. There, by the beginning of the second week of the uprising, rows of patients were lying in bed wrapped in plaster— the result of having had their bones broken by Israeli soldiers or border police officers. As well, even though it had been reported by the AP, no network showed pictures of the welts women had received in the Balata refugee camp as a result of beatings by the Israeli border police.[7] It was not until mid-January, when Israel's policy of beating Palestinian protesters had become the major news story, that wounds were shown with greater frequency.

The networks *were* competitive in the acquisition of images and information. Each TV news bureau had its share of scoops: ABC had the first interview with some of the young leaders of the uprising; CBS caught the scene of Israeli soldiers beating two Arabs with rocks after they had been captured; NBC was the first to report that Israel had killed the deputy chief of the PLO, Abu Jihad. However, in the overall presentation of news and the choice of what to present as news, a correspondence of viewpoint among the three major networks was almost total.

[6]AP, 24 December 1987, 17:59 GMT.
[7]See, for example, AP, 22 December 1987, 21:30 GMT.

Established routine was also the guiding strategy for the wire services. Although they work primarily with words, the news agencies, like AP and Reuters, operate with a broadcast medium's speed. They are the equivalent of information factories, assembling data twenty-four hours a day in multiple shifts, producing long lead stories on the day's events, updating material constantly, and disgorging an unceasing stream of feature stories and backgrounders. For example, on December 9, 1987, the first day of the intifada, the AP bureau in Jerusalem produced no fewer than eleven stories and updates, of which seven dealt with the outbreak of violence.

Until the advent of modern television, the wire services were the prime journalistic agenda setters for all of the other news media. Even today, the old saw "If it ain't been on the wires, it ain't happened" accurately reflects the attitudes of many editors. Not every editor has access to the *New York Times*, but every newspaper and radio or television station dealing with more than just local events is a subscriber to at least one news agency. The influence of the wire services is felt especially in foreign stories, which editors thousands of miles away from the scene of events may not have the knowledge or understanding to assess. Moreover, many leading regional newspapers in the United States, for example, the *St. Louis Post-Dispatch* and the *Milwaukee Journal*, have no foreign correspondents stationed abroad and have to rely heavily on the wires for stories about events taking place overseas.

Invariably, the first thing an editor does when he or she begins work each day is to check the wire service files for the previous few hours. Journalists with access to a news agency teleprinter or computer terminal usually check the reports on the wires before writing their own copy; and reporters in the field often will read the copy that has run on the wires before filing their own stories. In effect, the wires have become the modern-day chroniclers, providing the names, dates, and places where events have been and are occurring all around the globe. They are as close as any news medium has come to earning the citation of providing "all the news that's fit to print." For that reason, no self-respecting foreign ministry, intelligence service, or president's or prime minister's office is complete without a wire service terminal of its own. For foreign reporters with access to a news agency wire, the news services are a means for avoiding the tedium of basic fact checking. By providing a skeleton for the coverage of a running story, the wires can free the independent reporter to explore aspects of a story that otherwise would go uncovered.

In one sense, wire service reporters are among the most fortunate of all journalists. Newspapers, radio, and television service the broad news-consuming public directly. Their audiences are often amorphous, combining a vast range of socioeconomic strata with very different interests, backgrounds, and educational levels. The wires, on the other hand, have a very specific audience—the editors and reporters of their subscribers. Although much of their copy appears in print or as part of radio and television newscasts—and now, some of the agencies, particularly Reuters, are providing direct subscriber services to individuals—wire service reporters know that they are writing primarily for editors and reporters with roughly the same background and interests as themselves. Unlike the other mass media outlets, the wire services are in constant touch with, and receive constant feedback from, their primary readers, the subscribers. News agency bureau chiefs meet regularly with editors and other journalists to get a feel of what is expected of them; and they often are inundated with special requests that give them a sense of what their customers want.[8] The power of the wire services, therefore, comes not merely from the resources they can throw at a story or the speed with which they can disseminate material, but from the professional collegiality that infuses each report. In most cases, wire service reporters know exactly what is expected of them in terms of both style and content.

The danger, of course, is that the wire services also can become news gatekeepers, molders of a national editorial consensus on what is news and repositories and disseminators of story lines and conventional wisdom. Beyond that, the "ding" of the bell on a wire service's teleprinter—signaling an urgent story—is often enough to set off a filing frenzy and a bout of pack journalism anywhere in the world. In this sense, therefore, the wires not only report news, they make news.

Unquestionably, the most influential news agency in the United

---

[8]Ironically, wire service reporters regularly complain that except for "rockets"—demands that they cover a story a competitor has already published—they get the least feedback of all from their own head offices.

States is the Associated Press, a cooperative of its press member-subscribers. A study of foreign reporting in ten leading U.S. newspapers between November 6, 1987, and January 6, 1988 (which included the first weeks of the intifada), showed that the AP placed a total of 433 foreign stories in these newspapers, compared with 132 for UPI and 126 for Reuters.[9] Therefore, AP's performance during the intifada—and particularly during the first weeks of the uprising, when the press's agenda for the story was being set—is worthy of special scrutiny.

One thing stands out after reading all of the files sent out of AP's Jerusalem bureau during the first weeks of the uprising: extreme care was taken in preparing the reports. Although mistakes were made, they usually were corrected within hours. Beginning with the very first story AP filed, facts and figures usually were double-sourced and sometimes triple-sourced in the copy that was filed. Where possible, all of the sides to a story were given the opportunity to provide their own version. Where there were discrepancies or differences in the description of events among Palestinian, Israeli, or UN sources, each version was given and each source was identified. At least some historical context was provided as each new angle in the story developed. And credit was given to each press source whose material was used. The material was crafted to the highest professional and ethical journalistic standards. Nothing was overblown or hyped. Little that was substantial, accessible, and verifiable was omitted.

This very careful attention to detail, however, when combined with the essentially ephemeral nature of wire service copy, may explain why it took television's images to thrust the intifada to the top of the American press's agenda—and why the wires are less influential now in setting journalists' work schedules. In the past, when teleprinters held sway in editorial offices, "hard copy" provided on paper by the wire services would stay on an editor's desk all day, and anything unused would be thrown away at the end of a shift. Some of the better editors would reread the copy at the end of a shift and file some of it away for future reference. Today, with computer terminals, many editors never even see the material printed out on paper. Nor do they keep it for reference. It thus disappears into the ether. And even if it is archived in a data bank, many editors

[9]Michael Emery, "An Endangered Species: The International Newshole," *Gannet Center Journal*, Vol. 3, No. 4 (Fall 1989): 163.

prefer not to go to the time or expense of retrieving something just on a hunch. Thus, editors are losing the ability and even the will to ask the classic journalistic question "Didn't I see something about that (subject X) a few days or weeks ago, and doesn't it fit in with the information we are getting now?" With the rise of this phenomenon, the wire services' ability to influence stories that require perspective is eroding.

Compounding this phenomenon is the very nature of good wire service copy. From the outset, AP, for example, was well ahead of all of the television and newspaper outlets on what were to become some of the main themes of the intifada coverage—among them, the gratuitous and deliberate beatings of Palestinians by Israeli soldiers and border police;[10] the Israeli army's lack of control over the situation;[11] and the fact that the rioting might be more than just a small outburst of violence.[12] However, in getting the record straight and in providing the often great amount of data that gives validity to the wire service report, many of these trends and themes became buried in a mass of other details. What editors remember when faced with this mass of information is not a single detail or trend, but the event itself. Moreover, wire service copy is striking in its uniformity of style. There is almost no personal voice in the writing that would make one story or one aspect of a report stand out above the hundreds of others being filed from around the world. In order to make the copy as palatable as possible to as many editors as possible, and as protection against the problems of bias on the part of individual reporters, a report written in Poland reads much the same as one from Jerusalem. Thus, the wire services today may help set the press agenda on breaking events but not the press themes that develop out of those events.

One of the more fascinating things that emerges out of a study of media coverage of the intifada is how frequently major stories appeared first on the wires but either were not picked up at all or had to be "rediscovered" by another medium (usually after a staged media event) before becoming a subject for general press attention. For example, at a very early stage, AP highlighted the false rumors being spread by the rioting youngsters—like the "fact" that Israeli soldiers had poisoned the water

[10]AP, 10 December 1987, 11:06 GMT and 15:18 GMT.
[11]AP, 9 December 1987, 12:15 GMT.
[12]AP, 13 December 1987, 18:41 GMT.

supply in the Gaza Strip city of Khan Yunis,[13] or that soldiers were preventing the wounded in Gaza City from entering hospitals[14]—and pointed out the significant influence these were having in fanning the flames of the rebellion. Few of the other major press outlets reported on this decidedly significant phenomenon.[15]

On December 17, AP reported that Palestinians and UN refugee workers were complaining of food shortages in the refugee camps, the result of widespread commercial strikes and Israeli-imposed curfews. The story, as so often happened, evaporated into the ether and was rediscovered only by the *New York Times* on January 11, 1988, and by CBS on January 14, 1988. It became a major story for all of the media only on January 19, when the Israeli military helped create a media event on the subject: soldiers at roadblocks that day were ordered to prevent trucks with gifts of food from left-wing Israeli Arabs and Jews from entering the Gaza Strip.

Probably the strongest message to emerge from studying press coverage of the intifada is that in today's television age, being first, being fast, being accurate, and being professionally skilled and ethical may not be enough. Each medium must be able to use its foremost qualities to the maximum if the public interest is to be served. Print, for example, need not be tied to television's tyranny of time. It can devote considerably more space to a particular story than television or radio does. If permitted to, print reporters usually can take more time to gather information and to prepare their material than their counterparts in television, because they are not bound by the need to seek out appropriate images to accompany their text or to spend hours in an editing room preparing tape. In a medium where words predominate, and where the audience has the ability to review those words endlessly, nuance and ambiguity—the essence of real-life situations—can be given their fair share of time and space.

If the case of the intifada is any guide, print is still wrestling with the problem of how to deal with the new information age. Its practitioners are still carrying with them the baggage of bygone days—before television's

---

[13]AP, 14 December 1987, 19:44 GMT.
[14]AP, 15 December 1987, 13:24 GMT.
[15]A notable exception was the report by Dan Fisher, "Rumors Helping to Fuel Unrest in Gaza," *Los Angeles Times*, 17 December 1987, p. 10.

emergence as the primary press agenda setter and before news flow became a news deluge. Like television, it does not appear to have considered many of the implications inherent in this age of advanced technology and hyperquick information dissemination. It therefore has yet to find its real niche or to fill all of the niches left by television. Is it to be a medium of record, a collection of feature stories, a mirror on the world, or a vehicle for analysis? Should it try to compete with television in describing events, or can the unique skills of print reporters and the unique nature of print as a medium be used more effectively by abandoning some of the old, standardized print practices?

Most print outlets use a mix. Inevitably, however, because of the need for some sort of agreed format and routine, one or two approaches will predominate. The decision on which approach should predominate and which format should be used is a strategic one. Certainly, in this sense, the news organizations' strategies (or the lack thereof)—even more than the reporter's personal skills—affected the final product during the coverage of the intifada.

In the modern information age, particularly during a crisis period, readers can suffer from both information overload and, at the same time, a lack of the right kind of information—the kind that acts as a rational and measured counterweight to the strong emotional messages of television and provides the analysis that gives meaning and coherence to apparently haphazard news events.

To their credit, the four news outlets did not revert to what has become the standard cop-out for many news organizations facing these issues. They did not escape into purely violence-oriented stories or the use of soft feature stories that fill pages and give the appearance (but not much else) of news coverage. They did write about violence, and a goodly number of reports were feature stories, but the reporters also sought, to a greater or lesser degree, to find what lay behind the events they were covering. The question one must ask, though, is whether they went far enough in exploring the huge hole in coverage that television left in its wake.

Print's confrontation with the difficulties that were inherent in the intifada story highlights many of the long-term structural problems and considerations it, as a whole, is facing today. None of the staff reporters for the *New York Times*, the *Washington Post*, or the *Los Angeles Times*, for example, spoke Hebrew fluently. None of these large organizations was able to free up a parachutist who had worked extensively in Israel before, in order to bolster the coverage. Regardless of the medium they worked for, many of the reporters complained of running battles with editors who could not comprehend the nature of the ongoing story or the significance of a particular event.

AP, despite its vast manpower and technical capacity, is an example of how a lack of an overall organizational strategy for dealing with news crises, and therefore an inadequate allocation of resources, can affect the nature of its coverage. One striking feature of AP's coverage of the intifada was the relative lack of in-depth analysis. Although AP often was far ahead of other organizations in spotting major features of the intifada, during the height of the crisis period, despite a number of background stories showing how a particular situation had evolved, these features rarely were pulled together to show trends or to provide readers with a deeper understanding.

This was largely the result of in-house bureaucratic considerations that were reflected in both monetary and nonmonetary resource allocation. The AP foreign desk in New York works on three shifts, twenty-four hours a day, seven days a week. But often there is little coordination between the shifts—and what one shift may consider important, the next will ignore. In-house coordination was lacking. AP reporters also complain that executives never were available on weekends, when some of the most important events took place, to provide all-important guidance. AP relied heavily on established office routine to pull it through the intifada. But established routines, based as they are on past experiences, cannot always cope with the unknown. Someone within each organization must take responsibility for dealing with those situations for which there are no pat answers.

Although AP was fortunate in having a considerable body of reporters who had served either in Israel or in the Middle East, it chose to send them in in dribs and drabs to bolster the coverage, rather than as a task force. The AP staff in Jerusalem, bound to its primary mandate of meticulous fact gathering and fact checking, was overloaded. With so many different parties involved and so many different versions of events being proffered, there was little time to think about what the facts meant.

Nicholas Tatro, AP's experienced Middle Eastern and Israeli hand

and Jerusalem bureau chief, told me with some bitterness: "We either should have had more of the right kinds of bodies here, or we should have had more guidance from New York to take the supervisory load off us. As it was, we were a huge vacuum cleaner. I simply didn't have the time to sit back, look for trends, and assess what was going on."[16]

During a crisis, particularly one taking place in a number of different and widely separated locales, journalists often are happy just to get something to write and to get the description of an event right. One of the recurring faults of crisis coverage is the failure to stop and ask "What are we missing?"

The behavior of the three newspapers pointed up other underlying problems of crisis coverage. The *New York Times's* long-term commitment to the Middle East story has yielded stunning results, including three Pulitzer Prizes for its reporters in less than a decade. However, the intifada was to highlight a number of structural weaknesses in the newspaper's reporting strategy. The outbreak of the intifada could not have come at a worse time. It was a foreign editor's nightmare. The *Times's* prize-winning reporter, Thomas L. Friedman, was on leave, writing his book *From Beirut to Jerusalem.* His replacement, Joel Brinkley, was not scheduled to arrive in Jerusalem until the spring. Some of the newspaper's former Israel correspondents, like Peter Grose or Terence Smith, had quit; and those who had worked in Israel and were still in the *Times's* employ, like David Shipler and James Feron, were tied down in other jobs. More important, though, the *Times's* house rules were relatively inflexible, preventing it from adapting adequately to the situation.

John Kifner, an experienced Middle Eastern hand who recently had returned to the United States after many years abroad, was the foreign desk's choice to lead the newspaper's coverage of the intifada during the first months of the uprising. *Times* policy is to use copy only from its own correspondents—unless absolutely necessary. Kifner, despite his long background in the Middle East, essentially was thrown into a situation for which he was unprepared. Although he was an area specialist, he had worked in Israel only infrequently. He had few personal sources in the Israeli hierarchy and no time to develop the sources he needed, because *Times* policy demanded that he begin filing immediately.

[16]Nicholas Tatro, conversation with author, June 1990.

Kifner responded by doing what every quality parachutist in such circumstances does: he worked the streets. On the streets and in the small villages in the West Bank and Gaza, he was on even ground with all of the other reporters. Few of the other journalists around him had covered the occupied territories in any real depth during the previous few years. Most were in the same boat, scrambling to find out what was going on in a world that had changed completely almost overnight. Fortunately for the reporters, the Palestinian side of the intifada was largely a street story where traditional sources were of less importance, and reporters had more or less equal access to events and personalities. On this level of reportage, Kifner was better than most. However, the result of this approach to reporting was a serious imbalance in the coverage. The Palestinian side was covered in considerable depth, with a strong emphasis on the human side of the story. Kifner's dispatches included eyewitness accounts, interviews with a broad spectrum of Palestinians, and investigative reporting—including one of the very first interviews with a leader of the Palestinian underground.[17] But the *Times*'s reporting on the Israeli side was restricted to official public statements, speeches, and comments by Israeli journalists and a relatively small number of interviewees.

Kifner might have been able to overcome some of these problems had he been given the time to develop the Israeli sources that would have provided a greater degree of balance. But the *Times*, in addition to keeping to its policy of not using wire copy and demanding that Kifner file almost daily, decided on a stratagem that can only be described as "shuttle journalism." As backup to Kifner, the newspaper's editors sent in a series of reporters who stayed for a few days or weeks, worked the same sorts of streets as he did, and then left. This was not assistance, but duplication. There was no continuous backup that could have created continuity in the daily coverage and allowed Kifner to branch out into areas he had not been able to deal with because of the pressures of the daily assignment. Moreover, according to the paper's State Department correspondent at the time of the outbreak of the intifada, David Shipler, the newspaper's news desk was highly reluctant to print interpretive or analytical pieces on the news pages, preferring to leave that to the Sunday "Week in Review"

[17]John Kifner, "From Palestinian Rage, New Leadership Emerges," *New York Times*, 6 February 1988, p. Al.

section.[18] Thomas Friedman's occasional interpretive pieces were the exception, not the rule. As a result, the *Times*'s coverage included much of the "what" that was going on in the occupied territories but too little of the "why" Israel was acting as it was.

The *Times*'s coverage was further disrupted when its local Israeli stringer, Roni Rabin, who did much of the research and legwork for the reporters, left to join the AP just as Joel Brinkley was taking up his post at the beginning of April. While Kifner stayed on for a while to help Brinkley get settled in, that was not enough to overcome the discontinuity. The most notable result of this discontinuity in personnel was a loss of that most important of all organizational resources: institutional memory. It does no good, for example, to have a thick Rolodex of telephone numbers when the reporter does not know who the people on the white cards are or what kind of information they might be able to contribute.

Having come late to the story, lacking a background in the Middle East, and lacking the backup on which *Times* reporters rely heavily, Brinkley never really got into the story. The result was that the *Times*'s coverage for the next year of the intifada—with the exception of occasional pieces by Friedman—was notable for the paucity of insight, analysis, and nuance. And it was precisely at this time—when the dust had begun to settle, when the initial shock of the uprising had begun to wane—that a careful examination of what the rebellion meant in the long term was most important to readers.

The *Washington Post* was in an entirely different situation. It, too, had a policy of using wire copy only with great reluctance, and it also demanded that its reporter, Glenn Frankel, file almost daily. But Glenn Frankel had been in Israel for a considerable length of time, had a clear mandate and backing from his editors, and knew precisely the way he wanted to cover the story. His was an example of personal, reportorial strategic planning with backup by editors. The result was a Pulitzer Prize.

Frankel was fortunate in a number of ways. He had covered another popular uprising—in South Africa—before coming to Israel. He knew that when uprisings of this sort occur, there are no hard rules either in the way people behave or in how a story can be told. Unlike AP, for example, he and his editors accepted the premise that they could not be

---

[18]David Shipler, conversation with author, February 1989.

comprehensive and that there would and could be holes in the daily coverage. Unlike the *New York Times*, he was intent on analyzing what was happening.

He had come to Israel with a clear mandate from his editors to report on the Jews. His predecessors had done a lot of reporting on the Palestinians, and the *Post* had been subject to a considerable amount of criticism by Jews for what was perceived to be a very uneven handling of the Arab-Israeli dispute. Frankel, prior to the intifada, thus put a great deal of effort into developing Israeli sources. When the uprising erupted, he was well positioned to tell the Israeli side of the story in a way the *New York Times* correspondents could not. Although he had spent little time in the occupied territories, he benefited from the reputation his *Post* predecessors had built up among Palestinians and from the chaotic nature of the uprising. Like the parachutists, he was on an equal footing with everyone else who took to the streets to cover the story.

Frankel decided early on to adopt two basic tactics. As he told me later, he wanted to tell the story from the point of view of the "little person" as much as possible, and he wanted to stop every once and a while to double back and "sift the ashes" in order to ask questions there had been no time to ask while the events were taking place and to reanalyze the situation. The long-term strategy was to build up a body of knowledge of events and impressions over time—and then to take the first cut at history.

In retrospect, when his reporting is viewed over a period of more than a year, there is a sense of continuity, direction, balance, and insight. His Pulitzer was a justified professional recognition of a cumulative body of work. But from a newspaper reader's point of view, there are also obvious holes in the strategy he used. Although he had occasional support from Jonathan Randal, the *Post's* longtime Middle East correspondent, Frankel operated for most of the time with only a local stringer for backup. He had to file every day during the crisis period that lasted until May 1988 and could not but get caught up in dealing with daily breaking stories. He thus had little time until June 1988, when the pace of news developments began to slow, to sift the ashes on a regular basis. His tactics really could be implemented in full only after the height of the crisis was over. During the crisis period, he was at the same disadvantage as all of the other reporters who had to cover the daily story on their own—and he could not provide, in real time, enough of the all-important threads that would have tied the individual stories together and made sense of the chaos.

Undoubtedly, overall, in the first three months of the uprising, the most effective organizational strategy of any of the American print media was that adopted by the *Los Angeles Times*. What is striking as one reviews its reports during this period is the newspaper's ability to provide real-time factual information, in-depth background material, and real-time analysis—often all in the same article.

Like the *Washington Post*, it had a long-serving correspondent, Dan Fisher, in place. However, unlike the other newspapers, it regularly used wire service copy. Like the *New York Times*, it began by shuttling parachutists in and out. However, one of them, Kenneth Freed, did stay for most of the month of February and got to know the story—and therein lay one of the main keys to the newspaper's success.

Dan Fisher had begun his coverage alone. Even at the earliest stages of the uprising, he had packed his stories with detail and background information. But one of the problems any correspondent dealing with a crisis faces is that his or her slowly and painstakingly accumulated background material is used up extraordinarily rapidly. It is not unlike the situation soldiers find themselves in at the outbreak of a war. The material needed for battle leaves the warehouses at a faster rate than it can be replaced. At some point, the generals then have to decide whether to leave holes in the battle line—as the *Washington Post* did—or to change the battle plan itself.

The *Los Angeles Times* took the latter approach. The presence of a parachutist who could take on the load of doing the daily story freed up Fisher—even at the height of the events-driven news coverage—to do background research and analysis on a regular basis. In most cases, the analysis and background were not presented as special pieces, as was the case with the *New York Times* and the *Post*, but were integrated into the body of the text of the daily story or were placed immediately adjacent to it, thus continually providing both context and extensive background information in real time.

Unlike the *New York Times*, Fisher had Israeli sources and used them—although not to the same extent as Glenn Frankel. From Fisher's writing, however, he appears to have been more at home with Palestinian society than Glenn Frankel was. Unlike the television reporters, his language was cool and reserved, with the result that the event he was describing often had a greater lasting impact on the reader.

Surprisingly, at the end of February, the *Los Angeles Times* dropped its highly successful approach and withdrew its parachutist. Although the paper continued to use wire copy extensively, Fisher was put in the position of having to do many more "daily" stories. More important, though, the heart seemed to have gone out of the *Los Angeles Times*'s coverage. Although it produced a monumental question-and-answer tour de force on the Arab-Israeli dispute on April 3, it lost its decided edge over the other media outlets in the amount of analysis it could provide in the daily story.

Fisher's skills at sifting the coals and Frankel's approach to sifting the ashes highlighted what was probably the biggest hole in print's coverage of the crisis period of the intifada. Fisher's and Frankel's interpretive stories were what may be best called "close analysis"—the explanation of the daily event or the summation of the past few days' news. There were few attempts by print reporters, in the first months of the uprising, to try to tie these individual events together with thematic threads. For example, by mid-February, it was patently obvious that a political solution to the uprising was going to be difficult, if not impossible. It also was obvious that there could be no purely military solution. There was, however, a growing body of evidence—all of it reported as individual stories, but never tied together—that Israel would use the ultimate weapon any organized state has at its disposal, its bureaucracy, to impose controls on the Palestinians. The restrictions on food distribution in the refugee camps, the seizure of Palestinians' identity cards, the impounding of Palestinians' cars until their owners voluntarily submitted to interrogation or helped dismantle improvised stone roadblocks put up by the protesters, all were reported as separate events. They never were tied together in any of the stories to show that Israel had launched what amounted to a bureaucratic war of attrition. It was a classic example of the continuing problem of how to differentiate the forest from the trees while under pressure and how to judge the direction in which the entire ecosystem is going.

In comparing the basic approach to analysis by the print media with that of television, one contrast is particularly striking. Print invariably gave the job of doing analytical, background, and investigative stories to the most experienced and longest serving reporter in the area. Television, on the other hand, gave the job of analysis almost entirely to Washington-based reporters or to special home-based parachutists. It is no wonder, then, that print's overall analytical work was far superior to that of television.

The intifada raised a whole series of complex issues that had major implications for the future of both the Middle East and U.S. foreign policy. Those media representatives who had the personal background and who were actually in the field and not merely masticating ideas far away were the only ones in a position to present to the public realistic scenarios of where the uprising might lead. Print, however, is caught in a dilemma with which it has been reluctant to deal: how to approach the whole question of analysis during a crisis period is one of the major strategic questions it has left largely unaddressed.

Unlike television, which has allowed more and more editorializing to creep into its reports, the leading American newspapers have made substantial efforts in recent years to divorce reporting from editorializing and to reduce the amount of speculation in dispatches that are printed. Analysis lies in the gray area between descriptive reporting on the one hand and editorializing and pure commentary on the other. If trends are to be projected into the future and not merely presented as past history, there must be some element of speculation as well. One can understand why many organizations are unwilling to grapple with the issue of trend analysis. Trend analysis is a risky business for any organization—particularly those that are under constant public scrutiny, like the press. It leaves the media outlet open to charges of bias and agenda setting merely because, by definition, any trend that is projected into the future cannot have any direct evidence to support it and always will have someone ready to dispute its validity.

A common, but inherently dishonest, way of circumventing the problem is for the journalist to find someone with the same opinion and then quote him or her. This absolves the writer of any responsibility for the prediction. But when the thought is original and there is no one to quote, it also deprives the reader of the writer's insight. Even more dishonest is the not uncommon practice of journalists putting words into the mouths of fictitious anonymous sources.

To run away from dealing with the question of trend analysis is to act with cowardice. What is needed are appropriate in-house guidelines for the analytical reporter. It is quite apparent from the dispatches printed about the intifada that print editors have yet to define either the frames for all forms of daily newspaper analysis or when trend analysis, in particular, is appropriate and expected during a crisis. Also evident from the intifada coverage is that the decision on when to publish an analytical article and what sort of analytical article would be acceptable was very much an ad hoc determination. However, guidelines are precisely what is needed to help editors judge, among other things, how much time off from the running, events-driven story their reporters ought to have. Otherwise, correspondents cannot have the time to think and to explore and to question.

The pressure of events-driven coverage prevented print reporters from questioning many of the statements and tactics of the protagonists. Written skepticism by reporters was confined largely to the refutation of outright lies by the various parties or to the examination of Israeli policies that were patently not working. For example, most reporters wrote stories about the campaign of civil disobedience launched by, among others, Mubarak Awad and newspaper editor Hanna Siniora. In addition to refusing to buy Israeli cigarettes and other Israeli goods, part of that campaign was to include a refusal by Palestinians to pay taxes to the Israeli authorities. However, there was not a single interpretive article that questioned the wisdom of that part of the campaign or pointed out that the Palestinians who refused to pay taxes might be walking into a bureaucratic trap in which the Israelis held most, if not all, of the cards. Refusing to pay taxes was a strategic blunder in many ways. It enabled the Israelis to interrogate a large number of Palestinians under a legal umbrella. It permitted the Israelis to begin exerting new forms of control over the Palestinians. But probably most important, it moved the battle against the intifada indoors. The success of the intifada had been predicated on ensuring broad press coverage of major events. By allowing the Israelis to bring the campaign into government offices or into barbed-wire enclosures, where the interrogations took place and from which journalists were barred, the Palestinians undermined one of the pillars of the uprising: publicity.

One of the often ignored aspects of being a foreign correspondent is that the individual foreign reporter, especially during a crisis, is expected to cover the same wide gamut of events and issues as does the entire news desk at home. That, in itself, is an invitation to mental overload during a period of crisis. To compensate, there is always a temptation to fall into conventional wisdom as an escape from the daily psychic wear and tear— that is, to take that tiny step from routine daily practice to routine daily thought. One remedy is to take time off for thought and reconsideration of the meaning of events.

Time off from the daily story provides other benefits as well. During crises, traditional sources, no matter how honest, often are useless or unavailable because they are too busy, they choose to make themselves unavailable for one reason or another, or they simply don't know what is going on. The skilled journalist needs time to develop new and more applicable sources. In the case of the intifada, the best Palestinian sources were often hospital doctors and social workers—people with whom journalists had had little or no previous contact. Among Israelis, some of the best sources were the clerks, plumbers, and teachers, who were mines of information after they had done their reserve service in the occupied areas.

Moreover, unlike commentators and op-ed writers, analytical reporters need to get into the field without the pressure to write if they are to discover aspects of the story that they and others have missed and if they are to verify hunches. If the reporter is under constant pressure to produce copy, he or she invariably will go for the easy story or the story that is most familiar to them rather than the more important one that may take time to unearth. Only real corporate strategic planning can resolve the inherent conflict between the need for field work, the need for cogent consideration of the evidence already gathered, and the need to ask what is missing in the coverage. Unless these sorts of issues are addressed, readers will continue to be deprived of some of the most important and basic services a competent daily newspaper reporter can provide during a period of uncertainty.

The ultimate benefit to the public from a cogent, strategic approach, and print's ultimate strength as a medium for the gathering, processing, and dissemination of information, lies in diversity. During the intifada, the major print outlets managed to maintain a very considerable diversity in their approach to the events that were taking place. But there is a constant danger that under the pressure of events, the constraints of time, and the ability of spin doctors to shape perceptions, readers in the future may lose both the benefit of cogent analysis and the capacity to select from a menu of news-gathering approaches.

If one accepts the basic democratic premise that the ability of the public and of political leaders to compare different approaches and observations to events is what forms the basis for rational debate in public policy-making, then any monolithic press approach to an event is a danger to democratic political decision making. Since the broadcast media have, by and large, chosen the monolithic route, the responsibility for maintaining diversity has, almost willy-nilly, fallen to print. If print, as a medium, chooses to take up the challenge, each print outlet will have to make choices on what to cover and how to cover it. The question is whether these choices will be dictated by a vision based on forethought or by circumstances. Forethought is a powerful defense against pack journalism. Unforeseen circumstances drive individuals to club together for self-defense.

In an age when sophisticated news management by vested interests is beginning to spread beyond the confines of Madison Avenue and Washington's beltway, when a falling dollar has raised the cost of covering events abroad, and when the decrease in competition because of the increase in one-newspaper towns has eased the pressure on budget directors to spend money on foreign coverage, diversity is greatly endangered. It is all too easy for news executives to retreat into thinking that technical, graphic, or stylistic differences can substitute for diversity in content. To maintain an adequately high level of public debate, different approaches to raising the level of public discourse are required. The creation of a broad public data base, together with a commitment to encourage a variety of interpretations by those in the field about the meaning of events they are covering, the issues that are being raised, and where these events may lead in the future, is one of the most important challenges faced by print.

N · I · N · E

Journalists as Participants

Many journalists maintain that their job is to be nothing more than a mirror on the society or event they are covering. No concept of journalism could be more fallacious. Journalists have been participants in political and social processes ever since the profession began three hundred years ago. The very act of transmitting information from one individual to another makes a journalist an active participant in any story he or she writes. The moment a reporter describes an impression, condenses a long statement, or chooses between subjects for the lead paragraph in a story, he or she is no longer a mirror. The reporter is creating or altering people's perceptions of the world around them. The founding fathers of the United States understood this concept explicitly and for the common good chose to protect the right of journalists to be more than chroniclers by crafting the First Amendment to the U.S. Constitution.

Today, nowhere is this role of participant better symbolized than in the nightly stand-uppers by reporters on television news. Like the narrators of old radio serials, they summarize what already has happened, move the plot of a running story along with descriptive and bridging commentary, and provide inklings of what is to come as well as the moral message of the story, if any.

For more than two centuries—but especially following the growth in literacy and the advent of the penny press in the 1830s—the press in the United States, as an intimate of the political process, has played a remarkable and effective role in helping to set the national social and political agenda. The development of the telegraph in the 1840s made it possible for the first time to print that day's news, as well as to intervene rapidly with a public reaction to events taking place in Washington.[1] The telegraph created an information loop between the policymakers in Washington and the rest of the country. Feedback journalism was to become one of the outstanding characteristics of the American press system and American political life. The arrival of radio, and later, television, created a whip effect within the loop. Information could go out on the loop and a reaction could come back within a few hours. Satellite technology boosted the speed of the loop immeasurably by permitting interviewees thousands of miles apart to talk to each other and react to each other's statements in real time.

So close is the press involvement in the national decision-making process that it is very difficult at times to tell whether it is a separate "fourth estate" or a fourth, unelected branch of the U.S. government. The intifada is an example of how it wavers and waffles between these two roles, stepping back and forth through the often blurry line that separates the two concepts of journalism. At times during the intifada, some media outlets sought the power that a branch of government has—without the formal and legal accountability that is built into the American system of

---

[1]Two good histories of the early development of American political journalism and its influence can be found in Michael Schudson, *Discovering the News: A Social History of American Newspapers* (New York: Basic Books, 1978); and Thomas C. Leonard, *The Power of the Press: The Birth of American Political Reporting* (New York: Oxford University Press, 1986). An excellent short summary can be found in Timothy E. Cook. *Making Laws and Making News: Media Strategies in the U.S. House of Representatives* (Washington D.C.: Brookings Institution, 1989), 14–24.

governance. After coming under attack for having exerted that power, these same outlets retreated under the protective mantle afforded the fourth estate by law and tradition. During the intifada, television, in particular, sought both influence over foreign policy decision making and the prerogatives usually accorded neutral bodies in a political dispute.

As foreign policy decision making and policy implementation takes place, and as reporting on that policy is conducted in the United States today, it could not have been otherwise. The so-called free press of the United States is hardly free to do everything it wishes, even when it keeps within the strictures of libel law. And even when they work abroad in totally different cultures, most American journalists operate under what can best be termed "Washington rules." This unwritten and often unspoken code of behavior is the outgrowth of time, tradition, and circumstance. Virtually every reporter covering the national and foreign affairs beats in Washington absorbs these rules almost osmotically, as part of the process of being socialized into the capital's society. The most cynical of daily correspondents abides by it because it is one of the organizational imperatives of the American system of daily journalism. It is one of the demands editors make, and a journalist who breaks the rules does so at his or her peril. However, by keeping to the code of Washington rules— the U.S. equivalent of the Israeli system of co-optation and control— foreign correspondents and their editors cannot but run afoul of leaders of countries and organizations that operate under different political systems and different rules.

Rule number one states that wherever possible, any foreign event must have an American angle. This is very much the outgrowth of America's strong popular tradition of isolationism and lack of interest in foreign affairs. The American angle, no matter how peripheral, is therefore one of the most important items on any journalist's agenda. One of the basic assumptions of most of the mass-audience U.S. press is that any story abroad has to be made relevant to that mythical American information consumer, often named "Joe Six-Pack" by press practitioners. This is done either by stressing the basic human drama in an event, or by turning a foreign story into a local or national issue, or both. As one AP foreign staffer said, only partly in jest, "The first thing you learn when you begin working here [at the AP] is that your first paragraph better have a hard lead and your second paragraph better have an American angle—no matter how irrelevant." It is only natural that when this presumption becomes implicit or explicit in a foreign journalist's framing of a story, the press's focus will be broadened to include the corollaries that the United States government either has a role in or ought to have a role in directing the course of events in question. When there is no immediately apparent American angle, the press invariably turns to the State Department to get one by asking for a comment or interpretation and, if the story is deemed important enough, a U.S. government policy decision on the matter. If no policy decision is forthcoming, then the press often wages a public campaign to get one. In this sense, the State Department press corps, as a body, is prointerventionist. Since the network newscasts tend to deal primarily with national and international news and therefore are heavily focused on Washington, their news divisions tend to be even more interventionist than print outlets are. Such was the case during the intifada.

Rule number two states that after a comment or interpretation or policy statement has been elicited, it is fed back to the person responsible for dealing with the subject for a countercomment. All of this is in the interest of what usually is termed "fairness." If a countercomment is forthcoming, an information loop is established, with the journalist or his or her organization acting as the gatekeeper. If more than one party is involved, then an information matrix is established—with the journalist at its center—coordinating and often filtering the flow of data. This power, inherent in the journalist's job, is a source of fear for most governing elites.

This then leads to rule number three: that each governing elite will try to take control of this flow of information and to use the flow in its own self-interest. Information manipulation is part of the game. It is considered axiomatic that whoever tells a particular story first, or is the first to raise an issue, sets the agenda for everyone else in the area of policy-making. It is also assumed that while print may be the first to tell a particular story or to tell it in depth, television, even if it comes late to a story, usually will be the first to tell it to the nation. Therefore, the person or organization that is first in getting its version onto television will be the one to effectively control any public debate on the subject.

Washington spin doctors operate on the assumption that reporters needing to maintain the contacts they have established and faced with inevitable deadline pressures will acquiesce in the creation of what amounts to an information condominium. Each member of the condominium is permitted to protect its own prerogatives jealously, but each can demand services from the other. Thus, for example, a U.S. administration can raise any red herring as an issue and expect it to receive full coverage.

If there is a single hard dogma amid all of these rules it is rule four, which states that contact shall not be broken except under the most exceptional circumstances. To break contact is to lose one's position as a participant. To be shunned or ignored is the worst punishment one party can mete out to another.

Rule number five states that each party can raise almost any item for discussion if the party agrees to the basic premise that the only people with a right to participate in high-level public policy-making are narrow elites who speak to other narrow elites. Those senior reporters in Washington and editorial board members of major media outlets who agree with this premise are considered members of the elite. Gadflies need not apply. This is, in part, also a result of the routinization of news gathering. It simply is easier for a journalist to have to deal with a limited number of known sources. Members of legislatures usually are consulted only on foreign policy issues as either supporters or opponents of agenda items already raised by the elites. Constituencies are consulted only if they are "victims" of a particular policy or have a well-oiled lobby that can propel their representatives to the fore. Constituencies are mobilized by the press only as a punitive measure—and in particular, if one of the parties is seen to have broken one of the rules. In this sense, Washington rules support established hierarchies and are profoundly antidemocratic. So unusual is it for common electors to be consulted by journalists that the appearance of a defined constituency in news stories on a regular and repeated basis is the clearest public indication there is that a media outlet has launched a crusade to change some policy decision.

These basic premises are reflected in the structure of the news organizations themselves and in their daily working routines. In most news organizations (although not all), reporters who cover the State Department or the White House are considered higher up on the organizational ladder than those who cover Congress. It also is rare for a Washington-based correspondent to venture outside the beltway to seek out the mood of the general public—except during an election year.

Rule six states that if there is any dispute not covered by these rules, precedents set in the application of day-to-day practical politics in Washington shall apply. For example, prevailing U.S. social and political mores are invariably the prime measure used to judge the legitimacy of other foreign regimes.

From almost the very beginning of the uprising, Washington rules permeated the coverage of the intifada by the American foreign press corps, and often it was the application of those rules that created the most tension between the press corps and the Israelis and Palestinians. No journalistic medium, not even the *Washington Post*, for whom the U.S. government is a local story, kept as rigidly to Washington rules or used them to as great an effect as did television.

By its very nature, with an anchor sitting either in New York or in Washington introducing the story, television makes a foreign news story into a local one—at least visually. The story is further localized by the television reporter who appears in a stand-upper. He or she looks familiar, dresses like us, and uses our own language, no matter which strange and exotic place the reporter may be in.

The strong Washington orientation is not merely a response to the perceived need to cater to Joe Six-Pack. It is also a function of how television news operates in general. Senior television reporters today are media stars with the same face recognition by the public—and the same salaries—as many movie actors. Fame and recognition are the direct result of exposure on the screen. The more often a reporter appears, the better known he or she becomes, and the higher the salary that can be demanded. There is always, therefore, pressure from senior Washington reporters to get a piece of any good running story, no matter how unfamiliar or far away, in order to ensure continued personal public exposure. This, in turn, makes them highly reliant on government officials who know something about the events taking place, for the raw material that will get them on the air.

No less important are the bureaucratic turf battles between the New York and Washington bureaus. The two bureaus invariably are at odds over which should get more of the limited air time. Generally speaking, the New York bureaus control foreign news coverage. But for reasons of prestige and internal corporate power, the Washington bureaus constantly argue for more air time. Many Washington bureau chiefs maintain that almost any story can be told from the national capital, because there are so many sources in the government or in the nearby think tanks. For internal corporate peacekeeping purposes, the Washington bureaus often get their way.

It is no wonder, therefore, that the intifada was "Americanized" almost from the onset of the rebellion. From December 16, 1987, when the U.S. administration made its first comments on the Palestinian uprising, until December 24, when Washington shut down for the Christmas vacation, television broadcast no fewer than ten U.S.-angle stories or comments by anchors about the intifada—five by ABC, three by CBS, and two by NBC. When these reports were combined with the dispatches from the field, a classic Washington-style information loop was created.

Many print outlets, especially those with small or nonexistent foreign staffs, rely just as heavily on assessments by government officials for guidance on the importance of a particular foreign news story and the way in which the story should be played. This is true especially when the country involved has such an intimate and dependent relationship with the United States as Israel does.

The press's general reliance on the government for guidance gives the administration an enormous capacity to shape public perceptions, particularly of events occurring in places that are unfamiliar to editors. Merely by commenting, the administration can shape the nature of news coverage in places thousands of miles away. However, this is hardly a one-way street. Because of the existence of the feedback mechanism, the very act of asking questions, the comments elicited before a particular story is printed or broadcast, and the actual reporting of news from the field also influence policymakers in the way they think and approach a particular issue.

The number of comments elicited by the press from administration officials during the intifada makes it difficult to tell which was more important in molding the direction of press coverage—the events in the field or the administration's reactions to them. AP, for example, recorded no fewer than six separate official U.S. government statements about the intifada from December 15 to December 29, 1987. This information loop of field event, Washington comment, Israeli reaction, Palestinian reaction, field event, Washington comment, Israeli reaction, et cetera had a profound effect on the nature of the uprising itself.

By Christmas, for example, the feedback from Washington had made the Palestinians in the occupied territories realize that they had done something unprecedented. Indirectly, through the press, they had reached the highest levels of the U.S. administration. This realization was a key reason for the sustainability of the uprising in the critical first few weeks and months. The frustration and anger at the press expressed by Israeli officials during the first weeks of the uprising was in no small part the result of the realization that Israel had been drawn into this loop, had no means to control it, and could not escape from it. Moreover, for the first time, the Palestinians, whom the Israelis had tried to exclude from any participation in the diplomatic process, had been included in the loop on an even footing with Israel.

Incensed, blinded by their own conventional wisdom, and either ignorant of or oblivious to Washington rules, Israeli officials proceeded to make almost every mistake possible. This is hardly surprising. The system of co-optation and control had broken down and little prior thought had been put into replacing it with another comprehensive media policy. Most Israeli public relations activities in the United States outside the precincts of government were left to American Jews who understood the American political and media scenes. Israeli leaders, when they came to the United States, invariably met the media in highly structured environments—speeches to friendly audiences, press conferences, or interviews on the Sunday television talk shows. These leaders show all of the signs of having been totally unaware of the real day-to-day conditions and rules under which the U.S. media operate and were therefore equally unaware of the need to prepare adequately for the eventuality that some day, Israel would be inundated with journalists operating under those rules.

Rule number four states that thou shalt not break contact. Yet, during the middle of December, that is precisely what the Israelis did. Both Defence Minister Rabin and Foreign Minister Peres were out of the country, and no one in the cabinet wanted to talk publicly in their absence.[2] What few comments there were, were essentially reactive, not based on an initiative designed to place the Israeli position on the media agenda. The army refused to allow journalists to accompany Israeli patrols

[2]Peres arrived back in Israel on December 20, and Rabin returned on December 21.

or to speak to soldiers in the field—so even the Israeli human interest element was absent. By default, then, only the Palestinians put forth their positions forcefully to the press.

Obliviousness to rule five also had immediate effects. As a participant under Washington rules, television demands that the other parties to a story pay attention to its own agenda items. One of those items is the demand that there be drama in any long-running story. Yet another is that each party recognize and accept the importance of that most fundamental aspect of television news, image. During the previous two decades, U.S. politicians not only had acquiesced to this demand, but such spin doctors as Republican party media consultant Roger Ailes had made an art out of image manipulation. Moreover, the Reagan White House, which had been built on image, was both acutely aware of the subject and extremely sensitive to the image projected by others.

The intifada was an example of what happens when one party does not buy into television's agenda and concerns. The Palestinians quickly recognized the importance of image, and they played to it. By contrast, both the Israeli army and the Israeli government, although aware of this issue, took an almost perverse pride in ignoring and demeaning this central item on television's agenda. On December 21, in a speech at Tel Aviv University, Prime Minister Shamir stated: "Law and order come before putting on a pretty image." He was critical of the press for projecting "negative aspects [of the confrontation] out of all proportion. Against challenges like these and efforts to distort the truth, what we have to do . . . is not surrender to considerations of our image which are products of the media." But the scenes of Israeli soldiers gratuitously beating Palestinians were hardly "products of the media." Television may have manipulated taped images, but it certainly did not create them.

On December 23, Yitzchak Rabin stated, "I know that the description of what is going on in the territories, the way it is interpreted by the media, is not helping the image of Israel in the world, but I am convinced that above and beyond the temporary problem of our image, the supreme responsibility of our government is to fight the violence in the territories and to use all the means at our disposal to do that." What Rabin failed to recognize was that image and responsible government action are not necessarily mutually exclusive. As Margaret Thatcher had demonstrated innumerable times, a leader can take unpopular actions and still retain a positive image. And Israel's image abroad had long before become part of the government's and the army's "operational environment."

The Palestinians were rioting, in part, because they knew that not only had they been able to place their case before the world, but Israel's popular position in the United States had begun to weaken. For example, in a piece on Israel's image problem on NBC on January 2, 1988, Raja Shehadeh, a prominent Palestinian civil rights lawyer, stated, "The nature of Israel is that it cannot tolerate to have a bad image and it cannot tolerate to have people thinking badly of it." In the same program, Haider Abdul Shafi, the head of the Palestinian Red Crescent in Gaza, remarked, "Even if you wanted to make this sort of publicity here in Europe and the United States, it would have cost millions of dollars."

Whether plaintively, as in the case of NBC's Martin Fletcher, or with a stern warning, as was the case with CBS's Bob Simon, the television network reporters kept returning to the issue of image throughout their coverage—that is, to Israel's unwillingness to deal with it.[3] Print mentioned the subject of image only rarely, possibly because it is not a major concern of wordsmiths.

Rabin might have been right in his assessment had the other tactics he had ordered worked and actually put down the rebellion. But the tactics, based more on wishful thinking than on a clear assessment of the situation, did not work. Meanwhile, at the same time Israeli spokesmen were railing against the press and beginning to restrict the movement of journalists in the occupied territories, Israeli officials unwittingly were creating one media event after another, none of which advanced Rabin's stated aims. These media events sustained the information loop at a time when the revolt itself was beginning to falter. In the last week of December, for example, the Israelis began mass trials of the rioters—thus putting their entire system of military courts under press scrutiny.[4] At roughly the

[3]The issue of image was first mentioned on NBC on December 18, 1987, barely one week after the U.S. television networks had begun covering the uprising. Over a shot of Israeli soldiers beating a captured Palestinian, Martin Fletcher stated, "The Israelis are afraid their tough tactics are harming their image in the world." This may have been either an example of wishful thinking or an attempt at agenda setting, since the first official public comment on the issue by Israeli prime minister Shamir occurred on December 21.

[4]The first trials of individual Palestinians began on December 21, with almost no publicity. Heavy press attention began only on December 27, when the Israelis began bringing Palestinians to court en masse.

same time, they began publicizing their intent to deport some of the alleged organizers of the rebellion.[5] On January 3, the first deportation orders were issued. On January 13, the first four Palestinians were deported to Lebanon. On January 19, Rabin announced that the army's new policy would be to try to quell the uprising "with force, power and blows"—in other words, beatings instead of bullets.[6] These events, created as a matter of policy, were the work not of the press, but of Israeli officials. In fact, the press was used by Israeli officials to pass on the "message" that Israel was going to get tough.

As each media event occurred, it was inevitable, given the information loop that was in place, that both the U.S. government and the Palestinians would be drawn in to comment, and this, in turn, would increase the pressure on the administration to come up with an interventionist policy and give the Palestinians more and more opportunities to present aspects of their case. Once the intifada was well under way, barely a day went by without one major media outlet "looping the loop" by presenting a U.S.-based story on the intifada to accompany a dispatch from the field. In January alone, the *New York Times* looped the story twelve times,[7] the *Washington Post* nine times,[8] and the *Los Angeles Times* eight times.[9] ABC looped the story eight times,[10] CBS four times,[11] and NBC three times.[12] Significantly, most of the looping was done not after the Palestinians had initiated something, but after the Israelis had an-

[5]Defence Minister Yitzchak Rabin first announced his intention to begin deportation proceedings at a meeting of the Labor party caucus on December 22, where he stated, "We must try to concentrate more on the arrests of organizers and inciters—even if it involves hundreds [of arrests]. . . . And I think we must use expulsion. Otherwise we will lose control." (See AP, 22 December 1987, 19:35 GMT.)

[6]This policy, highlighted extensively by the foreign press, was to create a considerable amount of controversy among the Israeli public and confusion within the army on how the order should be interpreted. Rabin has since claimed that beatings were to be used only to subdue Palestinians and to prevent unnecessary bloodshed caused by the extensive early use of firearms. However, in later courts-martial of soldiers accused of using excessive force and of beating Palestinians after they had been taken into custody, the soldiers stated that the order was interpreted differently by senior officers and that there was an "environment" within the army that encouraged the use of widespread beatings.

[7]January 5, 6, 13, 14, 15, 20, 22, 24, 25, 26, 27, and 29.

[8]January 5, 6, 8, 15, 21, 23, 26, 27, and 29.

[9]January 5, 7, 8, 19, 23, 25, 27, and 28.

[10]January 3, 6, 7, 12, 14, 18, 22, and 27.

[11]January 6, 13, 14, and 28.

[12]January 14, 25, and 28.

nounced policies, like the deportation of alleged intifada leaders and the beating of Palestinian youngsters.[13]

Loops, once well-established, become extraordinarily powerful political mechanisms. By their very nature, they help clarify issues and statements that politicians often prefer to keep obscure. However, they also can reignite or inflame situations that may be calming down, because they put pressure on each party included in the pathway to act, or to react, or, at the very least, to appear to be acting each time the loop makes one circuit. As data circulate, the constant stream of questions, criticism, defensive and offensive actions, attempts at agenda setting, and self-justification from each of the parties make loops almost self-sustaining. The need to cope with, adapt to, and plan for future changes in the behavior of all of those involved can exhaust and weaken the parties. The intifada loop created a dynamic that enabled the rioting youngsters to sustain their uprising, led journalists to cover the story in great detail, forced the United States to intervene, made American Jews question Israeli government policy, united Arab-Americans behind a common issue, drove Israeli leaders to hunker down in defense, and eventually pressured Yasir Arafat to negotiate the terms of a dialogue with the United States. As occurred during the intifada, loops come to a halt only when exhaustion and stasis set in and there is a consensus among the parties that all of the available energy in the dynamic has been used up.

Here is a detailed example of how the loop worked on television. In the period immediately before the New Year's doldrums, the Israelis re-iterated their intention to deport Palestinians and the State Department repeated its opposition to this policy. Nonetheless, the occupied territories remained relatively quiet, and Israel had announced its intention to release one hundred prisoners as a gesture of goodwill. In an interview in *Haaretz* on December 29, Rabin stated confidently that "the riots in the territories will not happen again." But, as was to happen repeatedly during the intifada, a confluence of events—some planned, some unexpected—altered the situation dramatically.

---

[13]At times, there was a very self-conscious use of looping, as when Mike Wallace, on January 13, had Rita Hauser, a prominent American Jewish peace activist, comment on scenes of violence that were being projected on a television screen in front of her.

On January 3, Israel announced that it would deport nine Palestinians. That same day, an Israeli soldier in the village of Ram, north of Jerusalem, shot a Palestinian woman who was hanging up her wash on the balcony of her house. Rioting broke out immediately in the village and in two nearby refugee camps. The stories of the expulsions and the killing were covered in detail by both print and television. The reports included interviews with Israeli spokesmen and with the families of those who were to be expelled. That same night, ABC also ran a report on Washington's reaction to the situation that explicitly demanded a more active U.S. role in halting the violence. Among several interviews on the subject, Michael Hudson, a Middle East expert at a Washington think tank, stated, "The stakes are so high for the U.S. in the region that it would be irresponsible for an American government not to take the initiative." Here was an example of the loop working at full tilt—with the added dimension of television acting as an agenda setter, trying to change U.S. policy and bring the United States directly into the action. The Reagan administration still was resisting the temptation to be drawn into the conflict, and the next day, David Shipler, the *New York Times*'s diplomatic correspondent, noted that U.S. reaction to the expulsions "had been muted."

That would not last long. By January 5, the rioting had spread. The policy of deportations, combined with the killing of the woman, had restarted the uprising. In the Gaza town of Khan Yunis, one man was killed and eight others wounded. Israel, as it would do constantly throughout the intifada, had fallen into a trap of its own design. As NBC's Martin Fletcher commented that night, "Israel seems to be losing its grip." That night, the United States voted for a resolution at the UN Security Council condemning Israel's policy of deportation.

By the following day, the rioting had spread further and television returned to using Washington-based stories as a vehicle for more agenda setting. ABC ran a piece by John McWethy that noted both the $3 billion in aid Israel was getting from the United States and the frustration of Arab-Americans over the administration's policies. A piece by CBS dealt with reaction by American Arab and Jewish leaders, as well as by Senator Patrick Leahy, to the Security Council vote. In a stand-upper at the end, Bill Plante noted, "But as both sides in this dispute know, perception is often more important than official policy. And there is no doubt the daily scenes of violence have made it more difficult for the administration to back Israel."

On January 7, ABC, which was to lead all of the networks in attempts at agenda setting throughout the intifada, ran the loop almost single-handedly. The package that night, which ran an extraordinary seven minutes and fifty seconds, began with a highly charged introduction by Peter Jennings: "When the Secretary of State said today that violence has never brought peace to the Middle East, he was repeating what hundreds of politicians and statesmen have said before him for as long as anyone can remember. Today, the Israelis have shot and killed another Palestinian. The Israeli prime minister is thumbing his nose at the United Nations. The Israeli government and the Reagan administration are getting on each other's nerves." The introduction not only hyped and charged the loop, it served to introduce the main parties who would be included in this particular evening's circuit.

There followed a report from Dean Reynolds with pictures of the day's violence, including shots of Senator John Chafee being caught up in a riot during a visit to the Kalandia refugee camp. Prime Minister Shamir was quoted as saying that he would refuse to meet with UN special envoy Marrack Goulding, who was scheduled to arrive soon. The piece ended with an interview with Palestinian newspaper editor Hanna Siniora calling for a campaign of civil disobedience, plus more camera shots of violence. With this piece, the day's action by each of the parties in the field had been summarized and television's perceived need for drama had been served.

The Reynolds report was immediately followed by a story from John McWethy in Washington. McWethy noted that Secretary Shultz had gone out of his way to diffuse tensions with the Israelis, and included an interview with Israeli Ambassador Moshe Arad. There followed an interview with Khalil Jahshan of the Association of Arab American University Graduates, who introduced the main item for the political agenda—that the United States should be much tougher in putting pressure on Israel to "cease and desist" in its violations of human rights. Now the American angle, as well as the unspoken demand that television be allowed to help set the national agenda, had been included in the package, too. McWethy ended with a stand-upper in which he noted that Israel's relationship with the United States was "under great stress." With the reports on the day's events in the occupied territories, Washington's reaction, Israeli reaction, the Palestinian reaction, and the introduction of a major item for the political agenda—possible U.S. intervention—the loop had been closed.

It was now time for television, as a full-fledged participant in the loop, to argue on behalf of the item it had raised for the policy-making agenda. The ABC package turned from reportage to advocacy. The third report was a long special by Pierre Salinger. The piece combined intifada imagespeak, which by then was in full flower, with agenda-directed interviews. The combination drove home the point already made, that the Israelis and the Palestinians could not resolve their problems on their own. The report began with all of the classic shots: Palestinians shouting, tires burning, Israeli soldiers on the streets. An interview followed in which Seri Nusseibeh, a Palestinian professor of philosophy in Jerusalem, warned that "ultimately we will get to a total bloodbath."

Next came a segment on living conditions and shots of squalid refugee camps. Salinger noted that some Palestinians had seen living conditions improve under the Israelis, but most of those who had the advantage of an education could find only menial work after graduation. The comment was accompanied by shots of men working at sewing machines and cement mixers. An interview with Israeli researcher Meron Benvenisti brought home the point that you "can't bribe people with materialistic improvement."

The piece then cut to a series of imagespeak visuals drawn mainly from archival footage that was not identified as such: soldiers firing their rifles, women cowering near a doorway, Israelis beating Palestinians. Over a shot of an Israeli policeman kicking a Palestinian, Salinger noted that a recent public opinion poll had shown that 70 percent of Israelis had reacted favorably to "tough and often brutal" responses to demonstrators.

There then followed a series of intercut interviews. Israeli Cabinet Minister Dan Meridor stated, "Remember the U.S. advice to the Teheran government. 'Don't be too harsh.' I don't want a Beirut or Teheran near my home." Over another piece of unidentified file footage of soldiers patrolling in the streets, Salinger noted that "Israel is sitting on a time bomb." In the next interview, former foreign minister Abba Eban, a leading Israeli dove, stated, "This is a situation that cannot get better— like a malignant disease." Over a shot of the Israeli cabinet in session, Salinger noted that the Israelis claimed that there was no leadership on the Palestinian side in the occupied territories. To which Seri Nusseibeh replied, "That is Israel's fault. We have not had any proper leaders because, in general, any Palestinian who is in, or rises to, a leadership role is either put into jail by the Israeli authorities or deported." Dan Meridor responded, "Any Palestinian willing to talk to us was either killed by PLO terrorists or intimidated and scared away from talking to us."

The piece ended with a comment from Benvenisti: "It's a hardening of positions on both sides. I don't see any way out of it." The implication of the piece as a whole was that without outside help (that is, American intervention), the violence would simply go on and get worse.

By this point in the uprising, the loop had developed a self-sustaining centripetal dynamic of its own, sucking anyone who ventured near, like Arab-Americans and American Jews, into its vortex. The U.S.-based stories were not merely human interest or reaction pieces. Eventually, they became vehicles for constituency mobilization behind American intervention. The Israelis could see the consequences created by the loop but seemed to have no idea how to deal with it. As Avi Pazner noted, "It's very difficult to counteract the pictures."[14] Since they could find no way to co-opt the foreign press, which was in the midst of a filing frenzy, the Israelis sought to control press access to the story by preventing journalists and camera crews from entering areas where violence was occurring. On January 7, the chairman of the Foreign Press Association, Robert Slater, complained, "We are certainly disturbed by what appears to be an increasing number of incidents limiting our access to the story in the occupied territories."[15]

What the Israeli army did not understand was that merely limiting access would not halt the filing frenzy. Some visuals would always be available. The Israelis could not close off every potential trouble spot in advance. Jerusalem remained open for coverage. Outsiders, whether they were serious diplomats like UN envoy Marrack Goulding, interested politicians like John Chafee, or political opportunists like Britain's Secretary of State for Foreign Affairs David Mellor, would always be able to provide the media with an entrée into the occupied areas during their tours there.[16]

---

[14]AP, 7 January 1988, 20:45 GMT.
[15]Ibid.
[16]Mellor's official visit to Gaza on January 4, 1988, was a particularly interesting example of a modern, continued media event. With the cameras rolling, the minister suddenly began berating

There was also plenty of archival footage by this point, and intifada imagespeak was sufficiently well advanced so that icons and emblems could
take the place of images that could not be captured in the field. As a last
resort, studio graphics were available. Even more important, the uprising,
because of the information loop, had become as much of an American
story as an Israeli-Palestinian one. And the American story could and did
produce its own images. The only hope the Israelis had was either to alter
their tactics and policies in the occupied areas, or to counteract the images
produced by Israeli-Palestinian confrontations with photo-ops that would
present the Israeli government's side of the story, or both. However, to a
very large extent, the Israelis ignored both possible tacks.

In a sense, the intifada story resembled an atom in a cyclotron. Each
time it made one full passage through the loop, it gained both speed and
momentum. For the television networks, intifada imagespeak and home-
office packaging provided the guidance mechanism within the loop. Israel
might have been able to alter the parameters of the loop through negotiations with the press—as is done almost daily in Washington. But the
foreign press was viewed as essentially adversarial—an ally of the Palestinians—and therefore, no partner to negotiations. Moreover, the foreign
press, by late December, had become an important domestic tool for the
government—a scapegoat for failed policies, political inertia, and bureaucratic blunders. The situation reached a peak on January 9, when an
Israeli officer in Gaza charged that an ABC cameraman, Yossi Mulla,
had paid Palestinian children to riot in front of the camera. The allegation,
which had not been checked, was repeated on Israeli television by Avi
Pazner. Three days later, the charge had to be withdrawn. As the *Maariv*
newspaper put it on January 12, "An army officer who spread the
rumor . . . did not check the initial, unfounded information provided by
a soldier." The soldier had been influenced by "a lynch atmosphere against
reporters."[17]

---

an Israeli army colonel for the ill-treatment Israel was meting out to the Palestinians. Mellor
had the media stage to himself because he knew, in advance, that the colonel was forbidden by
regulations to reply, and that, in any case, the officer spoke little English and would have been
incapable of responding effectively to the verbal whiplashing. The incident was broadcast around
the world.

[17]This government-supported lynch atmosphere seriously backfired on the government during

For the remainder of the intifada, clashes between reporters and soldiers became routine. Reporters, photographers, and camera crews not only were regularly excluded from the scene of events, many had their film confiscated and some were even beaten. As with the beating of Palestinians, Israeli soldiers in the field used the tension created between the politicians and the press to vent their frustration and anger on journalists. By mid-January, the army and the government, confused and hurt by the press coverage, were virtually at war with the foreign press corps. However, it was a war without a strategy, with few tactics, and without any goal, other than to control press access to events.

A fascinating dynamic developed. Israeli spokesmen, bereft of any ideas on how to alter the flow of the loop, came to believe that they could not change things and virtually gave up trying to intervene to alter the course of the news flow. Their belief, and the actions or inaction that arose from that belief, thus became a self-fulfilling prophecy. The press, which by this time had become quite defensive about the criticism of its coverage, stopped seeking out official Israeli interlocutors—especially those who would use the opportunity to berate them for their work. This, in turn, meant that there was even less coverage than before of genuine Israeli concerns.

With each passage through the loop, Israeli credibility dropped further. Day by day, it reached what seemed to be its nadir, only to fall further a few hours later. For example, after foreign television networks had broadcast almost six weeks' worth of examples of gratuitous and deliberate beatings of Palestinians; after Defence Minister Rabin, on January 19, 1988, had publicly announced his policy of beating Palestinians; and after a *Haaretz* correspondent on January 22 had reported that he had counted 197 Palestinians who had been hospitalized in Gaza as a result of having received beatings in the past two days, Prime Minister Shamir blandly stated, "We don't have a policy of deliberately beating people."[18]

---

the 1991 war with Iraq. After the Iraqis began firing SCUD ground-to-ground missiles into Israeli population centers, the Government Press Office, for propaganda purposes, mobilized three camera crews to film the damage to civilians caused by missile explosions in the Tel Aviv region. Very quickly, however, the crews refused to go out to the site of the destruction, because they found that they were being beaten up by soldiers and rescue teams on the scene who were by then predisposed to preventing any television team near them.

[18]AP, 24 January 1988, 19:15 GMT.

On the same day, television did not have to look very far to provide a graphic refutation of Police Minister Haim Bar Lev's blatant lie: "There is no beating. This is an unfortunate term."[19]

By this time, there was a growing feeling within the State Department that not only did someone have to step in to halt the killings and beatings, but the United States had to move to save Israel from itself.[20] This feeling was, in part, the result of the heavy coverage given to the moral anguish American Jewish leaders were evincing as a result of the beatings policy and the continuing pictures of bloodied and beaten Palestinians. The intense press coverage given the American Arab and Jewish communities helped to create the kind of domestic constituency and consensus necessary for direct diplomatic intervention. A *Jerusalem Post* story on January 25 about a wall in Ramallah covered with bloodstains from Palestinians who had been beaten, galvanized journalists, liberal American Jews, and administration officials alike behind an interventionist policy. No less important, however, were the open splits within the Israeli cabinet over which policy to pursue in dealing with the Palestinians. These splits, it was hoped in the administration, would provide an opening for direct American action.

When Egyptian president Hosni Mubarak visited Washington on January 28, the administration already had geared itself up to break with past policy and intervene to try to halt the violence. The turning point in press coverage of the intifada, Israeli action in the field, Palestinian activism, and American intervention occurred on February 1. Once again, a confluence of events—some planned, others not—altered the course of the intifada.

As February began, the Palestinians in the occupied territories were at the height of their success. The intifada had become institutionalized and routinized, and the uprising's leaders, mainly by employing young "enforcer" squads, had the means to ensure compliance with their demands. In terms of the media, the underground leadership could count several major successes. The most important was that they had succeeded in turning the uprising from a media event into a press beat.

A press beat is a subspecialty of journalism, usually centered around

[19]See, in particular, CBS and ABC, 24 January 1988.
[20]Senior State Department official, conversation with author, January 1989.

a single institution, like the courts, or even a single building and its occupiers, like city hall or the White House, or around a particularly narrow subject, like medicine. Unknowingly, the Palestinians, because they had been able to sustain the rebellion for so long, had tapped into one of the fundamental organizational characteristics of all modern daily journalism.

A reporter assigned to a beat does not necessarily have to have broad knowledge. He or she is expected to know only what is going on within the confines of the beat itself. Thus, parachutists coming to the intifada story did not need to know the wider historical context of the Middle East dispute. They merely had to know how to get around the Israeli-occupied territories. Once the occupied territories beat was established, the Palestinians were able to focus journalists' attention primarily on their activities.

More important, however, the establishment of a beat routinizes a reporter's work. The essence of any beat is the anticipation and presumption by all of the parties involved that it is worthwhile for media outlets to commit long-term resources, because the beat will produce news. Beat reporters are usually the first to be called by their editors when the daily process of laying out a newspaper page or television news program begins. If the reporter is out in the field, space or air time often is reserved for them in advance in the expectation that the beat will produce a story. That is one reason why, even on days when there was a lull in the violence in the occupied territories, stories on the uprising continued to be printed or broadcast.

This phenomenon was apparent particularly in the activities of the video news agencies like Visnews and ITN (International Television News). These agencies are the video equivalents of organizations like Reuters or AP, supplying subscribers with tape and sound reports. Each had more than thirty subscribers in the Islamic world, and those subscribers were demanding a continual stream of material on the rioting—even when there was a general lull. Any incident, no matter how minor, had to be recorded in the normal dramatic fashion in order to satisfy the demand. Then, because they were available, many of these packages also were used by subscribers in the United States and elsewhere—especially if there was a shortage of other news or if a sudden hole in a news program had developed.

The establishment of any beat creates a particular dynamic between journalists and the subjects they are covering. A mutual dependence develops and journalists become subject to both subtle and coarse means of control by the people they are covering. This includes things like the scheduling of press conferences, the threat to withdraw the services of authoritative sources, and forbidding access to particular events. In the case of the intifada, the uprising's leaders were able to take control of much of the journalists' work schedules. By early February, for example, journalists had learned to anticipate that there would be riots following Friday services in the mosques. They therefore positioned themselves, in advance, at the mosque, expecting to get a story they could file. On the days in between, journalists' activities were guided to a remarkable degree by the leaflets that the underground leadership had begun to issue. Those leaflets, aimed primarily at the local Palestinian population, set out the days on which general strikes or particular protest demonstrations were to take place. Once again, journalists knew in advance where and when to position themselves to get a publishable or broadcastable dispatch.

The Israelis could have responded by creating a foreign press beat of their own as a counterweight to the one established by the Palestinians. But Israeli officialdom had, by this time, become so defensive and so xenophobic that it could neither think in nor react according to such strategic concepts.

February was the pivotal month. On February 1, the schoolchildren in the occupied territories who had been on their mid-winter break returned to their classrooms. The schools provided an ideal center for organization, rallies, and communication. The same day, the new U.S. peace proposal was leaked to the press for the first time[21]—establishing a political process in which the Palestinians could participate. It was also the day when Israeli soldiers, for the first time in more than two weeks, killed two Palestinians. Those killings provided the spark that set off a new round of rioting and reestablished the dramatic basis for further media coverage. Meanwhile, the Israeli army still was flailing around without a strategy— trying, literally, to beat the rebellious youngsters into submission.

[21]AP, 1 February 1988, 9:26 GMT; and Dan Fisher and Jim Mann, "U.S. Makes a New Mideast Peace Bid," *Los Angeles Times*, 1 February 1988, p. 1.

In fact, it was Israel that was taking a beating—particularly in the world press—and most of their wounds were self-inflicted. Yet, simultaneously, when they were at the apex of success, the Palestinians also were preparing the ground for the destruction of the media coverage of their own uprising. The signs of the impending destruction were there for all to see, but as so often happens when people are caught up in a crisis, the markers went unnoticed. The press, the Israeli politicians, the State Department diplomats charged with monitoring events and formulating policy in that part of the Middle East, and the Palestinians themselves were all so caught up in the momentary rush of the events that there was no one available and prepared to read the signs. In fact, if there was a singular failure of the press at that time, it was that no one stood back and began to question the conventional wisdom of the moment or to see beyond the obviousness of the events themselves. Like the other protagonists, the press, by feeding information back and forth between the various participants, had become a participant to such a degree that the journalists failed, all too often, to escape from their preoccupation with the events on the streets.

February was a time of considerable confusion for all of the parties. As the *Washington Post*'s correspondent, Glenn Frankel, had anticipated, there were shifting fronts of uncertainty. No one knew how or when new groups and individuals would be sucked into the cauldron or how they would react once inside. Israeli military commentator Hirsh Goodman probably described the atmosphere best: "It's not clear cut," he noted of the intifada as a whole. "It's not tanks coming across the Syrian border. . . . It's an amorphous *thing* that nobody can really touch and understand."[22]

On the night of February 6, Jewish settler vigilante groups began vandalizing the cars of Palestinians in Hebron. Their actions, in the midst of an already overheated atmosphere, sowed panic throughout the West Bank. Rumors of other vigilante actions spread by the loudspeakers on the minarets of the mosques, led the next day to the worst outbreak of rioting by Palestinians since the intifada had begun. The television cameras did not have to look hard for incidents of violence. The incompetence of the Israeli security authorities, as well as their continued policy of

[22]CBS, 17 February 1988.

breaking bones, became the basic themes of television's coverage. Typical was a straightforward piece by ABC's Dean Reynolds on February 8 concerning the commandeering of a bakery truck by the Israeli police in order to sneak into a Palestinian neighborhood. The rock throwers spotted it, smashed in the windows, and set the van on fire.

On February 11, a team of American doctors on a fact-finding mission entered the fray as well. At a press conference, they produced evidence of systematic beatings of Palestinians by Israeli soldiers. The evidence indicated an "epidemic of violence" by Israeli soldiers. According to one member of the team, Dr. Jack Geiger, "The numbers, rate and scope of the beatings and trauma we have seen cannot be considered deviations or aberrations. They come closer to being the norm."[23] That night, Secretary of State George Shultz telephoned Israeli prime minister Yitzchak Shamir to say that he was coming to the area personally in two weeks' time.[24]

As part of its initiative, the administration also began pulling new actors into the loop. Respected Israeli political analysts, both inside the government and out, were briefed in Washington and Israel by U.S. officials about the new policy and approach. The apparent intent was to build a constituency in Israel that would support the American initiative, or at the very least, one that would explain to Israelis why the United States was acting as it was. For example, on March 3, Zvi Rafiah, a former official at the Israeli embassy in Washington, after a visit to the United States, told reporters that U.S. leaders were alarmed because Israel appears "incapable, even incompetent, in resolving one of its most important problems, the peace process."[25]

Mid-February was also the time when the PLO decided to try to intervene. Its direct presence during the uprising had been noticeably absent up to that moment. The youngsters in the streets were derisively calling the organization's leaders "Cadillac revolutionaries."[26]

By the end of January, the PLO had begun to take a measure of

---

[23]The first press dispatch was on AP, 11 February 1988, 12:19 GMT, but virtually every U.S. media outlet gave prominence to the fact-finding group's report.
[24]AP, 11 February 1988, 23:25 GMT.
[25]AP, 3 March 1988, 21:14 GMT.
[26]The youngsters referred to the PLO leaders in this way in conversations at that time with the author.

control over the events taking place in the occupied territories. Through its communications links with the occupied territories and with the foreign press based in Arab countries, it was positioned to act politically on a broad international front and to exert a modicum of control over the front-line rock throwers and demonstrators on the streets. As had happened so often in the past, however, the opportunity would be frittered away.

Despite its technical capabilities, the PLO was probably the party least equipped to do anything substantive. Its conceptual sterility, organizational imperatives, and outdated modus operandi could not cope with the opportunities provided by the upheaval in the occupied territories. From the moment the PLO did begin to intervene directly, the intifada began to wane. Three decisions by the PLO in February served as signposts of what was to come.

Pressing to have a direct piece of the action and to make their presence known, the PLO leaders decided to try to launch a "ship of return"— with the consequences noted earlier. As a media event, it made few waves. Then, on February 19, fearful of the possible advent of a local leadership in the occupied territories, PLO headquarters in Tunis issued a statement forbidding any Palestinian in the occupied territories to meet with George Shultz. No decision did more to sabotage the local Palestinians' primary success of altering U.S. policy and drawing the United States into the fray.

On February 24, a man suspected of being an Israeli collaborator was lynched in the West Bank village of Qabatiyeh. As often happens during popular uprisings, the revolution had begun to turn on itself. Rather than cautioning against further acts of internecine violence, the PLO lauded the lynching and, in its future leaflets, called for more action against "collaborators." "Popular justice" soon became a norm. Within two years, more Palestinians were being killed by other Palestinians each month than by Israeli soldiers. As is often the case, individuals found a means to take revenge for personal, clan, and criminal disputes—all under the rubric of dealing with collaborators.

In retrospect, probably the most telling sign of Palestinian conceptual stagnation came from television. It was television's use of imagespeak that had brought the Palestinian case before the world. Throughout February, not a single new image or visual idea was added to intifada imagespeak. Repetition is a powerful element in imagespeak, but it also can create the visual equivalent of cant and cliché. Television could select or manipulate images, but it could not create them. The other actors had to do that on their own. For television, the visual Palestinian story was becoming as ossified as PLO statements had been in years past. The violence, which had begun as a cymbal crash heard around the world, soon would turn into a media drumbeat. Eventually, it became mere international-press background noise.

Satisfying news stories, those that maintain press and reader or listener interest, move the drama up to new levels. At each level, new issues, themes, icons, and emblems arise naturally to keep the news consumer's interest in the story. With George Shultz's arrival in Israel at the end of February, the Palestinians were given a golden opportunity to raise the level of the story to a political plane. Had the story reached that new plane, the intifada story would have been revitalized. There would have been a whole new set of images for television to work with, such as politicians shaking hands prior to a meeting or demonstrations by people in favor of or opposed to concessions by one side or the other. There would have been fresh sound bites as negotiators came out of meetings or stepped off an airplane. And as always happens in these circumstances, there would have been a new dramatic will-they-or-won't-they theme on which reporters could build their dispatches.

In keeping with the PLO's tradition of blowing every opportunity, the chance was lost. Instead, as the press recorded in great detail, at the end of his short February visit, Secretary Shultz delivered an almost pathetic speech in the American Colony Hotel before a large audience of the press and a nonexistent audience of Palestinian invitees, to whom the speech actually was directed. The most ironclad of the Washington rules—never break contact—had been broken.

In January, Seri Nusseibeh had voiced the need to raise the uprising from the street to the political level.[27] But he and other Palestinians in the occupied territories who could think in strategic terms could not make themselves heard, because of the heavy censoring hand of the PLO. But even if they could have challenged the aging professional revolutionaries at the helm of the PLO, they could not have been heard above the din of the thoughtless young radicals on the streets who had become drunk

[27]Seri Nusseibeh, conversation with author, January 1988.

on violence and addicted to political absolutes. By June, Nusseibeh could only lament that the Palestinians had not developed a political strategy. "I felt from the beginning," he said, "that it is not enough to wage war . . . you have to wage peace equally strongly. To do one without the other is to waste effort."[28]

Political upheavals, and the press filing frenzy that often accompanies them, do not necessarily come to a rapid end—particularly when a beat has been established. News events often develop a momentum that is hard to stop quickly, and there are always areas and issues that could not be covered in the heat of the moment and that still need exploration and treatment. During the intifada, though, it was the Israelis and the American diplomats, by their own actions, who kept the story alive for the next few months. It was, for example, the very arrival of George Shultz in the area that led to a renewed bout of violence at the end of February.

By February, the intifada as a social revolution in the occupied territories had gone as far as it was going to go. Those leading the uprising—either inside the occupied territories or outside them—showed that they had no reserves of originality, no strategy, few tactics, and only the most rudimentary sense of political direction. The Palestinians in the occupied territories were no longer initiators. By the end of George Shultz's trip, they had said what they were going to say and done what they were willing to do. From this point on, they could only react. For the next weeks and months, it was Israeli initiatives that gave the Palestinians the opportunity to react—and therefore to keep the story alive in the press. It was primarily Israeli-created media events, like the expulsion of Palestinian leaders, the beatings, and the murder of PLO deputy chief Abu Jihad, that gave the Palestinians in the occupied territories the stage on which to perform their by now repetitive stone-throwing and tire-burning dance before the cameras. George Shultz's frequent trips filled in the spaces the Israelis left out.

Any long-running media event is subject to cyclical media coverage. Themes and stories are discovered, analyzed, and then laid to rest as new issues and concepts arise. Cycles in television coverage tend to be far

[28]AP, 6 January 1988, 14:28 GMT.

shorter than those in the print media. Television, because of its emphasis on the episodic and dramatic elements in news, constantly demands excitement and novelty. Print can afford a more leisurely pace—gently nibbling at an event to achieve a degree of depth. But during a crisis, print, too, often is dragged along by the pressure of events, and the need to react to the atmosphere set by television's dramatic images.

The period from December through the end of January was the first cycle in the coverage of the intifada. It was the time when the story and background were established by both television and print, and imagespeak was developed. The month of February saw a second cycle emerge. A regular beat was established, almost all of the relevant players were introduced, and the basic roles of each party and the causes that had led to the uprising were explored.

The last days of February and the month of March saw the advent of a third cycle. As a mover and shaker and direct participant in its own right, television had, by this point, developed its own stakes in the outcome of events. Television's coverage throughout March and April was as much an exercise in Washington-style politicking as it was a journalistic enterprise. Television was operating as though it were a fourth branch of government. Daily newspapers, which throughout the crisis had maintained a more traditional posture as the fourth estate (at least on the news pages), did not have the same stakes and therefore approached the story very differently—more cautiously, and with considerably less hype.

Through its image manipulation and emphasis on the violence, television had played a major part in bringing George Shultz on his hastily arranged trip to Israel. Having played such an important role, however, it then was faced with the consequences of its pressure: the fact that there had been insufficient groundwork done because of the lack of time and the general recalcitrance of most of the parties to the conflict. As a result, none of the preconditions for successful negotiations were in place.

In a sense, George Shultz had been set up for a fall. The rush to create an image of U.S. action had led Shultz to risk a not inconsiderable amount of personal political capital and American prestige. On February 25, the day of Shultz's arrival in Israel, ABC's John McWethy described the Shultz trip as "maybe the toughest negotiation of his life." CBS's Wyatt Andrews was blunter. He noted that "a sense of overwhelming rejection is in the air." NBC's Martin Fletcher described the trip as having the appearance of "a mission impossible." Moreover, because of the lack of political and diplomatic groundwork, the Palestinians in the occupied territories could react to Shultz's initiative only with the tools they had at hand—an upsurge in violence that led to thirteen more Palestinian deaths during the course of the Shultz mission. Ironically, therefore, in its rush to get U.S. action to halt the violence, television had helped create more.

That upsurge in violence introduced the third cycle. The gong that signaled the change was a report by CBS on February 25. In it, Israeli soldiers were seen kicking two captured Palestinian youths and beating them with rocks for forty minutes. For two months, both print and television journalists had been reporting about Israeli soldiers battering captured Palestinians. But this one film segment seemed to galvanize the issue. Many of the details in Bob Simon's voiceover to the story were wrong. But that really didn't matter. The evidence in the pictures was indisputable and the impact of the images was extraordinary. What CBS had broadcast was not image manipulation, but clear evidence of criminal conduct. CBS replayed the pictures no fewer than five times in the next eleven days. Parts of the film segment were shown on Israeli television on February 26, sending shock waves throughout Israeli society and the Israeli military and political hierarchy. If previous television footage had placed Israel's international image in jeopardy, now its self-image was at stake. Worse, the soldiers involved were not right-wing activists or pathological bullies, they were young kibbutzniks—the pride of the Israeli Left and the nation's doves.

The commander of Israeli forces in the West Bank ordered his senior officers to watch the entire tape and warned against the army turning into "rabble." The Left warned that the intifada and the lack of peace were distorting Israeli society. Some, on the fringe right, threatened both the CBS office in Tel Aviv and Moshe Alpert, the Israeli cameraman (also a kibbutz member) who had taken the pictures. Camera crews in the field began to encounter increasing hostility from soldiers at roadblocks or on patrol. The previous isolated skirmishes between television crews and the army, and between the television networks and the Israeli government, was about to turn into all-out war.

The actions of both the television networks and the Israeli politicians who were calling for restrictions on press access offer a superb example of people pursuing policies contrary to their own self-interest, despite the availability of feasible alternatives.

At the February 28 cabinet meeting, Likud ministers in particular demanded that the press be excluded from the occupied territories. Moshe Katzav, the Likud labor minister, declared that "the presence of the media causes the riots. . . . If the media will not be there, I don't think there will be any more riots."[29] Katzav was repeating what already had become conventional wisdom in much of Israeli society—particularly on the political right. In a political blunder of no small proportion, that conventional wisdom soon was to be put to the test.

So long as the charges were kept to a polemical level and so long as the press was not excluded from the occupied territories, journalists really had no way of defending themselves and disproving the allegations. Foreign journalists could continue to be used as scapegoats for domestic political purposes. The dispute over who was right could continue to be used by Israeli politicians as a mask to divert attention from, and to cover over, failed policies.

To most foreign journalists, it was patently obvious in the wake of the CBS report that any restrictions on access would not be designed to stop the riots, as was claimed. Rather, exclusion from the scene of events would be intended to prevent journalists from posing embarrassing challenges to Israel's self-image and from disclosing discomfiting hard evidence of political and bureaucratic malpractice. This bit of professional journalistic conventional wisdom could not, however, be validated without an objective test.

By March, television's interest in the story had begun to wane. By introducing a new contest and a new dramatic subject in which television had high personal stakes, the Israelis would once again help to sustain the intense coverage of the uprising. By any measure of political self-interest, the construction and implementation of such a test was folly.

The anchors at ABC and CBS, Peter Jennings and Dan Rather, exhibited equal tendencies to folly. At a time when they knew how sensitive the Israelis were, at a time when they also knew that the Israeli government was considering implementing restrictions on access, and at a time when

[29]John Kifner, "Israeli Officers Ordered to Watch Tape of 4 Soldiers Beating Arabs," *New York Times*, 29 February 1988, p. Al.

one of the chief Israeli complaints had been that events connected with the uprising were not being put in their proper context, they nonetheless were surprisingly careless (or, as Israeli critics could claim, one-sided) in the wording of their introductions to stories from the field. On March 1, for example, Peter Jennings introduced a piece by saying, "A Palestinian doctor claimed the Israelis broke into a hospital, fired tear gas, and dragged out two boys and beat them." The next night, in an introduction to a piece on Israeli plans to cut press access, Dan Rather stated, "In the West Bank, Israeli troops fired tear gas into a hospital, then grabbed a teenager and threw him down a flight of stairs, sat on him, and beat him with a club." Both introductions were factually correct. However, they also were distortions of the truth. As AP had reported on March 1, Palestinian youngsters had been using hospitals and schools for six weeks as havens, hideouts, and staging grounds for rock and firebomb attacks.[30]

These two particular introductions were not one-time lapses. Such lapses had begun much earlier and would continue throughout the intifada. Peter Jennings in particular was prone to editorializing and putting spin on his introductions. For example, on March 4, in his introduction to a piece on the Israeli decision to close the occupied territories to journalists, Jennings stated, "The job of reporting there has been made more difficult. Not liking what the world has seen, borrowing a page from other countries like Iran, Iraq, and, yes, South Africa, Israel today closed most of the West Bank to reporters." Jennings's comparison of Israel with that list of odious regimes was, again, factually true. However, he left Britain and the United States off the list in spite of the fact that they had excluded the press during the Falklands and Grenada invasions.

Omission, however, was not the only form of distortion. On March 4, Dan Rather announced that "Yasir Arafat told CBS correspondent Doug Tunnell today that the PLO has met American conditions for joining any peace talks—including recognizing Israel's right to exist." The next night, the actual interview was broadcast. To Doug Tunnell, it was "a new message of moderation." Arafat stated, "We can accept easily the United Nations' auspices for a short period of time as a transitional period. We can understand the need of the Israelis and the American administration for this transitional period."

[30]AP, 1 March 1988, 19:29 GMT.

Tunnell: "Then you accept Israel's right to exist—[UN resolutions] 242 and 338?"
Arafat: "I am accepting all UN resolutions including 242 and 338."
Tunnell: "Unequivocally, tonight, Yasir Arafat accepts those resolutions."
Arafat: "Definitely."

In fact, Arafat's statements were neither new nor moderate. He had accepted "all UN resolutions" in many public statements over many years. In the interview, it was Tunnell, not Arafat, who used the expression "Israel's right to exist." Had Arafat used the term, he would have legitimized the Israeli government—something he was absolutely loathe to do. By keeping to his old, standard phrase "all UN resolutions," he was continuing to deny the Israelis legitimacy, because among those resolutions are those equating Zionism with racism and supporting the 1947 partition agreement, which, if implemented, would leave Israel without large chunks of its pre-1967 war boundaries. Both resolutions are classic Palestinian arguments for denying legitimacy to the Zionists.

At times during this extraordinarily tense contest between the Israeli politicians and the foreign press, the anchors' introductions bordered on the absurd—as though they had not even bothered to listen to the tape segments of their own reporters. On March 12, NBC's Connie Chung introduced a piece by Jim Bitterman by saying, "More Arab policemen who work for Israel in the occupied territories resigned today to protest Israel's treatment of Palestinians." But what Jim Bitterman said less than a minute later in his report was that the policemen had resigned "apparently [following] threats from the PLO."

The formal battle between the press and the Israeli authorities was joined on March 4, when Israeli soldiers set up roadblocks and prevented journalists from entering most parts of the occupied territories. Once again, at their own initiative, the Israelis had created a media event— except that this time their opponents not only had a stake in the outcome of the event, but they had powerful, nonviolent means to fight back. The event provided a "peg" for assembling all of the recent incidents of violence by Israeli soldiers and settlers against journalists. Rummaging through their by now extensive archives, all three networks retaliated by showing scenes of photographers being beaten, threatened, and jostled by soldiers and Jewish settlers; journalists being stopped at roadblocks; and soldiers covering the lenses of television cameras with their hands. ABC managed to get a camera crew into a village near Bethlehem by using a back road and was able to show that demonstrations had continued—even without the presence of the press. ABC's Dean Reynolds was able to conclude, "While the Israelis are trying to control the media, it is clear that they haven't been able to control the protests." NBC's Jim Bitterman noted, "Keeping out the media today did not keep the trouble out. . . . Whatever the image, an even worse picture could be created of a country doing away with the freedom of the press."

The total ban on coverage was lifted the next day. But just because their thesis had been disproved, that did not prevent Israeli officials from banning press access selectively. As ABC's Dean Reynolds commented the next night, "Israel is now fighting this conflict on two fronts—with the Palestinians and with the press." Large sections of the occupied territories continued to be declared off limits to journalists, with all of the closure orders being duly noted in the nightly newscasts. The image of a soldier putting his hand up to a camera lens—already in use in January— had virtually supplanted the uniform and rifle as the symbol of the Israeli army. The epidemic of almost hysterical hostility toward the press continued to spread, reaching unprecedented levels. It made little difference that the causal relationship between press presence and rioting had been disproved, and that not one of the more than one hundred Palestinians who had been killed to date had been shot while cameras were present.[31] It also made no difference that the uprising had erupted for political and social reasons. Rationality did not guide the critics. Perceptions did. And the perception among many was that the foreign press corps, and particularly the television networks, were "the enemy." Just as the uprising had, by now, developed a self-sustaining momentum of its own, so, too, had the wave of press bashing.

On March 15, Israeli President Haim Herzog declared, "The press— and I'm speaking primarily about foreign TV crews—has explicitly been

[31]The first death by shooting that was recorded on tape appeared on ABC on 4 April 1988.

a side involved in the events. . . . Cameramen [are] the main weapon [of the Palestinians]."[32] Among many Israelis, there was a desire for revenge. Right-wing Knesset member Geula Cohen probably best expressed the feelings of many: "It is better that the media will be in distress than me being in distress."[33] Clashes between journalists and soldiers and settlers increased in number. Photographers had their film confiscated and had to file for a Supreme Court injunction to get it back.[34] At the end of March, the occupied areas were closed once again to most press coverage—this time for three days. But once again, closure orders did not halt the rioting. Four Palestinians were killed on one day alone, and dozens of others were wounded.

Of course, the Israelis and the television networks were not the only ones engaged in folly. No major political event in the Middle East seems to be complete without one massive act of foolishness by the PLO. By the time George Shultz had arrived in Israel on February 25, a groundswell of media support for negotiations with the PLO had begun. The central theme was that there could be no settlement without the PLO and that the PLO was prepared to talk.[35] And after the Shultz mission failed, there was intense criticism of Israeli prime minister Shamir in Congress—even among some of Israel's best friends.[36] However, in what must be recorded as one of the supreme acts of folly of the intifada, on March 7, the PLO sent three raiders into southern Israel. They captured a bus full of women on their way to work, and in the ensuing battle with Israeli police, six Israelis were killed. The PLO media groundswell stopped dead.

The attack did not put a halt to television's attempts at agenda setting. In a classic example of Washington-style politicking, television began to help build and then publicize a broad American constituency in support of the Shultz plan. In a piece on CBS on March 12, Congressman David Obey stated, "A day doesn't go by without a call [asking] 'What are you going to do about it [the violence]?' " And CBS anchor Bob Shieffer commented that the Shultz plan "enjoys remarkably bipartisan support

[32]AP, 16 March 1990, 01:52 GMT.
[33]CBS, 2 March 1988.
[34]AP, 21 March 1988, 10:13 GMT.
[35]See ABC, 26 February 1988; CBS, February 26 and March 4 and 5, 1988; and NBC, February 28 and 29, 1988.
[36]See ABC, 6 March 1988; and "30 Senators Write to Shultz to Criticize Shamir Remarks," *Washington Post*, 8 March 1988, p. 26.

in Washington." At the same time television was pushing Shultz and his plan, it began a process of demonizing Prime Minister Shamir as the source of Shultz's embarrassment. On March 13, ABC's Jeanne Meserve noted that in Washington, "There is broad support for the Shultz peace plan and broad criticism of the Israeli prime minister." Earlier, Senator Lowell Weicker had stated, "What we don't need is for one man in the Israeli cabinet to slam the door in George Shultz's face."[37]

Shamir, of course, had brought much of this criticism on himself with a series of unbending and inflammatory statements that only served to highlight perceptions that he was politically catatonic. On March 11, for example, *Haaretz* quoted him as saying, "The only word I agree with in the U.S. plan is the name 'Shultz.' " As one senior Likud official lamented to me at the time, "He [Shamir] can't differentiate between what it is to talk to the party branch in Acco and the international community. He doesn't realize that what you say to one is heard by the other."

A not insignificant sidelight to this period was a campaign by ABC to delegitimize Shamir. Its reports on March 14 and 15, for example, emphasized the fact that Shamir had the support of only half of the cabinet and half of the Israeli people. This was true, certainly, but it ignored the fact that in a democracy, and particularly under the Israeli system of government, a leader needs only the support of half of the people in order to rule—or at least to block opposition initiatives.

During this period, only NBC's John Cochrane noted that Shamir was not alone in his opposition to the Shultz plan and that "King Hussein has not responded to it, Syrian president Assad has ridiculed it, and the PLO's Yasir Arafat has rejected it." In fact, the so-called Middle East peace initiative had broken down into bilateral Israeli-American negotiations.

All of this political activity in Washington failed to create any progress in the peace talks. And in the occupied territories, where Palestinians still were being killed almost daily, a certain fatigue and ennui had set in among the television reporters. As CBS's Bob Simon put it on March 15, "[There are] no new ideas, only old questions, and the growing feeling on both sides that there are no solutions." The next day, he described the violence as "an old and tired tragedy." By this point, despite the

---

[37]NBC, 8 March 1988.

seemingly determined efforts of Israeli officialdom to keep the intifada story alive, the television reports from the field had begun to get shorter and noticeably fewer in number, and they were being broadcast later in the newscasts (a sign of lessening importance). Nonetheless, the reporting of the violence did continue on an almost daily basis—in part because the intifada had become a beat, in part because the momentum to the story, built up over the previous months, still was driving reporters and editors, and in part because Israel's campaign to bar the press from the scene of events provided a peg on which to hang footage of the continuing violence.

Among the print reporters, the previous months' filing frenzy had begun to turn into filing fatigue. It took the return of George Shultz to the area at the beginning of April to regenerate the rioting and reinvigorate the story. But that did not last long. Beat journalism was beginning to turn into blip journalism. From mid-April onward, another cycle began. Only major events, such as the killing of an Israeli girl in the West Bank village of Beita, the killing of Abu Jihad, or King Hussein's decision to pull out of the West Bank, would engender the kind of intense coverage that had been the meat of the journalists' work in the previous months. Even George Shultz's final trip at the beginning of June did not create any significant media waves.

AP's coverage of the news in Israel in January and again in May 1988 is indicative of how coverage was being treated by all of the media. The wire services try to cover every event, major and minor. In January, despite two other major news events in Israel—the trials of Mordechai Vanunu, who sold Israeli nuclear secrets to the *London Sunday Times*, and that of alleged war criminal John Demjanjuk—AP could find the time and space for only twenty-one nonintifada-related stories. In May, there were fifty-nine such dispatches—almost three times as many—even though they dealt with such relatively lightweight subjects as a visit to Israel by Joan Baez and accusations against State Department counsel Abraham Sofaer that he had exported Israeli antiquities illegally.

The reduction in press interest in the story did not, however, halt the political attacks on the press. The Israeli army continued to impose restrictions on coverage, and journalists continued to be subjected to both verbal and physical attacks by critics. For Israeli domestic political purposes, television reporters, in particular, would continue to be participants in the political battles to come—whether they chose to be or not. The Foreign Press Association continued to log cases of its members being manhandled. Between December 1987 and June 1988, no fewer than 150 complaints of physical abuse of journalists had been registered with the Israeli authorities. "A sort of paranoia has developed about the media," Yariv Ben Eliezer, a professor of film and communications at Tel Aviv University, commented at the time.[38] Physical and verbal attacks by Arabs on foreign journalists also increased. The same kind of xenophobia and paranoia that had afflicted some Israelis began to appear among Palestinians. Camera crews, which once had been welcomed with open arms, were suspected by the Arabs of being Israeli spies; and camera crews began to find that Palestinian youths were barring access to events.

However, while Israeli popular and political attacks on the press were to continue unabated, the army, in a remarkable exercise in honest self-analysis, was in the midst of preparing a unique training docudrama on relations with the press. The twenty-two-minute film, distributed to the troops in mid-June, documented soldiers' brutality toward reporters and Arabs alike in the occupied territories. Entitled *The Camera Sees All*, the film ran through half a dozen of some of the worst and most dramatic incidents of army brutality that had been captured on tape, while saying that the dispatches of foreign reporters usually were fair and professional. "Do not make the cameraman put you on stage," the narrator admonishes. "These [scenes of troops beating unarmed Arabs and accosting foreign journalists] only make the viewer sympathize with the party who is done harm."

By September 1988, press coverage had entered a new cycle—one that was to last throughout the coming months. Print began to do what it traditionally has done best—nibbling deeper into the story and uncovering facets that had been ignored or misinterpreted during the height of the crisis coverage. Television, with no agendas left to set, withdrew from its role as a fourth branch of government, gave up intifada imagespeak almost entirely, and began doing what it does best—preparing micro-documentaries on selected subjects. The only major exception was ABC's hyped coverage of Yasir Arafat's November exercise in trying to meet American demands for a dialogue. But soon that, too, was corrected.

[38]AP, 2 May 1988, 17:42 GMT.

As one of the great, unresolved, but emotion-engendering regional issues of our time, the Israeli-Palestinian dispute will continue to attract media attention—and criticism of the media. Coverage of the intifada was not just an exercise in modern reporting of a major political event; it was also an example of the close interaction between the press and foreign and domestic politics. There are many lessons to be learned and many issues that remain to be explored.

Press coverage of the intifada raised a great number of issues about the workings of modern foreign correspondents. Most of these issues were not unique to the intifada itself. Many of them arise whenever and wherever a large body of foreign journalists congregate. Some problems and failings seem to be endemic to modern journalism, others are the product of the unique environments and historical moments in which foreign journalists find themselves. Why, for example, are some countries chosen for coverage and others not? Why does the press cover certain topics and ignore others? When two or more parties being covered are in conflict, is the reporting fair to each side? What is the place of the press in the modern political firmament? And how much of a story is shaped by a reporter's personality and views?

Editors choose to cover certain countries for a vari-

The Intifada and Practical Issues in Modern Foreign Reporting

ety of reasons. The most obvious factor is whether they are aware that a newsworthy story is taking place. Some areas of the world, like Chad or Somalia, are so isolated or their communications systems are so poor that little information about what is happening there reaches the outside world. No less important is whether the media outlet believes it can get access to the story. It does no good to spend thousands of dollars sending a reporter or camera crew to an area if the correspondent cannot get the information he or she needs. Thus, riots in Korea tend to be covered extensively, but not those in nearby Myanmar (Burma), where the military dictatorship controls both press movements and opposition politicians. The events at Tiananmen Square were covered extensively, in part because the Chinese government lifted restrictions on the press during the historic visit of Mikhail Gorbachev to Beijing.[1] The student rebellion broke out while press preparations for covering that visit already were in place. As soon as Gorbachev left, the Chinese authorities reimposed restrictions on the foreign press and pulled the electronic plug by shutting down satellite communications. Shortly thereafter, field coverage of dissent in China waned. A third, and often deciding, factor is whether the home country's interests are involved. The breakdown of the Communist system in Eastern Europe was covered extensively because the events there could not but affect American interests and the contest between the superpowers. South America gets relatively little coverage because changes in government there are not seen to have an immediate effect on U.S. interests.

Even by these standards, however, coverage of the Israeli-Palestinian conflict has been disproportionately intense, and the intifada once again raised the long-standing question of why a country as small as Israel gets so much coverage. Many answers to this question have been posited in the past. Of course, the Israelis did invite many news organizations to set up offices in Israel. And because there are a great many permanent foreign news bureaus in the country, it is inevitable that reporters will tend to cover events close to home. The country is one of the pleasantest in the Middle East in which to live. Generally speaking, it is safe. Restrictions

---

[1]For an excellent short summary of how the Gorbachev visit affected coverage of the Chinese student rebellion, see Leonard Pratt, "The Circuitry of Protest: Electronic Journalism in China, 1989," *Gannet Center Journal* vol. 3, no. 4 (Fall 1989): 105–16.

on the press are relatively few. There are excellent communications facilities. Many of the news stories are dramatic. Most of the leading Western
countries have important economic interests in the Middle East, interests
that can be endangered when there is open conflict between Israel and
its neighbors. Israel is the site of the Holy Land. Jews read and buy
newspapers. On the darker side, it has been suggested that anti-Semites
have a morbid interest in Israel.

But all of these reasons are incomplete somehow. Each can be at
least partially refuted. For example, Cyprus is at least as pleasant a place
in which to live. Jordan has excellent communications. Stories about the
Holy Land are not enough to keep a full-time correspondent busy. There
are plenty of dramatic stories in other parts of the world.

A more complete answer would seem to lie elsewhere. As one looks
down the list of the *Who's Who* of the foreign press in Israel over the past
two decades, one detail stands out. Virtually every foreign staff reporter
stationed in Israel has come from a media outlet in a democratic country.
Although Argentina, for example, has a large Jewish community, during
the period of the junta, it did not have a single reporter in Israel. Brazil
under the dictatorship, despite being both a burgeoning economy and a
largely Catholic country with religious interests in the Holy Land, sufficed
with one stringer.

And therein lies the key to this question.

Israel is both an open democracy and an as yet incomplete "state-
in-becoming." Because so many fundamental issues within the country
are unresolved, and because it always has had to face those issues while
under the threat of war, the country is, in a sense, a huge laboratory for
experimentation in popular rule under conditions of extremis. Most of its
struggles, and those of its leadership, are similar to those faced by other
democratic countries. Major issues include minority rights, how to maintain democratic institutions during a period of major threat from without,
the quest for national values, how to deal with "guest workers" and im-
migration, how to deal with civil disobedience and with the rights of a
free press during a period of upheaval or war. In a country as ethnically
diverse as Israel,[2] which operates without the benefit of a formal consti-

---

[2]A chief military censor once claimed to me that his roster of reservists listed 103 languages and
regional dialects spoken as mother tongues.

tution and bill of rights to guide its lawmakers and form the basis for a national consensus, each issue produces a major public debate when it is raised for discussion. Its population is literate, vocal, and highly opinionated. Most of the issues the country faces are not mere intellectual abstractions, but have a direct bearing on daily life. How issues of principle are decided has an immediate practical impact on the present and future of individuals and of the state as a whole. Over the years, Israel has had to deal with a very great number of major political and social issues simultaneously—each of which, on its own, could undermine the workings and legitimacy of its democratically elected government. As each issue died down or became temporarily quiescent, a new one, just as important and just as fundamental to the workings of a democracy, inevitably came to the forefront to take its place on the media stage. This created a series of ongoing political struggles over the direction the country should take. In struggle there is conflict. When conflict becomes public, there is drama—the meat of so much modern foreign reporting. When that drama can be related to events in the foreign reporter's home country, there is a media peg. Many of the most prominent disputes in Israel, whether they be the relationship between religion and state, peace with Israel's neighbors, housing or unemployment, or even constitutional law, are highlighted for all the world to see because they are carried out in the streets in noisy and even raucous demonstrations that are easy for cameras and reporters to record.

Many media critics have noted the intense coverage given to Israeli actions that involve human rights and the almost nonexistent coverage given to greater incidents of human rights violations in other states—especially in the Arab world. But given the circumstances, that is only to be expected. I do not think it is an example of press hypocrisy or double standards. There are few public debates in the Arab world over issues of human rights, and even fewer public demonstrations that would act as a peg for a news story. Those demonstrations that do occur invariably are quashed immediately by the authorities. There is also nothing comparable in those states to Israel's public and decades-long struggle to reshape its system of jurisprudence from that implemented by its former Ottoman and British mandatory colonial masters and designed to restrict civil rights, to one that incorporates modern Western concepts of human rights.

More important, a very special dynamic is at work when events in Israel are examined and reviewed by Western outsiders. I call it displacement. It is all too common for nations that have been unable to resolve issues of direct or immediate concern, or that have chosen to sweep them under the carpet, to raise those issues in a different and less domestically threatening environment. Rather than creating direct social tensions at home, the press in those countries tends to concentrate on similar issues raised by events taking place in what appears to be a familiar but geographically distant society. Israel's self-mythologizing certainly plays a part in this process. In its quest for international political and economic support, it has portrayed itself in particularly virtuous terms as a bastion of Western moral and political values, a moral as well as military ally of the United States and its value system. The fact that Israeli leaders over the years have chosen to present themselves not only as defenders of democracy in a sea of dictatorships and absolute monarchies but also as the heirs to the biblical and prophetic ideal, made displacement on Israel by Western democratic countries almost inevitable. Israel created anticipations and expectations in others that, despite its acute security problems—or maybe because of them—it could succeed where others had failed: it could find a formula for survival and prosperity that would overcome or circumvent many of the often distasteful aspects of realpolitik.

This sense of anticipation was probably best summed up by U.S. Supreme Court Justice William Brennan. In a speech delivered in Jerusalem on December 22, 1987, just two weeks after the start of intifada, Brennan first reviewed the failures of the United States in preserving civil liberties during times of threat to national security. He then stated:

> Prolonged and sustained exposure to . . . assorted security claims may be the only way in which a country can gain both the discipline necessary to examine asserted security risks critically and the expertise necessary to distinguish the bona-fide from the bogus. . . . [It] requires long lasting experience with the struggle to preserve civil liberties in the face of continuing national security threats. *In this respect it may well be Israel and not the U.S. that provides the best hope for building a juris-*

prudence that can protect civil liberties against the demands of
national security [my emphasis].[3]

It is this perception that "Israel is like us" and the anticipation that
it will "find a way and do the right thing" that, in part, leads to the
differential coverage given Israel and other states in the world.

The excesses of dictatorships are important news stories—and when journalists become aware of them and can get access to the scene of events,
they usually are covered, if often in lurid detail. Mass murders of civilians
by their own government, for example, often evoke revulsion in readers
or television viewers. But they do not produce the same popular gut
reaction as would a similar event taking place in a democratic country.
The United States, for example, faced extended displacement coverage
by European countries during the civil rights demonstrations in the American South in the 1960s. On the other hand, the mass murder of the
Kurds in Iraq after the end of the Iran-Iraq War did not preoccupy the
press for very long, in part because the Kurds looked and talked differently
than we do, but also, more important, because the killings could be
dismissed or ignored by the public as the perversions of an inherently bad
or even evil political system that they could not change. What happens
within nondemocratic political systems may be viewed as immoral or
disgusting, but it is not seen as inherently threatening to the established
order in which an American or Canadian operates. The rationale usually
used is that "It couldn't happen in a democratic country."
     This may explain, in part, why there was less coverage of the reign
of terror imposed by gangs of young Palestinians in many towns in the
occupied territories during the second year of the intifada than was given
to Israeli actions in the same towns the year before. The world of the
Palestinians was seen as essentially anarchic and without an established,
popularly elected chain of civilian authority—and therefore less immediately relevant to foreign, established societies. Israel's reaction to the
Palestinian uprising was relevant immediately because among democrats

[3]The full text can be found in Shimon Shetreet, ed., *Free Speech and National Security* (Boston,
London and Dondrecht: Martinus Nijhoff, 1990), 10.

outside Israel, there is always a deep-seated fear of how their own established institutions would react under conditions of stress—which civil
liberties might be taken away from them and how their law enforcement
units might react. An analogous case of relevancy—and one covered in
considerable depth at the time by the European press—was the massacre
of the students at Kent State University.

Displacement also has a historical component. National guilt over
some distasteful event in a country's own history can lead that country to
counsel "Don't do what we did." Similarly, attempts at self-absolution
also play a part. In the case of Israel, it is as though many countries with
extensive records of anti-Semitism and persecutions of Jews now say, in
effect, "See what it's like, now that you have your own state. Do you
behave any differently toward others than we did toward you?"

Under Washington rules, the American press actively supports the political
mores currently prevailing in the nation's capital. However, in many cases,
because the United States has no modern experience with some specific
problems that occur elsewhere, those mores are based on idealized concepts. The American press, reflecting those mores, then tends to use those
idealized standards in judging a society far away—particularly and precisely if displacement is taking place. During March 1988, for example,
there was intense coverage of the media restrictions adopted by the Israeli
army. There was no similar criticism in the United States of the media
restrictions adopted by the U.S. Army during the initial stages of its
invasion of Panama. The highly critical coverage by European journalists
of the civil rights battle in the United States came at exactly the moment
West Germany was beginning to face the problem of the *gastarbeiter* and
their civil rights, and France was seeing the rebirth of a radical, xenophobic
Right. As well, it always is easy to find mitigating circumstances in one's
own society to rationalize away why a particular reality differs from an
ideal. When displacement takes place, we are less likely to look the
other way because we, ourselves, do not have to face the practical consequences.

Displacement inevitably creates distortions in coverage. Despite some
appearances, Israel is not a Western country. Many of its basic premises
differ from those of North American and Western European nations. As

a result, when outside journalists come to examine the society with the preconceptions inherent in displacement, they often are confused, disappointed, and even disoriented. For example, in Israel, matters of personal status like divorce and marriage are within the province of the clerical leadership, not the civilian courts. A majority of its population has less than one generation's experience with democracy. Most of its citizens, whether they came from Eastern Europe or the Arab states, have no historical democratic ideals on which to fall back in times of crisis. Moreover, a growing proportion of its population, whether Arab or Jew, deeply believe in theocracy, not democracy. Even among many secularists there is a deeply rooted belief in the indivisibility of nationhood and religious identity—a concept quite foreign to Western secularists.

Although they may appear similar on the surface, many of Israel's institutions also differ in both style and substance from those found in the United States. Religiously based political parties are numerous and powerful, not merely fringe elements in the body politic. The courts operate without juries. And lacking a formal constitution, the courts operate on different premises.

The danger in habitual displacement is that it leads to false analogies, inadequate coverage, vicariousness, and eventually incorrect analyses and "surprises." Displacement carries with it an assumption that there is a universal norm for political and social behavior. That is, that there is an established order of things—a secular, democratic replacement for the concept of divine right and divine revelation. Those who use displacement tend to look for that which is familiar (including examples of their own idealized concepts of "right" and "wrong"), rather than the much more important elements on which we fundamentally differ with others. As a result, they generally end up imposing their own values on a situation that may not be at all analogous to anything in their own or their country's experience. This secular absolutism leads to a fallacious search for common ground and social bonding across cultures. It also leads to disappointment when a commonality of interests or a means for cross-cultural communication cannot be found. In anger or in disappointment, the central question becomes "If they are like us, why don't they behave like us—or as we would like to think we would behave under similar circumstances?"

An excellent example of how this attitude affects press reporting was the coverage given to the Israeli Supreme Court during the period of the intifada. Any and all cases, not merely those relating directly to constitutional law, can be brought before Israel's highest judicial tribunal. Thus, for example, unlike the United States, all Israeli murder cases, no matter what the circumstances, can be appealed to the Supreme Court in Jerusalem. Unlike its counterpart in the United States, it is both the country's highest arbiter of constitutional law and its high court of justice. During the intifada, it was called on to adjudicate on a wide variety of cases, from individual deportation orders to whether a military court of appeals should be established in the occupied territories. Foreign press coverage of the court's decisions was striking in one respect. Invariably, the decision was incorporated into the body of a more general story and not given an article all its own—no matter how important the subject. When I queried American colleagues why this was the case, the answer was usually that the justices "never come down with decisions of principle." This was hardly the case, and many decisions based on issues of principle were issued. But what the foreign journalists were saying was that none of the decisions were based on a principle enshrined in a particular constitutional law— a law that would make the case analogous to, comparable to, or directly relevant to their audiences' experiences with the U.S. Supreme Court. Lacking a formal constitution on which to base itself, the court, instead, judges individual cases of legal principle for which there are no precedents on what commonly is termed the "balance of interests." Thus, not a single deportation order issued by the Israeli authorities was canceled by the court, because security interests were believed to have outweighed all others. This kind of thinking was totally foreign and exasperating to American correspondents and they had difficulty in crafting it into a full story that would be meaningful to their audiences. Only the bottom line—the decision—was thought comprehensible, relevant, and important. Therefore, the decision to allow the deportation orders to stand became a single line or paragraph in an article.

Displacement and the belief that stories must be made relevant to audiences can explain only some of the omissions in coverage that took place during the intifada—and that continue to take place elsewhere in the world. Probably the most glaring omission was the failure to report on the activities of Jewish constituencies within Israel proper. That was precisely the same failure that had taken place in the occupied territories before the advent of the intifada. Journalists have a very strong tendency, for practical and other reasons, to seek out "authoritative" sources who are assumed to know what is happening or to be able to explain what has happened. Most of these sources are among the established elite and may or may not actually represent a real constituency. Prior to the intifada, the Palestinian constituencies, whether they were fundamentalist or secular nationalist, were in ferment. But their activities, complaints, and beliefs generally went unreported. Thus, although many signs of resentment were present, the rioting came as a "surprise." Once the intifada was under way and it was blatantly obvious that new constituencies had taken control from the old, established elites, the Palestinian common men and women who were out on the streets finally came in for their fair share of reporting. The same, however, was not true for Jewish constituents or for those Palestinians who quietly opposed the violence.

Only those Jewish constituencies that were capable organizationally of mounting staged media events—like the Peace Now movement or the Jewish settlers in the occupied territories—were given extensive press coverage. From the beginning of the intifada until the final collapse of the Shultz mission in June, not one story, either in print or on television, was devoted specifically to the opinions of Jews of Asian or North African origin, though these Jews form the majority of the voters in Israel, are the bedrock of Likud popular support, and do not think in American terms. This failure may explain, in part, the press's demonization of Prime Minister Shamir. He was presented consistently as the single block to a peace settlement. In fact, however, he was in power because he was the legal and democratically elected representative of a very considerable number of Israelis. He was not acting alone, but in concert with tens of thousands of like minds.

The failure to cover the activities of alien constituencies is a widespread phenomenon. One need only think back to the lack of coverage of the activities of the Islamic radicals in Iran prior to the street demonstrations that led to the overthrow of the shah. One can only speculate, but it may be that in addition to this general phenomenon, a special dynamic is at work in the press's coverage of Israel. The failure to cover the opinions and beliefs of Shamir's many supporters could have arisen because of a conscious or unconscious fear on the part of some reporters that if they emphasized the wide public support in Israel for policies that had been denounced in the United States, they might be accused of anti-Semitism. It may well have been easier and less risky personally to focus their personal displeasure and official American displeasure at the Likud's hard-line position by centering their attention on one man.

One of the more notable outgrowths of the failure to cover constituencies is the often repeated failure of many journalists to distinguish between a public personality and a genuine leader who is given both backing and resources by his or her followers. Journalists trying to cover a story from a distance are particularly prone to this phenomenon. A very good example occurred on ABC on January 27, 1988. Introducing a piece on a visit to Washington by Jerusalem newspaper editor Hanna Siniora and Gaza lawyer Fayez Abu Rahmeh, Peter Jennings stated, "Well, while the Israelis are searching for what they call a new Palestinian leadership, Palestinians will tell you that the leaders already exist—if the Israelis would only talk to them. Two of them were in Washington today to talk to Secretary of State George Shultz." There were two factual mistakes in this introduction. To begin with, Israeli officials had talked to both men at length over many years. More important, however, was the fact that, as Palestinians in the occupied territories would tell you, neither was considered a leader. Both were certainly public figures of some stature, but neither (and especially not the Christian Hanna Siniora) had anything even remotely resembling a constituency behind him.

Many reasons can be given for the failure to cover constituencies properly. The work takes an inordinate amount of time. One has to sit for hours on end over many cups of coffee in order to gain an interviewee's confidence. Then one may be subjected to a tirade or a speech that in cultural terms may be offensive to the interviewer. The payoff comes at that most precious of moments when, in the midst of a jumble of words, the interviewee answers a question that no one had known enough to ask.

However, in the age of ten-second sound bite broadcast journalism and quick quip print journalism, time, especially during a fast-breaking crisis, is always in very short supply. Editors, especially those operating under restricted budgets, are concerned about turnaround time, the amount of time it takes the reporter to file a story from the moment he or she begins running up expenses. Moreover, public opinion polling has made journalists lazy. It simply is easier to quote a poll or a so-called authoritative source than it is to do the hard legwork that covering a constituency entails. Authoritative sources often are wrong in their assessments. And as anyone who has ever been subjected to a poll will tell you, the questionnaires used tend to be formulated on the basis of preconceptions that frequently leave no gray areas and fail to ask many of the questions about hidden issues that are truly bothering people. This is because the questionnaires are crafted by analysts who also do not sit in cafés, car repair garage waiting rooms, or local clubs deliberately listening to others give answers to questions no one had known enough or bothered enough to ask.

Another form of constituency omission was the failure to talk to Jews outside the main cities of Tel Aviv and Jerusalem. This is a foreign variant of the failure of Washington-based reporters to move outside the beltway. Israel has an extraordinarily varied population, with immigrants from more than a hundred countries. Almost every ethnic group is politically active in one way or another, but not all reside in the two main cities. Furthermore, regional issues often color their approach to national politics and to the support they give national leaders. And in a country with such a finely balanced coalition government, those in the small towns and villages can have a disproportionate influence on government.

Journalists did travel to many of the small villages in the West Bank. But almost invariably, it was in search of the dramatic story. With the exception of a few references to the battle for popular support between secular nationalists and Islamic fundamentalists, there was little reporting on the internal debate raging within the Palestinian community between the various political groups, like Al Fatah, the Popular Front, and the Popular Democratic Front. This made it appear as though the Palestinians in the occupied territories were a virtually monolithic body—which they were not. It was not as though these battles were hidden entirely behind closed doors. All a reporter had to do was to read the graffiti daubed on the walls each night in almost every village, or listen to the often heated arguments between members of the different factions.

This failure to distinguish between differing ideologies and different political factions may account, in part, for another major failing. Television never, and print only rarely, identified interviewees according to their political affiliation. In the United States, not to refer to a major public political personality by his or her party membership would be almost unthinkable. And in an area as highly politicized as the Middle East, where virtually everyone carries around a large bundle of ideological beliefs and political prejudices, not to identify individuals by political affiliation cannot help but distort a reader's or viewer's perception of their remarks. Thus, for example, the Israeli who handled many of the cases of Palestinian arrestees and who was a frequent interviewee, Felicia Langer, typically was referred to as a "civil rights lawyer," omitting her affiliation with the Communist party. Her many public statements were not merely the product of her legal work, they were a public projection of her party's ideology. The same was true for virtually every Palestinian interviewee. Most of the interviewees who were labeled by their professional background were talking not only as supposed authoritative sources of facts but also as representatives of a particular ideology—which then shaped their presentation of the facts.

Another glaring hole in the coverage was the failure to report the activities of institutions. This, too, is a widespread phenomenon in foreign reporting. During the period of the overthrow of the Communist regime in East Germany, for example, virtually nothing was written about the inner workings of the Lutheran Church, although the church played a crucial role in helping to mobilize the protesters in Leipzig. People establish institutions like trade unions, women's leagues, or professional associations to represent their interests on a permanent basis. These institutions can be among the bodies most sensitive to the trends in the wider population. Prior to the outbreak of the intifada, the Palestinians had placed great stress on building up these institutions—and many of them were extremely active during the crisis period of the intifada. Yet, with the notable exception of reports on the *Shebiba* and two references to Palestinian institutions by John Kifner, no coverage was given to these highly important public bodies.[4] The Israeli military authorities recognized the importance of these institutions and spent a great deal of effort trying either to undermine them or to shut them down completely. And sig-

---

[4] John Kifner, "From Palestinian Rage, New Leadership Arises," *New York Times*, 6 February 1988, p. A1; and John Kifner, "New Leaders in Arab Unrest: Radical and Loyal to P.L.O.," *New York Times*, 26 February 1988, p. A1.

nificant Israeli institutions, like the Histadrut (the national trade union) and the Israeli Manufacturers' Association, were ignored completely. This is all the odder considering that so much of the Palestinian effort was directed at disrupting the Israeli economy.

The failure to cover Israeli and Palestinian institutions might have arisen for three reasons. The first is a general tendency in American reporting of foreign events to ignore institutions, because to many editors, covering them smacks of what is usually termed "inside ball"—material of interest to specialists but not to the average reader. The second reason is that most popular institutions—those not directly associated with governments—are designed to provide public services that governments cannot or will not provide. Only rarely is knowledge of a foreign language a criterion for those being hired. The staff, therefore, is naturally isolated from journalists who have no command of the local tongue. The third reason is the plague of vignettism that has overtaken much of American journalistic writing. In their search for the human interest side of the news to attract readers, many reporters today bend over backward to look for vignettes that they hope will somehow explain big and complex issues. Vignettes can and do highlight particular aspects of a larger problem, but on their own, they cannot explain them. Foreign institutions are barren deserts for vignettes—sprinkled only occasionally with small oases of human interest stories—and thus usually are ignored by many reporters as a waste of time.

Completing this list of major oversights was the failure of all of the media to read correctly many of the symbols being used. Every community, over time, develops a set of symbols its members use as a kind of shorthand to pass on messages. And in the case of the Jews and the Palestinians who have been in such intense and intimate conflict for so many years, symbols also are used as a form of communication between communities. The most obvious forms of symbolism, such as the flying of illegal Palestinian flags, were given their due share of coverage. But it was in the more subtle use of symbolism that some of the most important clues to trends lay—and these were given no coverage at all.

Two examples will suffice. During the months of January, February, and March, when the policy of beatings was at its height, there was a great deal of debate among the intellectual elite and the senior army officers in Israel. At issue was whether there might be a popular revolt in

Israel over the possibility that the young conscript soldiers themselves were becoming brutalized because of the orders to beat Arabs. A popular revolt would have had enormous political consequences. It was just such a popular revolt by the country's silent swing vote that eventually forced the Israeli government to withdraw from Lebanon.

For two decades, an almost foolproof sign of popular discontent and public worry with army policy in the field has been the Friday laundry lines in the tightly knit lower-middle-class neighborhoods. When Israeli conscripts or reservists come home on leave, their mothers or wives invariably wash their uniforms as soon as they enter the house. During normal times, these uniforms usually are hung out to dry on clotheslines that are hidden behind specially installed slats in most new Israeli apartment buildings. During times of stress, however, the uniforms invariably are hung out for all to see—a signal to the entire neighborhood that "I was worried, but my son (or husband) is safe." During the crisis period of the intifada, the uniforms were all hung out behind the slats—a sign that the concerns of the elites were not those of potential swing voters, because there was no perception of an immediate danger to those in uniform. The issue of Israeli youths being brutalized by their service in the occupied territories, while not an insignificant social issue, was, nonetheless, a political red herring.

Trees have a particular symbolic meaning in the unspoken language of the Israeli-Palestinian conflict. Since the very beginning of modern Jewish settlement in the area, the Jews have planted trees as a symbolic means of staking their claim to the land. In virtually every Jewish synagogue in the free world, for example, there is an annual collection made to buy trees to be planted in Israel. Tu Bishvat, Israel's Arbor Day, is a major festival, especially in schools. The Palestinians, too, take great pride in and care of their orchards, carefully tending, pruning, and plowing. For decades, the uprooting by one side of the trees of the other has been viewed both as a means of punishment and as revenge. A major question that was being asked, once the intifada got under way, was whether and how the Palestinians would try to bring the rebellion to the Israeli heartland. It was speculated correctly that they would eschew guns because they had been given so much media attention for limiting their weapons to rocks and firebombs. The use of live ammunition would only hurt their cause. Instead, they took their cue from the Israelis.

As part of its policy of punishing stone throwers and firebombers, the Israelis demolished houses and uprooted orchards. The symbolic meaning of these acts was the delegitimization of Palestinian landholding. The Palestinians had no equivalent response to the destruction of the houses, but they did have matches. After months of the Israeli army's uprooting of trees, it was inevitable and predictable that the Palestinians would respond. They did—setting huge tracts of carefully tended Israeli forests, scrubland, and farm fields alight in May. Most of the media ignored the tree uprootings entirely, preferring to concentrate on the more dramatic scenes of house demolitions. AP, in its chronicler's fashion, did record the uprootings, but it never explained their symbolic significance.[5] Only when the rash of forest fires broke out did the media awake to the issue. Even then, the fires were reported only as events, not as political messages.

Undoubtedly, one of the most controversial media issues raised by the intifada was that of what often is termed "fairness" and "context." Both are extremely loaded terms and were used extensively by both pro-Israeli and pro-Palestinian media critics to bash the press's coverage of the up-rising. The public debate over fairness and context is not a new one and may be unresolvable. The problem with both of these terms is that they are almost undefinable. *Context,* in the form used by media critics, usually means both background material and the relationship of the news event in question to other events, both past and present. The question is, how much background and history is it possible to put into a story without losing or confusing the reader or viewer? And how much is really necessary for a nonspecialist to make a reasoned judgment of the situation? In the case of the intifada, for example, context also could have included the part played by the Israeli-Palestinian dispute in the East-West superpower conflict that was still under way then. Or it might have included third world issues. Or the uprising might have been discussed within the general framework of all regional conflicts. There is, in fact, no limit to the amount of context one can find.

[5]See for example, AP, 3 March 1988, 00:31 GMT; 18 March 1988, 01:02 GMT; 31 March 1988, 20:50 GMT; and 28 April 1988, 21:53 GMT.

The same problem applies to *fairness*. What is fairness? Does it mean giving equal time to the fringe elements on both sides? That only polarizes the story. Does it mean giving equal coverage to those able to organize staged media events? That, too, usually distorts public perceptions. Does equal air time and newspaper space for both sides at any particular moment compensate for what may have been a lack of adequate coverage of one party in the past?

In general, media critics of the intifada coverage used both of these terms as a lever to try to get a disproportionate degree of press attention for their particular political agendas. Jewish activists, for example, called for a greater press concentration on the history of Arab attacks on Jews. Palestinian critics concentrated on the Israelis' denial of Palestinian national rights. Neither side, in fact, really was concerned with what might be fair. What they wanted was the biggest possible share of the media pie for their particular position. When their pleas and complaints went unanswered, public press bashing was the result.

A more reasonable way of looking at the problem is whether there was "balance" in the coverage. In other words, over time, were enough of the issues brought forth in a clear and reasonably objective manner so as to provide the reader or viewer with the means to make reasoned judgments about the situation? The answer is both yes and no. If one looks at the crisis period of the intifada from December 1987 to June 1988, the reporting, particularly by television, was unbalanced. As noted, there was an overemphasis on the dramatic and the visual in the television reports. There was image manipulation. And there was a very considerable amount of editorializing by the anchors that could not but distort public perceptions. Moreover, television's amazing lack of self-criticism, combined with its usual refusal to make on-air corrections of mistakes, left viewers with false impressions.

Compounding the problem was the fact that television was engaged in patrol journalism. The camera crews were sent out each morning to record events, but usually, because there were so many crews, most were not accompanied by a journalist. Cameramen are trained to collect images, not to be journalists. They often missed important implications that were inherent in the events they were recording. They also usually are not trained and do not have the time to do the kind of meticulous fact checking that is basic to a journalist's work. For example, reporter Bob

Simon was not present when, on February 25, 1988, the CBS camera crew took its famous pictures of Israeli soldiers beating Palestinians with rocks near Nablus. The pictures were taken using a telephoto lens from a distant hillside. That night, Simon, in his voiceover, stated, "Much is done in the Middle East in what passes for the heat of passion. This seemed cold, deliberate, methodical. It went on for forty minutes. . . . Hospitals in the West Bank and Gaza are full of young Arabs with broken arms. This is how it's done—multiple fractures with a rock. The boys did not scream. They did not beg." As was later confirmed, the soldiers had been subjected to several hours of taunts and rock-throwing incidents. The Palestinians in this case did not have their arms broken; the next night, they were seen walking without casts or slings.[6] And it would have been difficult to know from a distant hillside whether or not the Palestinian youngsters had screamed.

One of its greatest failings, and one of the major reasons for the imbalance in the coverage of the intifada, was and remains television's impatience with process. Its coverage continuously embodies that most American of preoccupations, the fast bottom line. Major social and political upheavals have a rhythm and pace of their own that do not necessarily coincide with television's need to use time for dramatic purposes. Moreover, when democratic governments are involved, the pressure to avoid normal time-consuming political processes acts to delegitimize the whole democratic process, of which the press in the Western world is supposed to be a guardian. The pressure by television on George Shultz to intervene was but one example. It was as though Shultz was expected to resolve a problem immediately that had defied resolution for generations.

There was, for example, not one in-depth piece done on what preconditions might be necessary for any negotiation to succeed. Instead, television pounded away at the same story lines that had gone unchanged for years—especially the themes of land for peace, U.S. recognition of the PLO, and divisions within the Israeli government. These themes were certainly not insignificant, but they did not tell the whole story by any means. They did not, for example, deal with how any Palestinian entity

[6]See CBS, 26 February 1988.

would be a viable economic unit, or with how, if a political deal were negotiated, Yasir Arafat might be able to impose discipline on the various factions within the PLO to prevent future terrorism.

In their defense, it should be noted that both print and television also were caught in the bind of having to report the running story—"news"—find the news niches that had gone unreported, and research the background, all at the same time. It is virtually impossible in such a complex story to do all of that without a large journalistic task force and enormous amounts of air time and newspaper space. Had the media outlets expended such resources, other areas of the world that were also in ferment at the time, like South Korea and Nicaragua, would have been under-reported—and that, too, would have distorted the significance of the intifada story. However, because of the relative shortage of these key resources, there was a notable tendency by the reporters in the field not to look beyond the immediate and to ride the crest of one or two aspects of the story until those aspects had worn themselves out.

In that sense, television's impatience with process is all the more notable, since it expected political and diplomatic action before it was even capable of placing all of the relevant information before the American public. At the height of the crisis, television also became so wrapped up in the atmosphere of upheaval that it tended to hype much of the coverage, precluding reasoned judgment by those who relied on it for an assessment of the situation. Moreover, by taking a leading role as a participant and not merely being a neutral mediator between the parties to the conflict and the American public, it had its own stakes and therefore could not, despite pretensions to the contrary, be a disinterested party in presenting all of the facts to the public in a sober manner. The demand that George Shultz take immediate action was, therefore, one very good example of a genuine conflict of interest between the real needs of the parties at conflict and the American public and television's own agenda. Television's demand for immediate and continuous dramatic action is inherently in-compatible with the need to create the conditions that will allow real political drama to take place.

One also cannot ignore another reason for imbalance—one over which the reporters had little control. Press restrictions and press freedom vary enormously from country to country, especially in the Middle East. Foreign journalists are essentially guests in each country and are required to obey the laws and regulations, no matter how restrictive they may be. Particularly in an international story, as the intifada was, there cannot but be an imbalance between the coverage of a country that allows greater press freedom and one that does not. In April 1988, for example, when the battle for press access to the occupied territories was at its height, NBC's Rick Davis was expelled from Jordan for a critical piece he had done on the country—thus ending any real coverage on NBC of the reaction by Palestinians in Jordan to the intifada.

Television news, because it feeds off images, is susceptible to imbalance particularly on international stories. Print reporters, theoretically, are less visible and less susceptible to overt pressure, because they can always slip their notebooks into their pockets and leave the country to file. So long as communications facilities are working, they always can fall back on telephone interviews, fax machines, and modems to get information. But television reporters use bulky equipment and have to work in teams. In general, they do not cover stories for which they cannot get moving pictures. The use of graphics as a replacement for tape is considered a very bad second option. This factor, when combined with a government's policies of press restrictions, cannot but create an imbalance in the coverage.

Nonetheless, if one looks closely only at the work of those reporters in television and print who were permanently resident in Israel during the first two years of the uprising, there was a very considerable degree of balance when their work is seen in toto. Once the excitement and the hype stopped, and once the journalists themselves had time to reassess the story, many important new issues were brought forth and the public was given, if not the whole story, a very considerable part of it. It is interesting, however, that when television executives trot out examples of their work to counter the charges leveled by media critics, they invariably use pieces that were done after September 1988. For it was only then that television stopped trying to be a fourth branch of government, returned to the arms of the fourth estate, and began providing more measured and balanced coverage.

Television's action while it was trying to set national policy had other consequences as well. It could not reconcile the traditional role of the journalist as watchdog with its own interests as a participatory institution. As a watchdog, it was obligated to present all aspects of the situation so that the democratic process, and the very idea of democracy, could be sustained. But as an institution with its own interests, it also was subject to using many standard political techniques—such as demonization—to further its own interests. This conflict of interest always has been a major problem for print, too, but never to this extent, never with such a power to shape public perceptions, and never with such little self-criticism.

Television, particularly during the crisis period, also set itself apart from the other journalistic practitioners, to the detriment of both. Symbolically, for example, when the Israelis began restricting journalists' access to the occupied territories, the icon used in television news pieces was always either a television cameraman or a still photographer being stopped by an Israeli soldier. Although print covered the difficulties that the television crews were facing, television did not once mention the problems that print reporters or radio reporters were encountering. While it was building political coalitions in Washington, television failed to do the same with other journalists in the field. It did not seek the assistance of the print reporters when real principles of press freedom were involved either. The very opposite was true. It broke with the other reporters who, protesting the closure orders, refused to accept pools. In its mad search for images, it consistently accepted pools, even under the most tightly controlled conditions. The intense competition between the networks also meant that even when major issues were raised by one network, they were not followed by coverage from the other networks. Thus, for example, neither ABC nor NBC made reference to the incident in which CBS had caught Israeli soldiers beating Palestinians with rocks.

In terms of press freedom, the cases of Glenn Frankel of the *Washington Post* and Martin Fletcher of NBC stand out. Both had their press credentials withdrawn by the Government Press Office after they filed detailed stories on how the Israelis had killed Abu Jihad. Neither ABC nor CBS was willing to give the event any play, despite the fact that such sanctions were a threat to the principle of press freedom.

The Frankel-Fletcher case raised another thorny issue. Television, during the crisis period of the intifada, had chosen to be a participant. It then had to deal with the consequences of its decision—notably, public criticism. But what happens when the press deliberately is made into a participant by one of the parties? Fletcher and Frankel, two of the most sober and careful foreign reporters working in Israel at the time, had their stories about the killing of Abu Jihad leaked to them deliberately by senior Israeli officials. The Israelis wanted the story of their derring-do to get out. When the heat was on, however, they then punished those whom they had used as a communications vehicle.

A far more dangerous example of forced participation was the use by the *Shabak* and the Jewish settlers of PRESS signs on their vehicles as a means of getting into Palestinian villages unhindered. After several incidents of this type, the Palestinians began ignoring the press signs entirely and would stone any vehicle approaching them. The lives of the journalists had been placed in danger deliberately. As one settler told me at the time, "We want you to suffer like we have." And as a very senior official in the Defence Ministry told me when I queried the use of press signs by the *Shabak*, "I don't care, if it's a matter of life and death, whether we use press signs or ambulances or anything else to get the job done." He refused to respond, however, when I queried whether it really was a matter of life and death, or mere convenience, that led the security forces to endanger the lives of journalists.

One of the more interesting findings of this study was the stark contrast between the writing of those reporters who had been through the crisis period and those who came later. By April 1988, the intifada, as a major news story, was beginning to wind down. Many of the excesses and imbalances of the crisis period of coverage had begun to disappear by June. More care was used both by print and by television reporters in the wording of dispatches. The language employed was more muted. There was less use of single sources for information, even when they could be named. By contrast, the language of those who were new to the story was far more exciting—as though the story was being discovered for the first time.

Had the story merely matured and really become less entrancing? Had the journalists now accepted that no matter what they did, the natural political process would take its own leisurely path and pace? Were the veterans overcompensating for the charges of hype and one-sidedness that had been leveled against them? Had the final collapse of the Shultz initiative ended intense American interest in the uprising? Or was this just a case of battle fatigue on the part of the veterans? One really cannot judge, but the sharp contrast in the two styles of writing does provide food for thought.

And Who Will Watch the Watchdogs Themselves?

While most of the practical professional issues raised by the foreign press coverage of the intifada undoubtedly are open to solution, many of the ethical questions probably are not—at least not as long as the type of coverage used today remains as it is. For this reason, most journalists refuse to raise these issues even among themselves or to discuss them publicly. When forced to do so, journalists usually are highly defensive. Ethical issues invariably arise within the context of professional routines, and it is by abiding by those routines that journalists have won their success and professional recognition. Since there is no professional code of behavior in journalism—just accepted practice—a threat to routine is a threat to the very essence of the journalist's personal, working, daily identity.

U.S. journalists like to portray themselves as the

watchdogs of democracy and the public good. Almost every American newspaper loves a good crusade. Unless it unduly riles advertisers, a crusade is good for prestige and good for sales. American journalists, as a body, basked vicariously in the glory of Woodward and Bernstein's investigative work uncovering the Watergate scandal. But what most people forgot was that they were only two of hundreds of reporters then working in Washington. Except for those two, none caught on to the story until much, much later. Journalists are as frail, egocentric, and open to conflicts of interest as anyone else. They want recognition and they want to be able to pay the mortgage. For the most part, those who succeed do so by doing what their organization's conventional wisdom demands of them.

But the fact is, reliance on conventional wisdom and past practice may be an insufficient guide, particularly during a crisis, when many standard rules no longer apply. For example, should in-house rules on second-sourcing of every piece of information apply when the only second source available, for reasons of incompetence or embarrassment, refuses to talk?

What makes the issue of ethics of such immediate importance, especially in today's world of high-speed interactive communications, is that the actions of journalists, for good or ill, do have consequences. It is not enough to say that journalists are a nonreactive mirror on the world, or that they are simply messengers, and leave it at that. Journalists, whether they choose to be or not, are part of a huge and complex information loop. Their level of participation in that loop is only a matter of degree. As was seen throughout the crisis period of the intifada, journalists do have the power to shape public perceptions and to influence public policy. With that power must go a measure of responsibility and a willingness to question standard operating procedures. In the new information age, as was demonstrated vividly during the intifada, the concept of accountability has taken on a whole new dimension.

In many cases, there are no easy answers to many of the ethical questions that can be raised. But the very act of asking questions leads to awareness and, perhaps, to more careful consideration of the implications of a particular act. George Shultz, for example, might have been spared personal defeat in his peace offensive had television, in addition to interviewing analysts who pressed for American intervention, also interviewed those cautioning against it because of the political risks involved.

In terms of public scrutiny of an ongoing media event, the intifada presented a best-case scenario. Both the Israelis and the Palestinians had vocal supporters in Washington with easy access to the media. Both also had active media watch groups ready to pounce on any real or imagined slight. Despite this heavy scrutiny, it remains a fact of life that journalists rarely are answerable to the public for their actions. The intifada was no exception to the rule that in the end, reporters are answerable only to their editors and to those higher up in the organizational chain of command. The question then arises: Who can make journalists accountable for their actions? In-house critiques are probably an insufficient means of keeping journalists aware of bias, conventional wisdom, or even inaccuracies that may have crept into their work. Editors cannot know everything that is going on in the field and may be subject to the same biases and conventional wisdom as the reporter. In general, media ombudsmen, no matter how concerned and honest they are, can deal only with blatant unethical actions, such as plagiarism or gross inaccuracy. Outside media watch groups, if they have the archives and skilled staff available, can play a very important role in pointing out some of the subtler ways in which news is distorted. But the very existence of these groups raises a profound professional ethical question: How sensitive should a journalist be to any organization with a political agenda and the resources to make itself heard? At what point does a correction of detail or a bit of supplementary information provided by such an organization begin to turn a dispatch into a propaganda vehicle for one side or another?

News packaging, especially in the ephemeral broadcast media, still is based largely on trust—a belief by the public that it is being told the truth and that it is not being manipulated by some unseen hand. That trust can be broken. Such is the case when subliminal messaging is used on a regular basis. As has been shown here, however, only meticulous *post facto* study and analysis can reveal whether such messaging, deliberate or not, is being used. By then, it is often too late to alter public perceptions or the course of events themselves.

Unlike a doctor, a journalist cannot be sued for malpractice—unless the issue involves libel or slander. The public has little recourse when professional sloppiness is involved. Errors in judgment and outright mistakes may be forgotten by the next day, but the subconscious effects on a news consumer caused by distorted coverage may be felt long afterward. Even if an event is recorded accurately in all of its details, if a multidimensional conflict is portrayed in two-dimensional terms, can that not but distort? Or if a small-scale conflict that is easily reportable is given prominence over a larger-scale problem for which access is limited, is there not distortion through disproportion?

An allied problem raises the question of what journalists should do when they know that they are dealing with incomplete information.[1] In a breaking story, it is generally accepted that a reporter can file a dispatch that does not contain all of the details, simply because those details are not available. (In such cases, it is important for the journalist to point out which parts of the story are missing, so that the audience does not jump to conclusions.) This problem will become even more acute as advances in communications technology further blur the line separating foreign and local journalists.

Foreign reporters, especially those working in countries where local press coverage is restricted by the authorities, do become local reporters once a satellite linkup or fax machine becomes available. Journalistic sloppiness that may create no reaction in their home countries can have immediate consequences in the country they are covering. The subjects of their reports, for example, may act in a way that is prejudicial to their own interests. In an environment where the public does not believe in the veracity of official public statements—such as occurred in the Israeli-occupied territories—mistakes that appear in the foreign media can have the same disproportionate effect on actions as local rumors do. But since locals are not considered direct consumers by the publishers or broadcast executives, those consequences are all too often ignored. The short-term gain in meeting a deadline by failing to check all of the details completely, or failing to inform the public which details are missing, can have long-term consequences for those directly involved.

It is not only lack of care in fact checking that can alter perceptions. The use (or improper use) of language also can distort. Imagespeak is a language—perhaps the first universal one. It can overpower even the most

---

[1] During the 1991 war with Iraq, this was a particularly acute problem in CNN's instant "radio with pictures" coverage.

cogently and carefully written verbal commentary. But that is not to underestimate the power of words either in print or on television. The spin that anchors often put in their introductions to intifada-related stories is a case in point. Their words, though relatively few in number, in some cases had a disproportionate effect on perceptions By their very position in the foreground on a television set, the anchors visually establish themselves as neutral mediators and final arbiters between the report from the field and the audience. Unlike the field reporter, whose words can be overpowered by the images, most of the anchors' introductions are not accompanied by moving visual images that could detract from their words. Any lack of care in the writing, or any coarse editorializing, can and does create false impressions among the audience.

In an area of the world like the Middle East, where language and poetry have a particular power over people's emotions and where diplomatic language has shades of subtlety that are almost indistinguishable to the outsider at first glance, lack of care in interpreting what others have written also can have major effects. Thus, after a short period of using the term *alleged collaborator*, many journalists switched to the simpler, but clearly odious, term *collaborator*. This switch effectively legitimized the killing of many Palestinians by other Palestinians.

This issue is compounded by the twin problems of clarity and ambiguity. It is important for a journalist to write a story clearly, so that the audience will understand what he or she is talking about. Unfortunately, not every story automatically lends itself to clear, declarative statements and straightforward story lines. In most major political events, there is a great deal of ambiguity as the participants try to make sense of, and to react to, the events taking place around them. It ought to be incumbent upon journalists to make note of the shades of gray. The problem, of course, is how much of the ambiguity can be included within a story without confusing the audience, and how much can be included within the confines of the air time or newspaper space available. The failure to listen closely to the subtle use of terms by Israeli and Palestinian leaders led to misjudgments and to the reading in of meanings that were not there.

It also is important for the journalist to help the reader or viewer distinguish between reality and a made-for-the media event. Crafted, rather than spontaneous, media events can be news: a press conference, for example, can be a news-making event and may be no less valuable in providing important information to the public than a personal interview initiated by a journalist. But many media events during the intifada were created not to provide new and important information, but purely to provide the images needed by imagespeak. And because the modern foreign press has the capacity to empower those who are underrepresented or without the means to make their cases heard within normally prevailing circumstances, reporters have a duty to be as critical of those whom they have empowered as they tend to be of those in titular power. The modern media has changed the David-Goliath equation by arming the underdog with the means to elicit international sympathy and, at times, direct assistance. If the press is to be a watchdog for the broader public, it also must watch over those to whom it has given a public platform. Previously, access to media technology was often a function of money. Only those with considerable finances could compete in the long term. Today, almost any underdog can acquire access to these technologies in return for a good running story. This, in turn, gives those who ultimately control the dissemination of information, like the television networks, unusual judicial powers and responsibilities.

Many of the major ethical issues today center around the advent of new technologies and new data-gathering techniques, especially those relating to television. Television, however, has been exceedingly un-self-critical. The arrival of the minicamera, and the choice by the television networks to distribute them to direct participants and to use the resulting footage, is but one example of how new questions of what is ethical journalistic behavior have yet to catch up with the rapidly changing technological scene. In the years to come, image manipulation, so powerful in helping to set the U.S. foreign policy agenda during the intifada, undoubtedly will become more sophisticated as new technologies develop. To date, television nightly newscast teams have not shown themselves to be unwilling to dabble with such concepts as dramatized portrayals of news events for which there are no images. This did not happen during the intifada, because dramatic images were plentiful. But it is a sign of the temptations that lie before the television news producers—temptations that are hard to resist.

One can only speculate, but it seems as though the trend in television journalism to quick cuts and short scenes may be making the audience more passive than ever before. Because of the rapid flow of images, the viewer is not given time to think or to question—only to absorb. Similarly, the trend to both visual and verbal vignettism has the effect of reducing complex issues to simple, emotionally charged parables, so that when the audience does react, it does so emotionally and not thoughtfully. Wide-scale public passivity or widespread emotionalism on major issues of the moment is a significant danger both to the democratic process and to the policy-making process. In effect, it leaves those in control of the media in control of the national agenda.[2]

One of the central charges made by Israeli authorities against television crews—and the main rationale for closing areas to television coverage—was that the very presence of cameras either creates or stokes riots. The charge implies that camera crews are at least partially responsible for death and destruction. There is little doubt that many of the Palestinian young-sters did play to the cameras. In fact, during the first few weeks of rioting in Gaza, the youngsters near the Shifa hospital regularly would put on a display of firebombing for the cameras just before sunset—and just before the camera crews' deadline. But the absence of cameras did not halt the rioting. The presence of cameras was one aspect of the rioting, but it was not the cause. Then, too, was there anything substantively different be-tween a youngster in the streets waving a Palestinian flag at a previously designated hour and an Israeli official speaking at a press conference, called in advance, with an Israeli flag behind him?

In fact, there is considerable evidence that at times, the presence of camera crews helped to reduce the level of violence. Israeli soldiers and

---

[2]One of the significant side effects of President George Bush's efforts to fashion an international coalition against Iraq in the months prior to the outbreak of war was that the effort took time. The time available helped overcome the pressures exerted by emotional agenda setters for im-mediate action, and it allowed dissenting voices to be heard and a full-fledged national policy debate to be carried out.

police officers were more cautious once they realized they were being recorded or witnessed. Israeli soldiers, after the initial and heavily criticized stages of the beatings policy, were reluctant to be caught on tape using gratuitous violence. One incident in particular that I witnessed remains vivid. I was in Gaza doing some interviews when a demonstration broke out nearby. Youngsters began throwing firebombs on a side street. At almost the same moment, a television crew and an Israeli army unit appeared on the scene, each coming from a different direction. The Palestinians continued to throw their Molotov cocktails, splattering the street with burning kerosene and glass shards. The television crew began filming. The army patrol, after making a headlong charge down the street in a command car, spotted the television crew and backed off. The youngsters eventually ran out of homemade firebombs and stopped. The army patrol withdrew, and so, too, did the television crew. In many ways, it was unfortunate that these nonevents never made it to the screen on the nightly newscasts. All the television networks showed was what the crews could capture of dramatic action, not what common sense dictated should be an anticlimax.

A far more important issue, however, is that the cameras became one of the tools used by security agents to control and arrest demonstrators. Intelligence and security agents have used journalists' published reports as one of their main sources of data throughout this century. In fact, no intelligence organization worth its salt does not have a department to sift through noncovert materials. With the arrival of television, and particularly of satellite coverage and VCRs, their work has been made immeasurably easier. Print journalists cannot make personal reference to each person taking part in a demonstration and press ethics normally demand that a person be identified by name only after his or her permission has been secured. Moreover, print reporters can use an indecipherable code in their notebooks if they choose. But there is no such thing as a code or an illegible scrawl on television. The television camera takes in the entire sweep of a riot, recording each person present. Both during the intifada and later, during the demonstrations in Tiananmen Square, intelligence agents regularly downloaded pictures of demonstrators that were being sent via satellite, in order to identify and arrest those who had taken part in the demonstrations. One Israeli official admitted to me that television's regular coverage had resulted in the arrest of hundreds of Palestinian youngsters. Willy-nilly, camera crews and tape editors became part of the security agencies' system of control. During the trials of alleged Palestinian demonstrators, video footage was used regularly as evidence.

Television reporters are aware that their material is being used, but they claim that anyone taking part in a demonstration is doing a public act and should be prepared, in advance, for any consequences that may result. That may be true when the demonstrators are aware that the tape machine is rolling. But what happens when a cameraman, sensitive to charges that the presence of the camera increases the level of rioting, arrives on the scene and deliberately hides behind a wall or under the chassis of a truck? Is that not the visual equivalent of a print reporter listening in on a conversation and then quoting the person by name without having first asked his or her permission? Not everyone caught up in the public adrenaline of a demonstration is sophisticated enough to understand the risks involved should a camera be nearby. And what of innocent passersby who get caught up in a sudden and unexpected demonstration—as happened frequently during the intifada? They, too, are recorded indiscriminately as part of the scene, even though they merely may be hurrying home to get away from the scene of events. And then there is the problem of the pan shots from a high perch as the camera peers into private back gardens, where many of the demonstrators took shelter. With television, the line between the press's right to record a public display and an individual's right to privacy can become blurred easily.

One of the basic prejudices and mistakes American journalists bring to foreign coverage is the presumption that even outside the bounds of the United States, they somehow are covered by the protective shield of the First Amendment to the Constitution. When one walks into the bureaus of the television networks, in particular, one can see the tapes of the archive all neatly arranged and catalogued on the shelves. This is almost an open invitation to security agents to try to seize the material, for the archives contain not only the "public" material that has been sent by satellite but also the "outs"—the television equivalent of that part of a journalist's notes that he or she, for one reason or another, has chosen not to use in a story.

The CBS bureau in Israel voluntarily gave the Israeli army the entire tape footage, including the outs, of the beating of the two Palestinians with rocks by Israeli soldiers in Nablus, in order to help the Israelis apprehend the culprits. Subsequently, the producer was reprimanded by his bosses in New York. But not all of the material the Israelis acquired from television was given voluntarily.

Israeli officials did seize material in the field, and it is only a short hop and step between grabbing tapes and films on the streets and doing the same thing in an office a few miles away. After the lynching in Qabatiyeh in February 1988, Israeli soldiers took away the tapes made by CNN. In a report on April 9, 1988, NBC's Martin Fletcher noted that because of the confiscation, "Now villagers think that cameramen are government agents." The CNN case was not to be the last example of confiscation. Later that spring, after Israeli soldiers had confiscated film from *Time* and *Newsweek* photographers, the Israeli Supreme Court, in a landmark decision, ruled that the film had to be returned to the photographers but that the army had the right to develop it and look at it first.[3]

The unwillingness or inability of journalists to confront the ethical and moral questions they were facing, combined with the failure to cover constituencies in depth, probably account for yet another major gap in the press's coverage of the intifada. Many of the important moral questions with which both Israelis and Palestinians were grappling went unreported. Yet some of these moral questions are universal—the weft and weave of the social fabric not only of the societies in the Middle East but of any group of people caught in a period of social and political instability anywhere in the world.

If we are to consider public policies rationally, we need to know what the consequences will be. If such policies create upheaval, we need to know what happens to people when the normal and accepted rules of society have broken down. What occurs within individuals when they are left with no socially accepted markers of behavior and there is a conflict between conscience and self-interest? If there is a true need for vignettism and human interest stories in journalism, it is surely in the area where an ordinary individual is forced to grapple with extraordinary events, retain his or her sanity, and be able to face any consequences of a personal decision with conviction. One of the few ways any of us have of preparing for the unexpected is to see how others have handled themselves under

[3]AP, 24 March 1988, 09:48 GMT.

unusual circumstances. Reporting on such personal, internal struggles is not voyeurism, but a public service to all.

The only moral questions covered by journalists were those that obviously were open to media coverage and could be linked to a current political event. Thus, the decision by a few Israelis not to serve in the occupied areas because of the policies of occupation and beatings became a significant and well-covered journalistic subject. Because they were easy to gather, so, too, did individual stories that some people, usually for personal political reasons, chose to expose in the local press. However, there was no concerted attempt to ferret out those stories that people did not choose to make public but that are important as lessons and models and offer a way to understand how our world works. During a period of upheaval, ethics and morality are not philosophical abstractions, they are the sparks for real-life dramas that take place within the individual.

Many examples come to mind, but two are particularly poignant and instructive. One cannot really judge whether what the individuals in each case did was right or wrong. One only can learn. My family and I were sitting at a table at a friend's house enjoying a barbecue on a hot May night in 1988 when another guest, whom I had met only once before, leaned over and began to unburden himself. He had just finished his reserve army duty as a medic at a lock-up for Palestinian prisoners. One of his tasks had been to sign the medical forms certifying that prisoners who were about to be released were medically fit. The certificates always were made available to the Red Cross. His personal actions, therefore, would become part of the public record.

One of the Palestinians who appeared before him had been badly beaten by Israeli soldiers and the wounds on the prisoner's hands had not yet healed. The medic was caught in a dilemma. Should he lie on the certificates in order to allow the Palestinian to go back to his family, or should he send the individual back to the overcrowded prison camp for two more weeks until the broken bones had healed? He had chosen the latter course but was still wrestling with the problem of whether he had done the right thing.

Somewhat later, Mohammed appeared in my garden with a small delegation of close friends and relatives. We had known each other for more than ten years and become friends. He was a fervent Palestinian nationalist who had lost all of his family's landholdings during the 1948

Israeli war of independence. He hated King Hussein and over the past twenty years had made a point never to visit Jordan. But he also did not believe in violence, and from his own personal experience, he knew that social upheavals lead to personal pain. After the serving of coffee and the usual pleasantries, he edged toward the issue he wanted to raise. "They are mixing things up for the people, you know," he began. The nebulous "they" was a term I had heard him use often. It referred to anyone in a position of authority, from Yasir Arafat to the Israeli buck private at a roadblock.

"It is the boys, you know," he continued. The men around him nodded in encouragement. Slowly, and with considerable difficulty, he finally came to the point. It transpired that one of his sons had been under enormous peer pressure to take part in stonings and firebombings. Mohammed had forbidden his son to do anything of the sort. He believed in political, not violent, solutions to problems. The sixteen-year-old son was caught in a bind that is all too common during a popular uprising. From whom should he take his cue—his friends, or his father? And from whom should he expect punishment? In the end, he chose to obey his father, but the other boys in the tightly knit village then took revenge. They had taken Mohammed's son, held him down, and shaved his head. The son had been marked for everyone in the village to see.

It may be that some of the most important professional and ethical lessons of the intifada are locked up in the minds of the much-maligned television cameramen and still photographers. They spent more time in the field than anyone else and got to see and experience the events in broader terms than any of the reporters. It was inevitable that they eventually would become directly involved in the crisis in the streets in one way or another.

What, for example, is a journalist to do when he or she comes upon a wounded person? Where does his or her duty lie? That was the situation in which ABC cameraman Edouard Bianco found himself in Bethlehem on March 20, 1988, at the very height of the Israeli press-bashing campaign. He was driving near Bethlehem when he heard shots. He drove toward the sound of the shots and saw one Israeli soldier lying on the ground in a pool of blood and another firing wildly into the air. The former had been shot in the head by a Palestinian. Bianco grabbed his camera and told his sound man to get help. But what was he to do? "I was afraid to go near the guy who was firing," he relates. "He was acting really wildly." Bianco felt he couldn't go near to try to provide any assistance, so he just recorded the scene from fifty yards away. "It's what I was trained to do," he says. When he got back to the office, he broke down and cried.[4] The next day, without checking the facts, Knesset member Geula Cohen charged that because Bianco had succeeded in taping the event so soon after it occurred, he must have known in advance about the shooting. Other critics claimed that Bianco should not have taped at all but should have helped the critically wounded soldier.[5] Should he have endangered his own life by trying to overpower the soldier who had gone wild in order to try to provide assistance, or was the public better served by him having recorded the event? I certainly cannot judge.

[4]Edouard Bianco, interview with author, September 1990.
[5]AP, 21 March 1988, 10:13 GMT.

The intifada was unique to a particular time and a particular place, but lessons with wider implications and applications can be drawn from it. Undoubtedly, one of the major lessons is that in today's world, international politics, domestic politics, and the press are inexorably linked. As the Chernobyl disaster and the intifada showed, nations can deny the press access to the scene of an event but they no longer can prevent their own residents and those of other countries from gaining knowledge of the event through fax, radio, and satellite dishes. The marketplace of information and ideas is thick with sellers. The global village, predicted for more than two decades, has arrived. No longer can politicians hide behind the excuse that what they do within their boundaries is their country's and no one else's business. Both they and the press will be subject to a greater degree of inter-

T · W · E · L · V · E

Conclusions

national accountability. With the advent of hyperspeed communications, what happens within their area of jurisdiction and authority can be a matter for concern and action around the world. It is not inconceivable, for example, that within a few years, supersophisticated satellite cameras will become available to the press, and the whole issue of access and the press's dependency on the goodwill of others for access will change completely.

With this increasing interlinkage, politicians no longer can afford to create policies without developing a media strategy to go with them. The stakes are too high. One can take things one step further and say that since the media have become so much a part of the politicians' and generals' operational environment, it may well be that media strategies not only will have to accompany policies, but will form an integral part of each policy—with media specialists as permanent members of the policy-making teams.

The Israelis chose not to develop a media strategy during the intifada and then had to cope with the consequences. Their prestige and standing in the United States and the world deteriorated. Their well-rotted, vestigial system of co-optation and control collapsed, and nothing was created to take its place. With the collapse, Israeli officials and apologists reacted like wounded animals, lashing out at the press indiscriminately but doing very little to ameliorate their own situation. The press bashing may have struck sympathetic chords within the country, but it did little to counter perceptions elsewhere in the world of intransigent and incompetent Israeli behavior.

In terms of media coverage, the Palestinians blundered into a short-term success of quite remarkable proportions and then marched boldly into failure. Having used violence and the foreign media's predilection to cover dramatic events in order to gain world attention for their cause, they did not know what to do next. After two months, they could go no further. A genuine cry of pain was replaced by strutting and bluster, while the organizational imperatives of the PLO smothered opportunities for real political advancement, and the Palestinian rebellion turned in on itself.

The kind of press coverage given the intifada was not some journalistic aberration. Rather, it was the product of more than two decades of an intense and intimate relationship reporters had developed with both the

The press will have to come up with clear strategies of its own if it is not to be carried along by a rush of events, many of which will be staged or contrived, each time a new crisis breaks. To cope and to preserve their independence, journalists will have to alter many of their standard routines. If they do not, they will be unable to prevent themselves from becoming an even greater unwitting arm of governments and vested interests than they are now. In the marketplace of ideas, the packages presented to the press will be smoother, slicker, and more image-oriented. As a result, it will take more work on the part of journalists to distinguish for their audiences between intellectual substance and self-serving flim-flam. Moreover, the new information age, which promised us a plethora of information sources as a protection against monopolistic information services, has brought with it a new problem: disinformation on a scale never seen or heard before. A single source, like a government, speaking deliberately in a multitude of voices through multiple spokespeople, each propounding a different message, can create confusion by making all of the available data sound like mere noise. When disinformation of this type is practiced by several sources, the result is data cacophony.

The intifada came as a surprise to the Israelis, the foreign press, and even the Palestinians themselves. Journalists had access to the occupied territories for many years, and the signs of ferment were there for all to see. But those signs largely were ignored. And so the press, if it lays claim to being a public watchdog, must bear some of the blame for not pointing them out in advance. One of the continuing failures of modern journalism is that all too often, journalists ask themselves what stories *can* be covered rather than the more important question of what *should* be covered. They respond to what they think the audience wants to know, not what it needs to know.

Some teachers of public management claim that any crisis can be averted with proper trend analysis and planning. But the real-life fact remains that humans don't necessarily see all of the signs around them or read those signs correctly. For that reason, surprises will continue to fall upon us. Having failed to read the signs, the main question becomes how those involved should react once a crisis arises.

One very notable conclusion that comes from a study of the intifada

Israelis and the Palestinians. The skepticism and even cynicisr
the veteran journalists displayed did not arise full-blown when
began, but was the result of a process that had been going or
Most notably, the titular leaders and their close associates on
had lost credibility. The credibility of the young Palestinians
cupied territories began at a high level but deteriorated withi
of months as the uprising became institutionalized and new ves
groups arose. While the intifada was supposed to be a total s
Palestinian society, at least in their relations with the press,
Palestinians eventually were doomed to repeat the mistakes of t
By the summer of 1988, the youngsters no longer had any
signs to sell in the marketplace of ideas, and interest in thei
peter out.

Throughout the intifada, the press was hardly a mirror.
it was more like the translucent ground glass screen in the vi
a camera—capturing a series of scenes that were never tota
often devoid of subtlety and shading, and always dependent
focusing the lens. As so often happens in symbiotic relatic
reporters used the parties to the conflict for their own purpos
used by those parties in return. The intifada was but one of i
examples of how the press not only covers news, but create
how it not only describes national and international agend
helps to set them.

The relationship between the media and politics is a d
If current trends, first developed in Washington, continue,
attempts to manipulate the media will become standard pr
where. In that sense, the behavior of the Israelis and the
during the intifada may be one of the last examples of beni;
the political possibilities that the manipulation of the press
vision came relatively late to the Middle East. The older
Israeli and Palestinian leaders grew up when television was
and never really understood how and why the modern me
does. The intifada taught some of the more thoughtful and
members of the new generation of leaders a hard lesson t
least, will not forget.

This media-reality therapy among political leaders, w
on around the globe, undoubtedly will pose new challenges f

was the propensity of all of the parties involved, once the rebellion was under way, to fall back immediately into familiar and routinized patterns of behavior—without considering that changed circumstances required a concomitant alteration in their modus operandi. Most of the reactions by the Israeli authorities, the press, and the PLO were knee-jerk in nature— designed to ameliorate short-term problems. But they often were counterproductive in the long run. One can see only isolated examples of clear strategizing by any of the parties. The success of the *Los Angeles Times* at the beginning of the uprising may be the clearest guide to how all of the sides to a crisis can best react.

Conventional wisdom says that one always should assign the best and most experienced person available to handle a crisis situation. But it would appear from the case of the intifada that that may be a mistake and a misuse of a precious commodity. It seems from the evidence that a wiser decision would be to release the best and most experienced person from having to deal with day-to-day events. There are almost always other competent people available who can deal with the problems of the hour. The most knowledgeable and experienced person is probably most usefully employed providing background material and, more important, taking the role of the outsider, standing back, and asking the questions that others who have been caught up in the sweep of events—and the hype that accompanies them—have forgotten to ask. Probably the first such question ought to be whether the currently accepted story line is, in fact, still valid under the altered circumstances.

That same person, then, also would be in a position to provide other, no less important, services. One of the significant phenomena of the intifada and other long-running crises is that because people get caught up in the situation of the moment and the jumble of events, there is no one left to analyze where we are in the process—and if there is a noticeable process at all. This is important particularly when short-term pack journalism strikes. Real strategizing requires not only responses to immediate concerns, but consideration of what is required in the long term. It is here that the print media, in all of their forms, can best serve the public interest. Hard copy on paper enables people most easily to review reports of events at leisure and to analyze them with care.

The role of knowledgeable outsider has become all the more important precisely because we now have moved firmly into the age of imagespeak. For imagespeak is not only used by the television networks, but by handlers for politicians and vested interests as well. Imagespeak has brought into people's homes a new form of discourse—just as epic poetry, drama, essays, fiction, the plastic arts, and rhetoric did in days past. In this sense, the development of imagespeak today is little different from the period in fifth-century B.C. Sicily, when the art of rhetoric invaded courtrooms. Plato complained bitterly that the rhetoricians failed to seek truth and were content only with the *impression* of truth. But Plato's arguments did not halt this form of discourse, and it has become a fundamental part of modern public policy-making.

Real protection for society came only through education and public analysis of the techniques of rhetoric. So, today, it would be fruitless for societies to try to limit the use of imagespeak. What is needed is a thorough study of the techniques of visual manipulation and an examination of the context in which it is used. Then we must teach visual literacy to all who would learn. If television coverage of the intifada is a guide to the future, then visual literacy already has become a precondition for cogent public debate and policy-making.

Visual literacy also would appear to be a prerequisite for modern professional foreign policy analysis. As was shown, trends in the political development and eventual stagnation of the intifada could be traced merely by looking at whether and which new icons and emblems were being incorporated into intifada imagespeak. In this sense, visual analysis of the images crafted for television or portrayed by television may become as important as—or more important than—the traditional textual analyses of speeches and statements.

Despite the competition between the various networks, U.S. television as a whole holds a near monopoly on the presentation and dissemination of moving images of events taking place in foreign lands—whether those images are created and manipulated by the news organizations themselves, whether they are the product of carefully constructed media events, or whether they are totally falsified.[1]

---

[1]New digitized video editing machines equipped with electronic paintbrushes and palettes, already in use, are capable of altering moving images in quite remarkable ways. Of greater concern is the fact no means exist for testing whether the images have been altered and how. For example, a video editor today can take a scene of a soldier standing with a gun and flawlessly superimpose

Television wields a power to broadcast those images with few formal or legal restraints. The antidote to some of this power—and to television's unitary concept of news presentation—lies not in censorship or in restricting access, as the Israelis tried to do. The solution lies in education.

So important is the subject of visual literacy that it ought to be taught from the first grade, together with reading, writing, and arithmetic. Undoubtedly, it will take years before visual literacy is taught in primary schools with the same intensity as verbal literacy. In the meantime, one of the major public services all of the media could perform is to create an aggressive, investigative visual manipulation beat—one that would point out to the public when and how their perceptions are being manipulated by people with special agendas. Such a beat would be no different, say, from that of the statehouse reporter who dissects a politician's speech. For those who can control the conditions under which images are captured, and even more so, the processing of images, may be able to wield forms of power that we cannot even imagine today.

---

another image in order to make it look as though the gun is being fired. (See Daniel Sheridan, "The Trouble With Harry," *Columbia Journalism Review* (January/February 1990): 4 and 6.

The manuscript for this book was completed prior to the launching of Operation Desert Storm. Undoubtedly, the war will bring in its wake a goodly number of intensive studies on the performance of the media during the months leading up to the outbreak of fighting and the period after the tanks began to roll. Nonetheless, some preliminary comparisons with the coverage of the intifada can already be drawn and conclusions made.

If the intifada presented the major American news organizations with a best-case scenario in which to work, the war in the Gulf was definitely a worst-case scenario. Both the Iraqis and the U.S. military, from the start, set out to co-opt and control the press. The Iraqis' techniques were as coarse and heavy-handed as their system of governance. The U.S. military's effort was a bureaucrat's textbook exercise in modern press manip-

Epilogue

ulation: rigid, narrowly conceived, and oblivious to recent developments in the media's coverage of events.

The control mechanisms used by both sides covered just about every aspect of news gathering and dissemination. The intent of the U.S. military was to provide a sterilized view of the war—one that would not undermine crucial support on the home front. The aim of the Iraqi military was to marshal not only domestic support, but also international backing for Saddam Hussein. Both sides recognized that this was as much a media war as a war on the battlefield.

Unlike the Israeli authorities at the onset of the intifada, the military on both sides of the Arabian Peninsula divide started out with enormous advantages. The press could be and was placed in a state of almost total dependency on the bureaucratic authorities. Visas were issued with considerable care and could easily be withdrawn. The military authorities on both sides could and did maintain physical control of the terrain in which the journalists sought to operate. The foreign reporters could not lean on their local colleagues for information and support because the Iraqi and Saudi governments were effective dictatorships with total control over the local press, and with the means to cow the local population into saying little more than what their governments permitted or demanded.

While the U.S. accredited more than 750 American journalists, they kept a tight rein on the movements of the press. Most news gathering, with the exception of very soft feature stories, was restricted to pools. Initially, only three pools, containing seven to eighteen journalists each, were formed each day. Eventually, under pressure from the media, twenty-one pools were formed daily. But this meant that even under the best of circumstances, only about one-seventh of the press corps was actually allowed to go out into the field on any given day. The rest were left to rewrite the copy and rework the tape provided by others. The military escort officers accompanying the pool journalists decided who would be interviewed, what would be said by the interviewees, and what the journalists would be allowed to see. In Iraq, the restrictions were even more severe, with the press rarely being briefed in depth and almost never allowed to meet with troops. Kuwait, the very focus of the war, was totally out of bounds.

Once the reporters returned from the scene of events, they were subject to censorship. The censorship by both sides was far more intense than that applied by the Israelis during the intifada; in many ways it resembled, the kind of self-serving blue-pencilling the Israelis had abandoned by the mid-1970s. Despite protestations to the contrary, the U.S. military censored not only items that had a direct bearing on security, the conduct of the war, and the safety of human lives; blue pencils were also wielded purely in support of the U.S. military's public image—and its budgetary wars in Washington. A typical example was a dispatch by Frank Bruni of the *Detroit Free Press*. After visiting a Stealth Fighter air base and talking to pilots returning from bombing raids, he described the planes as "fighter-bombers" and the pilots as "giddy" after their safe landings. The base commander demanded that the aircraft be described only as "fighters" and the word *giddy* was altered to "proud." At the time, the Air Force was trying to salvage its B-2 Stealth bomber project, which had run into heavy criticism in Congress, and wanted to differentiate between the two types of aircraft. The pilots were invariably being portrayed by the military as cool and skilled technocrats. Apparently, descriptions of emotions like giddiness were at odds with the image being projected. But military censorship wasn't always needed. Many journalists themselves exercised a considerable degree of self-censorship, preferring not to describe scenes or events that might get them into trouble with the authorities and endanger what little access they had.

The vast majority of the reporters who covered the war with Iraq were parachutists: men and women who spoke no Arabic and who were ignorant of the area in which they were working. And with the end of military conscription in the United States, only a minuscule pool of reporters had even a passing acquaintance with the ways in which armies operate. Most were thus heavily reliant on their military briefers and extremely susceptible to manipulation. In the years prior to the war, the American public demanded little information on the armed forces, and the military invariably shut out attempts by those few journalists interested in the subject to learn the concepts and precepts of modern warfare. Coverage of military affairs meant only coverage of the Pentagon bureaucracy, with no attention paid to the men and women serving in the field. While a few journalists in the Gulf had served in other trouble spots like Vietnam, Pakistan, and Nicaragua, their military experience was limited almost entirely to relatively small-scale skirmishes between conventional forces or guerrillas. Almost none of the reporters had ever covered a set-piece conventional war on a large scale and few knew how to interpret what scraps of information they could glean. As during the intifada, the parachutists were ill-equipped to deal with some of the fundamental political and military issues the war brought in its wake or to spot some of the most important trends. This was particularly noticeable during the weeks immediately prior to the outbreak of fighting, when the coverage was not events-driven, when the few real stories available had been done, and when the press had more than ample time to analyze what was happening all around. Instead, the filler material used during this period was primarily personality-centered, with individuals in the military—from frontline saxophone players to generals—becoming media stars overnight.

This inherent unpreparedness may explain, in part, why the U.S. military, having succeeded in gaining physical control over the movements of journalists, very quickly also took control of their story lines. Undoubtedly, one of the primary story lines was the almost wondrous exactitude of the weaponry available to the allied forces. The precision weapons were extraordinarily accurate. But no weapon, no matter how good, works correctly every time. However, on television and in print, the laser-guided bombs, for example, were always shown to have worked perfectly—with the military refusing to concede even a normal 1 or 5 percent failure rate, and the journalists failing to question the supposed perfection. All the American television networks ended up running patently absurd stories blaming those deaths of allied soldiers from friendly fire entirely on human error, not on the prized and precious equipment. Likewise, both print and television bought into and blandly accepted the story line promoted by the administration praising Israel for its "restraint" in not retaliating after SCUD ground-to-ground missiles hit Tel Aviv. In fact, the United States had the Israelis by the political and military jugular throughout the crisis period. They refused to give the Israelis the International Friend or Foe (IFF) codes used by allied aircraft over Iraq. Had the Israelis tried to retaliate from the air, they might not only have seen their own planes shot down but, more important, they might have shot down an allied plane. The Israelis also remained totally dependent on U.S. satellites and U.S. goodwill for early warning of SCUD attacks. And they needed money from Washington to pay for their own war alert and its accompanying costs. Finally, the United States refused to share real-time intelligence data on what was going on on the battlefield—so the Israelis could not know what had already been destroyed and which targets remained intact.

On the political side, the war highlighted once again just how easy it is for journalists to fall back on old story lines. The attempt by the Soviet Union to cobble together a cease-fire in the hours before the onset of the land war was reported by many journalists in the same, old-fashioned, superpower competition/Cold War story frame that had been discarded only months before. Many journalists cast doubts on Soviet motives and gave primacy to the proposition that this last-ditch effort at diplomacy was only an attempt by the Soviet Union to position itself for the postwar period. Moscow was undoubtedly trying to create a postwar role for itself. But the diplomatic effort may also have been a genuine effort to avert more bloodshed and to assist in the building of the new world order of which President Bush constantly spoke. In any case, every other country involved in the war was also positioning itself to try to grab some of the political and economic spoils, so the Soviet Union was not unique in this regard.

The war also provided a salient example—and a lesson to politicians—of what happens when the political echelon creates a story line that resonates emotionally, has the line accepted by the media, and then after displacement has occurred, tries to abandon the child it has borne. Throughout the conflict, President Bush tried to emphasize that this was a just war and that the United States had entered the conflict in order to support American values. Although other U.S. interests, especially economic considerations, were certainly more important in the decision to go to war, under Washington rules, the administration's rationale was given considerable media play. The story line of a war being fought in pursuit of moral values took hold. When President Bush urged Iraqi citizens, as a just moral and political cause, to overthrow the demonized Saddam Hussein, it was almost inevitable that the same rationale used by the White House to justify the recapture of Kuwait would be used by the media as its primary criterion for judging the administration's reaction to the Kurdish and Shiite rebellions.

Unsurprisingly, coverage of the Shiite battles—and the Shiites' defeat—was relatively short because a Shiite victory was not seen to be in American interests or in support of American values. The fate of the Kurds was another matter. Only the Kurds were able to project the image of victim—not alone of Saddam Hussein, but also of an American policy that supported the cause of wars of national salvation only verbally and superficially. As a result, the plight of the Kurds was given far more extensive coverage than that given the Shiites, and far more coverage than had been given to Kurdish civilians attacked in 1988 by the Iraqi army using poison gas. This time, the Kurds were no longer viewed as totally alien, but were perceived by the media to be acting according to the political and moral value code that the administration appeared to have laid down for itself but had been unable or unwilling to abide by. Displacement took place. Unlike the anti-American Shiites, unlike the Israelis during the intifada, and unlike the Kurds' situation in 1988, the Kurds were now seen as a people abiding by a moral code that had been legitimized in Washington. They were thus able to make their revolt into an American media story, hitching their long-standing rebellion to what had become a domestic American political issue: the system of political morality being preached in Washington. To this central issue were added the U.S. agreement to allow the Iraqis to fly helicopters and to use them as gunships against the rebels, the memory of the 1988 gassing of Kurdish civilians (the threat of poison gas being used against American troops had been a central issue of the war coverage and had become a domestic U.S. policy issue), and press revelations of previous U.S. abandonment of the Kurds. Once this happened, a loop was created, the administration's story line began to backfire on it, and it had to face a barrage of media criticism over American culpability in the Kurds' fate. In running the loop, television was aided immeasurably by the availability of dramatic visuals of Kurdish refugees starving and living under plastic sheets.

Recognizing that this was a war in which images would prevail in shaping public opinion, the American military went to extraordinary lengths to control the television images being projected. In keeping with its policy of presenting a sterile view of the war, particular emphasis was put on recording the nonhuman, sleek, smooth textures of the fighter aircraft and the precision of television-guided bombs as they glided slowly to their targets. Interviews with soldiers, even on the eve of the ground war, portrayed only tough, calm men and women in uniform. There were no signs of the real, human, gut-wrenching fear that inevitably accompanies any soldier about to risk death.

But the military had neither the imagination nor the conceptual skills to go beyond control over image selection. Its control mechanism did enable it to use the television press as a tool by turning the journalists into active participants. Probably the best case in point occurred when crews were permitted to tape the amphibious training exercises of "Operation Thunder," the ruse used to fool the Iraqis about the allies' real battle plans to sweep around the Iraqi western flank. Journalists, blockaded on almost every other front and desperate for anything resembling a real story, gave the maneuvers extensive coverage. The publicity was a critical part of the allies' program of tactical deception. Nonetheless, the military made very little use of modern, subtle forms of imagespeak. Despite their relatively high degree of success in co-opting the television networks, the military authorities' underlying suspicion of the press precluded any attempts to co-opt the television reporters into producing the kinds of sophisticated imagespeak reports that had had such an impact during the intifada. The video material made available during the Operation Thunder deception was one of the few cases in which the U.S. military allowed the networks to "run" with the material and create a primitive form of Iraqi-war imagespeak. In general, though, reports with high production values appeared only after allied troops entered Kuwait City and television journalists could escape the encumbering embrace of their military shepherds.

Controlled and censored, the press was almost totally dependent upon the military for basic data. What was all too often served up to the press was a combination of misinformation, disinformation, incomplete information, euphemisms, and lies. One of the more fascinating conclusions that arises from the behavior of the American military during the war is that while the new information age has, as expected, ushered in a huge linear growth in the amount of information available even under situations of duress, the advent of the new information technologies has permitted a geometric growth in the amount of disinformation being disseminated. Surprisingly, unlike the intifada, the press made little effort to point up the contradictions inherent in the U.S. disinformation campaign. Virtually all statements emanating from the military, whatever their value, were reported almost without comment—so long as they could be sourced in one way or another. Thus, for example, after a SCUD missile was fired toward Israel, an American military spokesman suggested that "it might have fallen in Jordan." The observation was dutifully reported by the press. The SCUD might have landed in Jordan, but it hadn't. And the U.S. military knew that. The missile had landed in the Israeli-occupied territories near the city of Nablus. None of the journalists present at the briefing even asked whether the rocket's warhead might have landed somewhere other than in the Hashemite kingdom.

Despite all the restrictions, there was a telling difference in the relationship between the press and the military authorities during the intifada and during the Gulf War. Both the Iraqi and the American military authorities regimented and restricted journalists' activities to a far greater degree than the Israelis had during the intifada. But while there were some verbal protests from journalists, and some journalists made strenuous efforts to get out to the front lines on their own (a CBS crew led by Bob Simon was captured by the Iraqis while it was out on the front lines trying to circumvent the strictures placed on the media by the U.S. army), the press as a whole acquiesced to the strictures that were applied in the Gulf. There was little of the open media warfare that had occurred in the Israeli-occupied territories. Until the postwar flight of the Kurds began in earnest, there were also very few attempts at independent political agenda-setting. Criticism was muted.

This seeming double standard was the product of several factors that distinguished the war from the intifada. American journalists had real stakes in the war's outcome. They and their audiences were citizens of the country at war. For the most part, the mass media viewed themselves as a mirror of the national consensus, and even as part of the consensus. The journalists were covering an American effort for a home audience that was, in one form or another, directly involved in the conflict. The war, viewed by large sections of the American public as the antidote to the miasma and ensuing malaise of Vietnam, was an extremely popular one in the United States. The press felt impelled to go to great lengths to show that it was not trying to undercut the national effort or its audiences' expectations and anticipations that the post-Vietnam period would finally come to an end. Old saws that the press had somehow been responsible for the Vietnam debacle were once again trotted out at the beginning of the war by the American Right, and the fear of an antipress backlash may have been at the back of the minds of many editors. A desire to avoid controversy, to be part of the national consensus, and to create a situation in which there would be a priori expiation for any publicly perceived sins of the press, may explain some of the heavy editorializing engaged in by some of the television anchors. Most important, however, unlike the intifada, the war was short. A rebellion among some journalists over the restrictions under which they were operating had begun by the time the land war was launched. A process of delegitimizing the military and political authorities because of the disinformation campaign had also commenced—at least among the braver and more savvy reporters. But both these trends were abruptly ended by the speed with which the land war was waged and brought to a halt. The system of co-optation and control thus remained largely intact.

The war pointed up once again, however, what happens when controls are so intense that the press is insufficiently questioning or critical. If, during a crisis, the press has but one public duty, it is to enable the individuals in their audiences to routinize their lives during a time of upheaval and uncertainty by accurately describing events in depth, pointing up the issues and the stakes involved, and most important, debunking false anticipations and creating real ones. During the intifada, the number of Americans directly involved in the Israeli-Palestinian crisis was minuscule. Relatively few individuals in the United States had their lives disrupted by the stone throwing and tire burning. The same was not true during the Iraqi war. The bombing of a bunker in Baghdad, which the Americans claimed was a command post and the Iraqis said was a bomb shelter, shocked the American public because the press had failed in its role of creating real expectations. So intent had the U.S. military been in not showing the real face of war—dead bodies—and so sterile had the coverage been, that the U.S. public was unprepared for the reality it faced once blood and gore were flashed on their television screens. No less important was the fact that as soldiers' mail began coming home from the front in such numbers that not all of it could be censored, their families were able to distinguish the often huge gaps between what was being described by their loved ones and what was being described in the press. Had the war gone on longer, and had the campaign of official disinformation become the subject of greater coverage, the misinformation campaign could have had the same catastrophic effect on national morale as it had had during the Vietnam war.

One very notable phenomenon of this war was the unique role played by CNN. Unlike the other three networks, it had never been known for a strong emphasis on production values or overt agenda setting. Its format of "radio with pictures" meant that it suffered less than the other networks from the dearth of video material available. Its extensive international connections, the replay rights it had sold to other foreign television stations, and its desire to project a sense that it was playing to an international audience, had positioned it as the primary international looping mechanism. One quite extraordinary example of looping was a satellite interview conducted by an American anchor, Bernard Shaw, sitting in Baghdad, talking with Israel's Deputy Foreign Minister, Benjamin Netanyahu, sitting in the CNN studio in Israel.

It was the recognition of CNN's unique role as an international facilitator, together with the personal courage of the CNN crew in Baghdad, that persuaded the Iraqis to give it almost press monopoly status in the Iraqi capital for much of the war. For an extended period, CNN was the only American media outlet capable of reporting on both sides of the conflict—at least those parts that were available for coverage. Just being in Baghdad to report, however, enraged some elements on the American Right—just as the very presence of reporters in the Israeli-occupied territories had sent some elements of the Israeli Right into spasms of criticism. Peter Arnett's coverage of the Iraqi side of the war was the subject of public denunciation by those who did not want to recognize that there was another side, another point of view, or another version of events. As so often happens when issues are presented in black and white, journalists who attempt even to explain the positions of those portrayed as the bad guys are charged with aiding the enemy. Despite the tight restrictions placed on Arnett by the Iraqis, his reports were, nonetheless, a useful addition to the body of public knowledge.

CNN recognized its unique position and responsibility as an international disseminator of news serving both an American and an international audience. Unlike the three prime commercial television networks, CNN only rarely played on the emotional, and sometimes even jingoistic, strings that could be found on the other networks.

The intense CNN coverage of the conflict led, however, to another phenomenon. Its constant updates altered the public's perception of the reality of the conflict in a significant way. The round-the-clock reports made it appear as though the public was getting all the information it needed. Metaphorically, however, the reporting resembled a spectroscopic line. Like a spectroscopic study of a chemical, each report was but a narrow slice, a thin color band, of the total spectrum—and there were enormous gaps between the slices. Like most of its competitors, CNN failed to point up where many of these knowledge holes lay. Particularly during a crisis, a major part of a journalist's job is to point out not just what is known, but what is unknown. For example, in virtually every recent war in the Middle East, the critical factor that decided whether soldiers would stand and fight, or break ranks and run, has been whether the noncommissioned officer corps of the relevant army remained intact. As the air war progressed and the land war drew near, no one sought to raise as a public issue whether the Iraqi NCOs were becoming demoralized. Had the first sergeants and the regimental sergeant majors not broken, allied forces would have met far stronger resistance and casualty figures would have been far higher.

As with the intifada, this war also saw the introduction of several new technologies. The most notable were the introduction, on a wide scale, of light, mobile television satellite stations that could be packed into a single van; direct satellite telephone hook-ups, which were used to great effect by the CNN crew in Baghdad after the normal communications systems were knocked out by U.S. missiles and bombs; and the video cameras positioned inside some of the smart weapons that some of the allied military forces used. Each of these technologies played a significant role in shaping the coverage. One technology, still in its relative infancy, was employed in the very first stages of the Iraqi invasion of Kuwait, but its use was abruptly curtailed once the alliance was formed. Detailed pictures of the front provided by the Soviet Cosmos satellites and the French SPOT satellite were purchased by television networks during the opening days of the conflict. But once the alliance was formed, access to the images was curtailed.

The months-long delay in the start of the actual fighting, caused by the massive military buildup, forced journalists to take a measured pace in reporting the crisis. This meant that the story could pass through five of the requisite six stages of reporting that make for effective public policy-making and consensus building. Initially, the story was events-driven. But because of the time available, it could go through the process of being topic-driven, interest-driven, issue-driven, and resolution-driven before the land war began. This enforced pacing of the story played a very significant part in building national support for President Bush's decision to recapture Kuwait.

As usually happens in crises of this sort, media critics on both the Right and the Left in the United States charged that their positions were not being given a fair hearing—and that their opponents were being given a disproportionate amount of air time and print space. Whatever the merits of the claims and counterclaims, the national debate was sufficiently extensive that, unlike Vietnam, most of the domestic political positions and points at issue had been brought to the fore for discussion before the final decision to go to war was made. This slow, media-directed process played a critical role in unifying the vast majority of the American public around the war's aims and objectives. It also accounts, to a very large extent, for the lack of a postwar political backlash—despite the allies' failure to destroy large chunks of the Iraqi army. The only significant backlash concerned U.S. policy toward the Kurds—and that intense criticism arose because U.S. behavior toward them differed from the consensus that had evolved out of the national debate.

One of the more interesting phenomena of the national debate was the ability by interested parties who felt that they had not been given a fair shake by the media to use a new technology and a newfound access to alternative media services in order to bring their positions before the American public. In the period immediately prior to the outbreak of fighting in the Gulf, in some areas of the United States, local television cable services and public access television stations became the equivalent of that most American of institutions, the town hall meeting. In a quite extraordinary example of participatory democracy in which journalists were not permitted to act as idea gatekeepers, special-interest groups, such as antiwar Ramsey Clark's Deep Dish Video, could and did get local cable and public access channels to air information or propaganda packages that they had prepared. This domestic phenomenon, which will probably become more widespread in the future, has important implications for international relations in general, and foreign reporting in particular. With the rapid growth in cable television services around the world, and with the increasing interconnections among cable services in different countries through the use of satellites, the type of advocacy politics practiced by interested groups that use cable services will undoubtedly become part of the news-making process. For the first time, this may create new international information loops outside the control of the journalists and political elites. The use of cable services, when combined with the increasing spread of computer billboards, and direct satellite broadcasting may create a new, visual form of the traditional political leaflet. As was shown in this book, traditional leaflets played an important part in shaping both public attitudes and reporters' activities and schedules during the intifada. The new video form of political advocacy, especially if it uses sophisticated imagespeak, cannot but increase the impact of such modes of communication and create challenges to both political elites and journalists in the future. For the first time, political advocacy groups may be able to communicate directly to audiences worldwide in real time—and circumvent established media outlets. Reporters then, inevitably, will have to redefine their niche and their public mandate.

If I could draw but one conclusion from a comparison of the press coverage of the Iraqi war and the intifada, it is that the nature of the reporting done in any crisis is not just a function of access or technology or professional skill. More than anything else, it is the product of whom the decision maker or the journalist chooses as his or her target audience. Once that choice is made, each participant in the event becomes a captive of his or her own perception of what the chosen audience wants, expects to hear and see, or can be made to believe. Theoretically, this gives the target audience enormous power. In principle, it is in a position to set the criteria by which success in the enterprise will be judged; the rewards for success that will be meted out; and the penalties that will be levied for perceived failure. In fact, however, it is the decision maker's or the media outlet's perception of what the target audience wants that counts. During the intifada, for example, the three main television networks decided that their audience wanted dramatic entertainment and stories with high production values. During the Iraqi war, the perception was that the audience wanted support, and so the network anchors, particularly Dan Rather, behaved much like cheerleaders. Perceptions of its audience's diverse character and demands shaped CNN's "generic" coverage of the dispute. During the intifada, the Israeli army's target audience was broad and diffused, and as a result, there was little direction to the military's public relations efforts. Among the U.S. military in the Gulf, the target audience was very specific—Capitol Hill—and the American public was used merely as a vehicle to reach the legislators. Perceptions of tactical field necessity and the budget wars in Washington led the U.S. military to ignore the potential effects on national morale of its disinformation and misinformation campaigns. The information/disinformation system employed by the military was a tactical success. However, it may turn out to have been a long-term strategic failure because it once again made many journalists skeptical of the military's veracity.

The major print outlets found their niches by concentrating on those aspects of the campaign that newspaper editors perceived were not being covered by television. And there were many such niches, especially those analytical stories for which television could provide no images. Television did make extensive use of analysts, but most of these experts were academics or former military personnel who had not been out in the field and were incapable of doing the kind of routine journalistic digging in which quality print reporters excel. No less important was the ability of the print press to provide readers with a detailed review of the previous day's events. This detail, spread over several pages, acted as a significant antidote to the rapid television cuts and the imagespeak that was used.

A significant new development was that major local and regional newspapers lost a traditional monopoly during the war and faced a new type of competitor: the local U.S. television stations. The more well-endowed local stations sent their own crews over to Saudi Arabia to work on the hometown news stories. This type of coverage had once been the exclusive territory (and part of the raison d'être) of print journalists working abroad. The local stations, however, perceived that by sending in their own parachutists, and by expanding their coverage in this way, they could gain a larger market share.

The inference one can then draw is that the target audience can, if it chooses to be active, alter the nature of reporting by altering the news-makers' and journalists' perceptions of what will "sell." Thus, the audience can be a direct participant. It can point out inaccuracies, inadequacies in coverage, and bias—and demand change. One unanswered question, though, was whether significant portions of the American public wanted full reporting. Some polls taken at the time of the war indicated that instead of more hard, but difficult-to-digest, information, many people merely wanted their prior perceptions reinforced. The problem that in-terested audiences faced if they wanted to intervene to alter the nature of the coverage was that there were few mechanisms they could use to make their voices heard in real time. Almost all the audience-reaction stories were crafted in one of three ways: polls, stories on public reaction initiated by journalists, and letters to the editor. Each of these techniques was limited in scope and had a time-delay mechanism built in. Each had to pass through a journalist-gatekeeper. Polls and stories initiated by jour-nalists were generally narrowly focused and concentrated largely on simple issues such as whether people were for or against the war. Call-in programs that might have allowed greater audience participation were few and far between. (National Public Radio's afternoon call-in program with Daniel Shorr was a notable exception). Such national call-in programs were a significant part of the Israeli broadcasting networks' coverage and played a major role in allowing Israelis of all ages to bond together by venting their deepest concerns in their own words. Real-time audience reaction to events also resulted in important and publicly useful changes in infor-mation-dissemination policies. For example, it was the publicly expressed fear that many people could not hear the air raid sirens when they slept that led to the creation of an open "silent" radio channel during the night hours. During the hours of midnight to six A.M., the radio station remained silent except to broadcast the sound of sirens during a SCUD attack. People could go to sleep knowing that they would be woken in time to seal their rooms and put on their gas masks.

Despite the enormous efforts invested, the information marketplace created by the Iraqi war crisis was filled with a considerable amount of very inadequate and shoddy goods. Undoubtedly the press coverage and the manipulation of the press will become a model for many spokespeople and news practitioners. That would be unfortunate. As in all democracies and free marketplaces, the responsibility for highlighting the failures and demanding changes lies with the public. For there to be better reporting by journalists and more responsibility on the part of spokespeople, however, the media consumer must be willing to demand not merely what he or she wants to hear and see. The lesson of this war, as well as of the coverage of other major foreign events, is that quality control of information products and services ultimately depends on cogent criticism by activist media consumers. The very act of providing audiences with a vehicle to voice their concerns in real time is not merely a public service, it also gives the press the kind of legitimacy that allows it to pursue other journalistic tasks. To achieve a higher level of quality, however, audience activism, in itself, is not enough. Audiences must also be willing to accept the often sour medicine of truth when it arrives.

Index